THE MASS

THE GREAT CHALICE OF ANTIOCH

A discovery of great significance and supreme importance has been made within our own lifetime. The great Chalice of Antioch, which was hidden from the world for some 1,300 years, was recovered in 1910. Some Arabs, digging the foundations for a house, broke into a subterranean chamber in ground to which the city formerly extended, and which local tradition described as once the site of a Christian Church. In clearing out the rubbish, with which the room was filled, they came upon a silver cup–a large bowl on a very short stem. It was seen to be the work of a consummate artist in metal. The cup was double: an inner cup of plain silver, without ornamentation of any kind, was loosely held in an outer cup, which was elaborately ornamented. The design of the pierced work of the outer cup shows us twelve vines springing from the base, and the grape-laden branches of these form a framework for a number of portraits.

Two of these are seated figures, identified as representing Our Lord in His youth and in later life. The others are figures of Apostles and Evangelists. The symbolism associated with the figure of Our Lord is undoubtedly the Eucharistic symbolism of the early Church known so well to us by the paintings of the catacombs. But it is of much earlier date than these. There are indeed those who suggest–not as a matter of proof, but of probabilities–that the inner cup is no other than the cup of the Last Supper, and that the splendidly-ornamented outer cup is its shrine.

This Great Chalice of Antioch is, beyond any doubt, the work of an artist who lived in the Apostolic Age and must have personally known some of those who had spoken face to face with Our Blessed Lord. It is the earliest of the monuments of the Catholic Faith, earlier than the Gospel of St. John. Its shape and its workmanship and several details of its designs mark it undoubtedly as belonging to the first century, and almost certainly to no later date than its third quarter.

Is it, then, the Holy Grail? Who can say! Of this, however, we are sure, soon after the Day of Pentecost there were many converts at Antioch, especially in the large Jewish colony of this Greco-Roman city which ranked second only to Rome itself in wealthy splendor and the number of people. It was there that the converts to the new Gospel message were first popularly known as "Christians." St. Peter spent some years there, and left St. Ignatius as its Bishop when he went to Rome.

When Julian, the Apostate, was at Antioch, he tortured Theodorus, "the guardian of the treasures" of the great church (that is, its cathedral) to force him to reveal where he had hidden some treasures that the persecutor wished to seize, and finally put the faithful guardian to death. The Persians sacked Antioch in the sixth century. In the following century the city fell into the hands of the Moslems. During all the centuries that passed, the great chalice lay hidden from the eyes of men. And now it speaks to us its testimony to the faith of the Apostolic Age and its identity with that of Holy Church in our own.

THE GREAT CHALICE OF ANTIOCH

International copyright, 1923, Kouchakji Frères.

FR. JOSEPH DUNNEY

THE MASS

Et ait illis: Desiderio desideravi hoc
pascha manducare vobiscum (Lk. 22:15)

ANGELUS PRESS
2915 FOREST AVENUE
KANSAS CITY, MISSOURI 64109

Nihil Obstat *Imprimatur*
Arthur J. Scanlan, S.T.D. Patrick Cardinal Hayes
Censor Librorum *Archbishop of New York*
September 8, 1924

Library of Congress Cataloging-in-Publication Data

Dunney, Joseph A. (Joseph Aloysius), b. 1881.
The Mass / Joseph A. Dunney.
  p. cm.
Originally published: New York : The Macmillan Company, 1924.
Includes index.
ISBN 978-1-892331-49-6
1. Mass. I. Title.
BX2230.3.D86 2007
264'.02036--dc22

2007019829

© 1924 by The Macmillan Company.
This Angelus Press edition published in arrangement
with Scribner, an imprint of Simon and Schuster, Inc.

All rights reserved. No part of this book may be reproduced or transmitted
in any form or by any means, electronic or mechanical, including
photocopying, recording, or by any information storage and retrieval
systems without permission in writing from the publisher, except by a
reviewer, who may quote brief passages in a review.

ANGELUS PRESS
2915 FOREST AVENUE
KANSAS CITY, MISSOURI 64109
PHONE (816) 753-3150
FAX (816) 753-3557
ORDER LINE 1-800-966-7337
www.angeluspress.org

ISBN 978-1-892331-49-6
FIRST PRINTING–August 2007

Printed in the United States of America

To me nothing is so consoling, so piercing, so thrilling, so overcoming, as the Mass, said as it is among us. I could attend Masses forever, and not be tired. It is not a mere form of words–it is a great action, the greatest action that can be on earth. It is, not the invocation merely, but, if I dare use the word, the evocation of the Eternal. He becomes present on the altar in flesh and blood, before Whom angels bow and devils tremble. That is that awful event which is the scope, and the interpretation, of every part of the solemnity. Words are necessary, but as means, not as ends; they are not mere addresses to the throne of grace, they are instruments of what is far higher, of consecration, of sacrifice. They hurry on, as if impatient to fulfill their mission. Quickly they go, the whole is quick, for they are all parts of one integral action. Quickly they go, for they are awful words of sacrifice, they are a work too great to delay upon, as when it was said in the beginning, "What thou doest, do quickly." Quickly they pass, for the Lord Jesus goes with them, as He passed along the lake in the days of His flesh, quickly calling first one and then another; quickly they pass, because as the lightning which shineth from one part of the heaven unto the other, so is the coming of the Son of Man. Quickly they pass, for they are as the words of Moses when the Lord came down in the cloud, calling on the name of the Lord as He passed by, "The Lord, The Lord God, merciful and gracious, long suffering, and abundant in goodness and truth." And as Moses on the mountain, so we too, "make haste and bow our heads to the earth and adore."–***Cardinal Newman***

TABLE OF CONTENTS

PART ONE

CHAPTER		PAGE
I.	THE SIGN OF THE CROSS	3
II.	CONFITEOR	10
III.	THE ALTAR STONE	20
IV.	THE INTROIT	29
V.	KYRIE ELEISON	35
VI.	GLORIA IN EXCELSIS	40
VII.	DOMINUS VOBISCUM	44
VIII.	COLLECT	54
IX.	EPISTLE	58
X.	GRADUAL	62
XI.	THE GOSPEL	67
XII.	CREDO	77

PART TWO

XIII.	THE OFFERTORY	91
XIV.	LAVABO	104
XV.	SUSCIPE SANCTA TRINITAS	118
XVI.	ORATE FRATRES	125
XVII.	SECRETA	134
XVIII.	THE PREFACE	138
XIX.	THE SANCTUS	146

PART THREE

XX.	CANON	155
XXI.	TE IGITUR	159

TABLE OF CONTENTS

CHAPTER		PAGE
XXII.	MEMENTO	164
XXIII.	COMMUNICANTES	169
XXIV.	HANC IGITUR — QUAM OBLATIONEM	175
XXV.	CONSECRATION	186
XXVI.	UNDE ET MEMORES	199
XXVII.	MEMENTO ETIAM	213
XXVIII.	NOBIS QUOQUE PECCATORIBUS	221
XXIX.	PER QUEM PER IPSUM	236
XXX.	PATER NOSTER	246
XXXI.	LIBERA NOS QUÆSUMUS	272
XXXII.	FRACTIO PANIS COMMIXTIO	276
XXXIII.	AGNUS DEI	283
XXXIV.	DOMINE NON SUM DIGNUS	297
XXXV.	COMMUNION	314

PART FOUR

XXXVI.	POST COMMUNION	321
XXXVII.	ITE, MISSA EST: BENEDICTIO	330
XXXVIII.	THE LAST GOSPEL	336

APPENDIX

THE VESTMENTS OF THE MASS	347
THE MASS OF THE CATECHUMENS	367

FOREWORD

It would be easier for the world to survive without the sun than to do so without the Holy Mass.
St. Padre Pio

Even God Himself could do nothing holier, better or greater than the Mass.
St. Alphonsus

The happiness of the world comes from the Sacrifice of the Mass.
St. Odo of Cluny

The Mass is the greatest treasure of the Church, as the Ark of the Covenant was for the ancient Jews. If you remember, in the Old Testament, the Ark was a precious tabernacle overlaid with the purest gold, containing in it the tables of the Ten Commandments, the rod of Aaron and a pot of manna. It was before this Ark where Moses conversed with God. One could say that the Ark was the place Heaven touched earth. When the Jews lost their love for the Ark, when they no longer appreciated it for what it was, God took it away from them.

Most of us do not appreciate what we have until after it is gone, for example, our health, good parents, and close friends. The Catholic Mass also falls into this category. God allowed Catholics to lose this precious treasure, much like He allowed the Jews to lose the Ark of the Covenant in the Old Testament, so that they would *learn to appreciate it*. In the 1950's, we had a very good pope (Pius XII) and there were many converts. Catholic churches were so plentiful, especially in our major cities, that one could go to Mass and confession whenever and wherever he pleased. However, when things are too easy, we grow lax. Familiarity breeds contempt. And while we hope no Catholic held the Mass in contempt, perhaps we no longer saw it for what it is: the most necessary thing on earth, the *only* perfect thing. In the 1960's, in a span of just six years, the ancient Latin Mass was taken away. From 1963-69 there were a great many changes: parts of the Mass were lopped off (prayers at the foot of the altar, the Last Gospel), more and more of the Mass was said in the vernacular, genuflections were omitted. Finally, the altars were turned around, a huge change because the emphasis changed. Before, the priest was offering a sacrifice to God for the people. He did not have his back to them, as much as he was facing the Lord in His tabernacle, or on the cross. But now, with the altar turned around, the Mass was "man-centered": the priest was presiding over guests at a memorial supper, conversing with them throughout the ceremony. It was no longer considered a sacrifice but a gathering of the community, where, it was said, the presence of the people made God present. Hence they emphasized the phrase "Where two or more are gathered, there I am in the midst of them." And, since the presence of the community was necessary, the "private Mass" disappeared and the word *sacrifice* was eliminated when referring to the Mass. Finally, in 1969, the *Novus Ordo Missae* was awkwardly promulgated, and the vast majority of Catholics never again saw nor heard the Latin Mass. The sacredness and solemnity of the ancient Mass was gone. Pop music was introduced into the Liturgy, lay men and women entered the sanctuary, kneeling was

FOREWORD

frowned upon; communion in the hand was introduced. Some Catholics finally awoke, asking themselves, "What happened to the old Mass?" Like the buried Ark of the Old Testament, it was nowhere to be found.

After years of agony with the *Novus Ordo* Mass, they became aware that there were some priests who were unofficially celebrating the Latin Mass. There was even a retired French archbishop who had publicly refused to go along with all the changes. Marcel Lefebvre was his name. He was making the old Latin Mass his banner and calling upon Catholics to return to the Faith of their fathers, much like Mathathias, father of the Machabees, had done two hundred years before Christ. Some fervent Catholics, when they rediscovered the traditional Mass, found that nothing else compared to it. *This* was the pearl of great price; the hidden treasure (Mt. 13) of which Our Lord had spoken. They sold what they had and moved to be closer to daily Mass.

When compared to the Tridentine Latin Mass, the *Novus Ordo* seemed empty, almost frivolous. Again, like the Ark of the Covenant when it was placed in the temple of the pagan god Dagon, the old Mass was clearly doctrinally superior and more powerful. The new Mass simply could not stand up alongside the old. This book helps explain why. There is a hidden depth and meaning to the Latin Mass that many Catholics have never grasped or have forgotten.

I had two friends in California (Latin Rite Catholics) who loved the Eastern Rite liturgies. They would visit churches and monasteries where they could witness first-hand some of the ancient customs of the Greek Church and their solemn liturgies. On several occasions I tried to point out that the Latin Mass was just as attractive, just as deep and meaningful, but they only rolled their eyes and smiled. They could never agree with me. They should have read this book.

Fr. Joseph Dunney wrote this book in 1924, and it has been out of print for over fifty years, yet it is a veritable treasure trove of information on the Latin Mass. Though written in the style of a book for Catholic schools, every chapter reads like a meditation on a part of the Mass. As such, it can benefit every Catholic over the age of eleven. Let the youth use it to learn the value of the Holy Mass; let adults use it to understand the depth and the riches of our greatest treasure, worth more to the world than any other activity or pursuit.

Back in the thirteenth century, the king of France, Louis IX, would daily assist at two or even three Masses. Members of his court complained that he was spending too much time in church, that there were more important matters to which he must attend. St. Louis pointed out that they would not complain if he were spending that time in hunting or entertaining, or some other worldly pursuit, so why were they angry that he should attend Mass?

It's the same today. Let someone go into work an hour early and he's praised for being industrious and dedicated; but if he goes to Mass daily, he's judged to be wasting his time. A busy mother may spend hours on her chores and hours more on her children, driving them all over the state for sports or music, but she does not even dream of going to daily Mass. "There's no time." "It's too far."

When Catholics first rediscovered the Latin Mass, they were delighted, and many continue to assist daily at a Latin Mass. But, human nature being as it is, with the passage of time, our initial zeal has begun to wane, other things in life becoming more pressing. We need to come back to the realization that the Mass is what matters; our Catholic Faith must hold again the first place in our hearts and minds.

This book should help us do that. It is not just about the Mass. It also has many lessons for life on virtue and character; it is loaded with examples from the Holy Scriptures and the lives of the saints, and is an excellent source of instruction on religion and Church history. I pray that it will find a place in every priest's office, every Catholic school, and every Catholic home.

Fr. Daniel Cooper, SSPX
July 2007

PART 1

THE MASS

I

THE SIGN OF THE CROSS

The priest on entering the sanctuary goes to the foot of the altar, genuflects, and goes up to the altar. There he places the veiled chalice on the Corporal, moves over to the Epistle side and opens the Missal. Then he returns to the foot of the altar, where in an audible voice he begins Mass with the sign of the cross.

You will notice that the first thing the priest does on entering the sanctuary is to genuflect before the crucifix. The image of the crucified Saviour on the altar is specially intended to remind all that Mass-saying is a special mind-making of Christ's passion. Sir Thomas More said:

In the presence of the crucifix, the priest says his mass, and offers up the highest prayer which the Church can devise for the salvation of the quick and the dead. He holds up his hands, he bows down, he kneels, and all the worship he can do he does — more than all, he offers up the highest sacrifice and the best offering that any heart can devise — that is Christ, the Son of the God of Heaven, under the form of bread and wine.

Remember the facts about Blessed Thomas More, martyr, and his extraordinary devotion to the passion of our Lord. "It was his custom to hear Mass every day. Once, when he was the king's chancellor, messengers from the king came to fetch him while he was hearing Mass. But Sir Thomas would not stir till Mass was finished, not even when a second messenger came and a third. 'I will first perform

THE MASS

my duty to a better man than the king,' he said. And the king (Henry VIII) was pleased when he heard of it, for at that time he was still a good Catholic."

The early Christians employed the cross in private as their most sacred symbol. It represented their Master, who was all in all to them; it represented all the faith — the person of Christ. Sometimes they wreathed it or ornamented it with flowers, as evidence of victory and triumph of the risen Christ. In the Catacombs and in all the earliest records it is constantly used in connection with the monogram of Christ. Several shapes of crosses were used, some of which may now be studied.

ANCIENT CROSSES

These crosses, found in the Catacombs, indicate various conceptions of the early Christians.

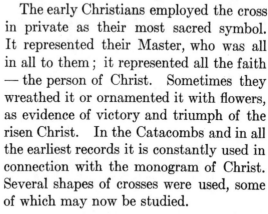

1. Crux immissa, Roman cross, a transverse beam crossing a perpendicular one at some distance from the top. According to tradition this was the form of our Saviour's cross. This appears correct from the fact that the "title" was placed over the head. This Roman cross sometimes possesses one or even two additional cross limbs, shorter than the main or central one. The upper bar stands for the title over the head of the Crucified One, the lower equals a support for His feet.

2. The Greek cross has four arms of equal length, thus ✚

3. The crux commissa, or Tau cross, is general from perhaps the earliest period: a transverse beam placed on the top of a perpendicular one, resembling the Greek letter T. A sepulchral inscription from the third century in the Callixtine Catacomb runs thus: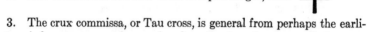

THE SIGN OF THE CROSS

4. Crux decussata, or St. Andrew's cross, like the letter X. This was a very ancient form, ✕ with its intersecting arms. The cross which appeared to Constantine was of this form with the Greek letter R in it so as to represent the first two letters of the word Christus.

5. A crucifix is a symbolic cross with the corpus (body) crucified form of our Lord on it. On every Catholic altar is a crucifix or a representation of the crucifixion.

In the Catacombs, where the early Christians assembled in times of persecution, and where they buried their dead, you can see to this day the signs of their devotion to the holy cross.

Nothing shows better how the Christian feeling leads truly to contemplate our Lord's sufferings and death. Christians owe it to Christ to love His cross. We see how the early Christians loved it, marked it on their monuments, kept it close to their hearts during persecution, long before it came into public use at the time of Constantine. In the latter part of the fourth century, a Christian poet tells of a Christian shepherd who secured his flock against disease by marking between their horns, *signum mediis frontibus additum*, "the cross of the God men worship in great cities."

>Signum quod perhibent esse crucis Dei
>Magnis quoi colitur solus in Urbibus
>Christus, perpetui gloria numinis, . . .

Do we trust in the cross and make the sign of the cross often and with devotion? Think what it means and why you do it. As you make the sign of the cross you say: "In the name of the Father and of the Son and of the Holy Ghost, Amen." That means, "in their Name, for their sake," you are going to do something. Everything you do should be done for God. You should try to remember to offer your acts — all of them. Not only with the morning offering, but by consecrating each big thing, each separate undertaking: rising in the morning, eating your meals, leaving your home.

ANCIENT SYMBOLS

This quaint carving, used to designate the Apostles and the cross, was taken from the frieze on an old tomb.

In olden days people used to do that much more often. They used the sign of the cross to show that what they did was for God's sake; when they lighted a candle, it honored Christ as the Light of the World; when they rose from bed; when they left the house to go to work; when they wrote letters, they put a cross on the top of the page. Many times did they bless themselves, an act very pleasing to God.

The sign of the cross is to be made reverently and carefully at Mass. Hearing Mass is the biggest, most important thing you can do. Be sure, then, to begin it right, with the sign of the cross, with real love in your heart, with the thought of pleasing Him who hangs on the cross you see on the altar.

Everywhere in the Mass the cross is used. Not only in the beginning of the Mass, but throughout the sacrifice the priest makes the sign of the cross: 1, for himself; 2, over the book; 3, upon the oblations (water and wine); 4, over the precious body and blood of our Lord; 5, with the host when giving Communion; 6, lastly over the congregation at the Last Blessing. But most frequently does he make the sign of the cross after the Canon has begun. This use of the cross was considered very important as a reminder

THE SIGN OF THE CROSS

that our Saviour is with us in the Mass which is Calvary all over again. Since the Mass is the mystical Calvary, the congregation must never lose sight of the importance of the cross. It should stir our hearts, excite our devotion. What silent eloquence, therefore, in those signs! They teach our mind, they impress our heart, they sustain our will. After the Consecration they tell us that we stand by the cross, where stood Mary and St. John and the other faithful ones when Christ died on Calvary. The use of the cross was held to be of such great importance that once St. Boniface (750 A.D.) consulted Pope Zacharias to find out how many times it should be used (in blessing) at the Mass. The Pope sent him a copy of the Canon with the crosses inserted at their proper places. Take your prayer book, look through the Canon, and notice the seven groups of them.

1. Te igitur ✠ ✠ ✠
2. Hanc igitur ✠ ✠ ✠ ✠ ✠
3. Consecration ✠ ✠
4. Unde et memores ✠ ✠ ✠ ✠ ✠
5. Per quem ✠ ✠ ✠
6. Per ipsum ✠ ✠ ✠ ✠ ✠
7. Pax Domini ✠ ✠ ✠

Then, at the end of Mass, comes the cross of the Last Blessing.

We ought to love with a real love that cross of Christ. Somebody has described it as "an eye-word which ever clothes itself with richer and fuller meaning, so that at one glance we take in more food for mind and heart than the ear could receive in an hour." The head inclined speaks to us of the infinite patience of Jesus; the hands outstretched speak of the width of His love, inviting all, embracing all; His heart laid bare to our eyes breathes love and asks a return. Indeed, the whole form of Jesus on the cross radiates love. Does it not call on our imagination by its vividness, awaken feeling by appeal to our senses, stir us to remembrance of the painful details of bodily suffering undergone for us by our Lord? "The sweetness of the divine love as revealed in the crucified humanity has spoken more in one single word to many a pure childlike heart than all the gathered experience and reflection of the wisest could utter."

While dealing with so important a theme, it will help to make ourselves acquainted with the different postures the early Christians used in their worship. These are five:

1. They stood upright, as among the Jews this was the most common posture (Matthew vi, 5; Luke xviii, 11–13).

2. They bent the head forward. This bowing of the head was meant to show their reverence.

3. They bent the back forward, to indicate their unworthiness.

4. They knelt on both knees. "The knee," says St. Ambrose, "is made flexible, by which, beyond other members, the offense of the Lord is mitigated, wrath appeased, grace called forth." Note the practice among early Christians, reflected in Ephesians iii, 14; Acts vii, 59; ix, 40; xx, 36; xxi, 5.

5. Most profound of all postures they prostrated themselves at length, as a profession of deep humility in drawing nigh to God in prayer.

The sign of the cross and the genuflection are our first acts upon entering the church for Mass. Let us be ever ready to give the right reason for them, and "for the faith that is in us." No one who is properly instructed in his religion should be at a loss to explain these and many other liturgical movements to an inquiring non-Catholic. The act of bending the knee to worship, for example, is called genuflection (*genu* = knee, *flectere* = to bend). The Catholic on entering church at once bends his knee because:

1. He knows that Christ is really present in the Tabernacle, therefore he adores Him.

THE SIGN OF THE CROSS 9

2. This act is a very marked expression of humility in drawing nigh to our Lord; it is also a token of penitence and sorrow, of felt unworthiness to be in the presence of Christ.

3. St. Jerome says: "It is according to ecclesiastical custom to bend the knee to Christ." Genuflecting thoughtfully, therefore, the intelligent Catholic considers the depths in which mankind was sunk, when the Son of God came down to earth, sounded all the depths of human sorrow in order to uplift mankind and redeem our race. That is why we kneel at the Credo words: *Et Homo factus est.* Our Saviour was the good Samaritan Who bent over the human race, wounded and half dead on the roadside (Luke x, 33).

All these points should stir us to increased reverence. "In reverence," says Ruskin, "is the chief joy and power of life. Reverence for all that is gracious among the living, great among the dead, and marvellous in the powers that cannot die."

1. Do you know the prayer before a crucifix by heart? 2. Have you a crucifix in your bedroom? 3. Do you kiss the cross on your beads? 4. Write a theme on the meaning of the crucifix: it has been the noblest theme of art, for its beauty is exhaustless. Every variety and combination of the arts of sculpture, mosaic, painting, and engraving have been applied to this subject from the earliest time to our own day. Do you know of any such work? 5. Character is shown in the choice of pictures as much as in that of books or of companions. Explain.

II

CONFITEOR

Having made the sign of the cross, the priest joining his hands before his breast begins the antiphon, Introibo. That said, he recites the psalm, Judica me, Deus, as a prelude to the Confiteor. With joined hands and humbly bowing down, the Confiteor is said: then the absolution is given and other prayers recited before the priest ascends the altar steps.

At the foot of the altar the priest and altar boy recite this beautiful antiphon and psalm.

P. Introibo ad altare Dei.

A. Ad Deum qui lætificat juventutem meam.

P. Judica me, Deus, et discerne causam meam de gente non sancta; ab homine iniquo et doloso erue me.

A. Quia tu es, Deus, fortitudo mea: quare me repulisti? et quare tristis incedo, dum affligit me inimicus?

P. Emitte lucem tuam et veritatem tuam: ipsa me deduxerunt et adduxerunt in montem sanctum tuum, et in tabernacula tua.

A. Et introibo ad altare Dei: ad Deum, qui lætificat juventutem meam.

P. Confitebor tibi in cithara, Deus, Deus, meus: quare tristis es, anima mea? et quare conturbas me?

P. I will go in unto the altar of God:

A. Unto God, who giveth joy to my youth.

P. Judge me, O God, and distinguish my cause from the nation that is not holy; deliver me from the unjust and deceitful man.

A. For Thou, O God, art my strength: why hast Thou cast me off? and why do I go sorrowful, whilst the enemy afflicteth me?

P. Send forth Thy light and Thy truth: they have led me and brought me unto Thy holy mount, and into Thy Tabernacles.

A. And I will go unto the altar of God: unto God, who giveth joy to my youth.

P. I will praise Thee upon the harp, O God, my God: why art thou sad, O my soul? and why dost thou disquiet me?

CONFITEOR

A. Spera in Deo, quoniam adhuc confitebor illi: salutare vultus mei, et Deus meus.	*A.* Hope thou in God, for I will yet praise Him: who is the salvation of my countenance, and my God.
P. Gloria Patri, et Filio, et Spiritui Sancto.	*P.* Glory be to the Father, and to the Son, and to the Holy Ghost.
A. Sicut erat in principio, et nunc, et semper, et in sæcula sæculorum. Amen.	*A.* As it was in the beginning, is now, and ever shall be, world without end. Amen.

Hundreds of years ago the above prayer was composed by a poor exile, enlightened by God's holy spirit. Nothing could be more appropriate for this time and place than the very plea of this psalm. First said by the pious servant of God, the Judica Me is a prayer from a heart heavy with sadness. It bespeaks a longing to return and take part in the service of God's temple, a heartache to pour itself forth in public worship, a burning desire to go to the altar of God Who alone can wipe away every tear. The author of the psalm had been cast among heathen enemies who taunted him about his God. It is almost impossible to exaggerate how much the good man suffered. He recalls the time when he served at God's altar. He grieves he is so far away from the temple. To add to his grief his foes scoff at him.

BEDOUIN PLAYING THE LYRE

The Hebrew psalmist, praising God upon his harp, was following a custom centuries old.

It was very common for the enemies of the chosen people to do that. Thus when the Jews were exiles in Babylon, the natives took malicious joy in heckling them. "Sing us a song of Sion," they scoffed.

Another time the exiles, looking back to their old home, wept in this sad strain.

> By the waters of Babylon,
> There we sat down, and wept
> When we remember Sion.
> In that land, on the willows,
> We hung up our harps.
> It was there that our tyrants
> Demanded of us songs,
> And our tormentors a song that was merry
> "Sing us a song of Sion!" (they said)
> How could we sing God's songs
> In a land that was strange! (Psalm cxxxvi)

Who can forget that psalm, so doleful, so pathetic in every line? What the pagan Babylonians did to the chosen people when they were in exile, that same thing do scoffers and bitter critics nowadays attempt when they malign Catholics who are true to their faith in Jesus Christ and His Church.

The one thing for all of us is to keep close to our Lord, confident that He will vindicate us against all the world. God and yourself make a majority that can overcome a host of enemies. It pained the exile in the Judica Me to know that he was debarred from worshiping God before the tabernacle. Only sin can debar us from that great privilege. We are far from perfect. We need many helps from our Lord. But, most of all, we need His constant friendship; his forgiveness for all our sins. Better beseech the Lord, like the psalmist, to bring us back to His good graces, back to Sion. And let us use every means to please him who is our God, the health of our countenance, the joy of youth. This we can do by approaching God with a humble, contrite heart and with a confession of unworthiness upon our lips.

We shall need to have this spirit of a contrite heart, which God will never despise. We must ask, too, for fullest for-

SEMITIC CAPTIVES (PROBABLY ISRAELITES)
They are playing on lyres, guarded by an Assyrian warrior. Echoes of that sad captivity are found in IV Kings xv and xvii.

giveness from God before whose altar we kneel. Hence the Church urges us in the Mass to say the Confiteor. That is just what the priest does here in the Mass. And when he has finished the altar boy says the same prayer:

A. Confiteor Deo omnipotenti, beatæ Mariæ semper Virgini, beato Michaeli Archangelo, beato Joanni Baptistæ, sanctis Apostolis Petro et Paulo, omnibus Sanctis, et vobis, fratres: quia peccavi nimis cogitatione, verbo et opere: mea culpa, mea culpa, mea maxima culpa.

A. I confess to Almighty God, to blessed Mary ever Virgin, to blessed Michæl the Archangel, to blessed John the Baptist, to the holy apostles Peter and Paul, to all the saints, and to you, brethren, that I have sinned exceedingly in thought, word, and deed;

14 THE MASS

Ideo precor beatam Mariam semper Virginem, beatum Michaelem Archangelum, beatum Joannem Baptistam, sanctos Apostolos Petrum et Paulum, omnes Sanctos, et vos, fratres, orare pro me ad Dominum Deum nostrum.

through my fault, through my fault, through my most grievous fault. Therefore I beseech the blessed Mary ever Virgin, blessed Michæl the Archangel, blessed John the Baptist, the holy Apostles Peter and Paul, all the saints, and you, brethren, to pray to the Lord our God for me.

P. Misereatur vestri omnipotens Deus, et, dimissis peccatis vestris perducat vos ad vitam æternam.
A. Amen.

P. May Almighty God have mercy upon you, forgive you your sins, and bring you unto life everlasting.
A. Amen.

Signing himself with the sign of the cross, the priest says:

P. Indulgentiam, absolutionem, et remissionem peccatorum nostrorum, tribuat nobis omnipotens et misericors Dominus.
A. Amen.

P. May the almighty and merciful Lord grant us pardon, absolution, and remission of our sins.
A. Amen.

The Mass speaks to us of the need of contrition and confession. These are made manifest at the earliest moment. The priest, standing before the lowest step of the altar, recites the liturgical confession; bowing down, he prays to God for forgiveness of his sins. As we say the same prayer let us recognize that we are co-actors in this divine drama, "the most wonderful and impressive drama in the world."

The individual soul, conscious of its weakness and its unworthiness, approaches the high court of Heaven. Saints and angels numberless are ranged about the throne of the great King. And the soul, throwing itself down in the presence of that splendid company, makes its humble avowal of guilt, to God, to the Most Blessed Mother, to individual angels and saints, to all the assemblage of the blessed. It bows lower and lower, the dramatic contrast of its own sinfulness with the purity of the just making itself more and more vivid. And from the beautiful climax of "mea culpa, mea culpa, mea maxima culpa," it rises to a series of invocations, fittingly concluding with an appeal for intercession before the Lord our God.[1]

A great English statesman used to say that the worst curse on his age (nineteenth century) was that it had lost its sense of sinfulness. To have this "spirit of insensibility: eyes that they should not see, ears that they should not hear" is a terrible thing. It means that pride has made people so blind to their real selves that they are thoroughly self-satisfied; they imagine they are perfect, that there is no room for improvement. Such pride is simply "borrowed majesty, stolen arrogance."

Let no one boast that he is faultless or without sin. We need the help of God and His angels and our patron saints to keep us upright. For all have faults and frailties and if we confess our sins, God is just, and will forgive. God is ready to forgive us when we are honest and open in our acknowledgment of guilt. Heaven knows we have need of repentance and confession. Certainly God likes us to show the sorrow of our inmost being. Wise Mother Church likes to see us do just that. Even though it is not easy, still

MARY MAGDALENE

[1] Brother Leo, "Religion and the Study of Literature," pp. 74, 75.

it is part of the way we secure forgiveness. Somebody truly said: "It is impossible to forgive one, in the strict sense of the term, who excuses himself for the injury he has done us; or who does not acknowledge, at least inwardly, that he is inexcusable." Hence the necessity of frankly admitting to God our sins, offenses, negligences.

Nothing is more necessary in religious life than a practical realization of our sinfulness, as also the knowledge that sin is more than the folly of self-hurt; it is an offense against God. It is natural to confess sin and unworthiness before engaging in so solemn an act as the Mass. God's anger against sin and the sinner is a deep, awful truth. Thus one must appeal to His gentleness and mercy, one should seek forgiveness. This is done in the Mass when the priest bends low and makes open confession of his sins.

The custom is not in any way new. The Jewish priests of the Old Law confessed their sins before offering sacrifices, in such terms as these: "Verily, O Lord, I have sinned, I have done amiss and dealt wickedly: I repent and am ashamed of my doings, nor will I ever return to them."

There is, of course, nothing unseemly in the priest making this public and official confession. It is right, proper, and becoming to do this, since it is a self-cleansing in preparation for the great sacrifice with its graces. When the priest says the Confiteor, he assumes an attitude of humility, he appears as a humble penitent, acknowledging his sins and striking his breast, the usual gesture of sorrow; after which he petitions God, and asks all to petition Him for the one thing he most needs, forgiveness. For only in this spirit of humility and with a contrite heart will he be able worthily to offer the holy sacrifice. The same feeling prompts the people to say the Confiteor, in which you not only say "I have sinned," but you say "I confess that I have sinned,"

CONFITEOR

implying that you feel the need and know the nature of the act of confession.

The liturgical confession, as it is called, is made at the lowest step of the altar. It was a form of general confession (before everybody) and was called the "Confiteor." The double form is used in Mass — that is, the priest says the prayer to the people, the people say it (through the server) to the priest. In so doing they are following a very ancient practice. "Confess your sins one to another: and pray one for another, that you may be saved" (James v, 16). That is just what is done before the priest ascends the altar steps.

If we keep our sins in sight, we will be less likely to fall easily into them again. If we say the Confiteor from the bottom of our heart, God will cast our sins behind His back; if we remember them, God will forget them. And if we truly love Christ, the deeper will be our regret that we should have offended Him by our gross and selfish conduct. "A faithful saying, and worthy of all acceptation, that Christ Jesus came into this world to save sinners, of whom I am the chief" (I Epistle to Timothy i, 15). If we are truly aware of our sins, that will be our feeling. The parable of the Pharisee and the publican makes clear how greatly God is pleased by the honest, heartfelt acknowledgment of sin. Study that parable in Luke xviii, 9–14.

From now on, two things must be kept in mind:

1. The priest stands throughout the Mass. As a rule the ancients prayed standing and mostly with upraised hands. But the congregation kneel for the most part, because kneeling came to be considered a more fitting attitude of worship for all in whose name the priest was offering sacrifice. In one history of the Mass, we read:

> As a general rule the churches of early days had no seats for the people to sit on, as that position was deemed ill in keeping with the gravity be-

coming the house of God. As the services, however, were much longer than at present, those who, through feebleness of health or other causes, could not stand, were allowed the use of staves to lean upon, and in some rare cases even of cushions to sit upon — a practice which is yet quite common in the churches of Spain and in many of those of the rest of Europe. It was the rule to stand always on Sunday, in memory of our Lord's glorious resurrection, and to kneel the rest of the week. As kneeling is a sign of humiliation, it was the rule to observe it during the penitential seasons and on all occasions of mourning. According to St. Jerome, St. Basil the Great, Tertullian, and others, these rules were derived from the Apostles themselves. Whenever any important prayer or lesson was to be read, and the people had been kneeling beforehand, the deacon invited them now to stand, by the words, *Erecti stemus honeste;* that is, "Let us become erect and stand in a becoming manner." During the penitential season the congregation was invited to kneel by saying, "*Flectamus genua,*" and to stand up afterwards by "*Levate.*" The same custom may yet be observed in Lent and on some other occasions.

2. Many times you hear psalms or parts of psalms recited in the Mass. Even before the Confiteor the priest recited the "Judge me, O God" (Psalms xlii). The early Christians made great use of the psalms, learning them by heart or repeating them over, or singing them while at work. St. Paul tells his early Christians to "speak to themselves in psalms and hymns and spiritual canticles, singing and making melody in your hearts to the Lord" (Epistle to the Ephesians v, 19). They would sing snatches of psalms, certain verses easy to be understood. These verses came to be the recognized form, and were gradually taken over and used in the Mass and in the liturgy generally. The priest would begin the verse and the people would take it up and finish it. Thus you find fragments of the psalms incorporated in the Mass liturgy.

Forever and ever, Amen.
Our help is in the name of the Lord, who made heaven and earth!

CONFITEOR

Apart from the verses found in the Mass it were well for every Catholic to form a literary and spiritual acquaintance with the Psalter or Book of Psalms. They form the framework of the Church's liturgy and they are the flower of a great literature. Dom Cabrol, one of the greatest of living authorities on the Roman liturgy, says:

> The psalms, as is well known, belong to the lyric poetry of the Hebrews, who, in this branch of literature, have never, in the opinion of excellent judges, been surpassed by any people, not even by the Greeks. No other lyric poet soars with so strong and bold a flight as David or the prophets, nowhere do we find strains more full of vigour, more heartfelt or more profound. These divine psalms breathing forth such varying accents of prayer and praise, of humble supplication, of true contrition, and of every emotion of the human soul in the worship of God, have been repeated by each generation of Christians, and in them the saints have found the truest expression of their aspiration. Study, then, this book.

How many young Catholics have, we wonder, ever dipped into the Book of Psalms? As an illustration of some of the gems there, take the following:

Psalm xxii	The shepherd's song to God
Psalm xxxiv	The war song of Israel
Psalm xliv	A wedding song
Psalm lxxi	A prophecy concerning Bethlehem
Psalm lxxxiii	A pilgrim's chorus
Psalm cxxx	A song to be sung before your examinations
Psalm cxxxii	A song of good fellowship

III

THE ALTAR STONE

After the absolution the priest says further prayers; then, extending his hands, he goes up the steps, bows down over the altar, and kisses it.

The Confiteor once said, there comes this touching petition recited by the priest and the altar boy:

P. Deus, tu conversus vivificabis nos.
A. Et plebs tua lætabitur in te.

P. Ostende nobis, Domine, misericordiam tuam.
A. Et salutare tuum da nobis.
P. Domine, exaudi orationem meam.
A. Et clamor meus ad te veniat.

P. Dominus vobiscum.
A. Et cum spiritu tuo.

P. Thou shalt turn again, O God, and quicken us.
A. And thy people shall rejoice in thee.

P. Show us, O Lord, Thy mercy.
A. And grant us Thy salvation.
P. O Lord, hear my prayer.
A. And let my cry come unto Thee.

P. The Lord be with you.
A. And with thy spirit.

Going up the steps of the altar, the priest again pleads for forgiveness in order that he may be made worthy to approach the great sacrifice. Even he, as the rest of us, is helpless without God's mercy.

P. Oremus.
P. Aufer a nobis, quæsumus, Domine, iniquitates nostras: ut ad Sancta Sanctorum puris mereamur mentibus introire. Per Christum Dominum nostrum. Amen.

P. Let us pray.
P. Take away from us our iniquities, we beseech Thee, O Lord: that we may be worthy to enter with pure minds into the Holy of Holies. Through Christ our Lord. Amen.

THE ALTAR STONE

Nor has the end of the plea come yet. The moment the priest reaches the altar, he bends low enough to kiss the altar, and prays that the saints will intercede for all the faithful:

Oramus te, Domine, per merita Sanctorum tuorum, quorum reliquiæ hic sunt, et omnium Sanctorum, ut indulgere digneris omnia peccata mea. Amen.	We beseech Thee, O Lord, by the merits of Thy saints, whose relics are here, and of all Thy saints, that Thou wouldst vouchsafe to forgive me all my sins. Amen.

Outwardly these words are accompanied by the act of the priest bowing low and touching the altar with his lips. Not only now, but several times in the Mass the priest kisses the altar. We should know that this is done: because the altar stone is a symbol of Christ; because it contains relics of the saints.

Later on in the Mass we shall be gathered around Jesus. He shall rest on that altar stone which will be enriched with His presence. Thereon He shall offer His life to His heavenly Father. The stone is a symbol of Christ; that is, it teaches our mind much about Him, and helps to keep before us some of our Lord's most vital lessons. The altar stone stands for Christ. It was Christ Himself Who said that He was

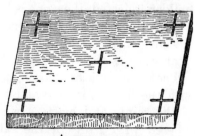

AN ALTAR STONE

The relics of martyrs repose in the *loculus* (under the center cross), which is sealed, then covered.

"the stone which the builders rejected." The Jews were the builders, whose duty it was to erect a spiritual temple. They failed to do so. Then our Lord came. Of Him the prophet had spoken: "Behold, I lay in Sion a chief corner stone, elect, precious. And he that shall believe in Him, shall not be confounded" (I Epistle of St. Peter ii, 6). From old days it was told that the Messias would be the corner stone of the spiritual temple. This temple would be built up of His people ("living stones") to take the place of the old Jewish temple with its imperfect sacrifices. Christ came to unite all men, Jew and Gentile, just as the corner stone unites the two walls. Thus our Lord willed to unite the Jews and Gentiles in the true faith. Christ was God's Son, sent to redeem and unite all men. But the Jews rejected the message of the Redeemer, wherefore our Lord rebuked them and told them how futile would be their opposition to His teaching (Matthew xxi, 33–46). The head of the corner is the most important position in a building, so that Christ (in Matthew xxi, 42) represents Himself, as what He really was, viz., the foundation upon which God's kingdom was to be built despite His rejection by the self-blinded people of Israel. "The stone which the builders rejected, the same is become the head of the corner. This is the Lord's doing: and it is wonderful in our eyes" (Psalms cxvii, 22–23). No wonder the priest kisses the altar stone as the symbol of Christ.

The second reason why he does so is intimately connected with the first: for in that altar stone are contained relics of the saints and martyrs who stood close to Christ and suffered with Him for the sake of the kingdom. In the center of the altar stone a hole is dug, in which rests the relics of the saints, placed there by the bishop. Then it is sealed, covered with linen, marked with five red crosses, and set into the table of the altar. Quite likely the origin of the relics on the altar is traceable to the days of persecution when the Christians heard Mass in the catacombs which were full of the graves of the early martyrs. The stone coffins of the martyrs were used for altars, and so the

THE ALTAR STONE

priest often said Mass on the table of the coffin in which reposed the body of a martyr.

Speaking about these tombs, an authority says:

Another form of interment was that in the table tomb or *sepolcro a mensa*, an oblong chest either hollowed out in the living rock, or built up of masonry slabs of stone or large tiles, and closed by a heavy slab of marble lying horizontally on the top, forming a table. The rock was excavated above the tomb to form a rectangular recess. When the niche assumed a circular form, which is the more frequent though not the earlier shape, it is known by the name of arcosolium. Both forms of tomb are met with in the galleries among the loculi, but their more usual position is in the sepulchral chambers, or cubicula, which opened out of the gal-

TABLE TOMB

ARCOSOLIUM

leries. The table tomb sometimes stands in front of the wall, projecting from it, like the altar tombs of our own churches. Examples of this arrangement appear in the tombs of the presbyters Eusebius and Gregorius in the papal crypt in the cemetery of St. Callistus. More frequently it is set into the wall, and stands in a recess, as we see in the tomb assigned by De Rossi to St. Zephyrinus, which formed the original altar in the same crypt and that of St. Cornelius in the same catacomb.[1]

Since that time the custom grew of always having relics under the altar table. The Church, you know, clings to the old customs because they link us with the olden days, waken in us the historic sense, and show us how our Church is the mother of the ages.

If you have ever been in a cathedral church, you have noticed the cathedra, or the chair of the bishop. In the catacombs, even to-day, you can see the seat cut in the tufa

[1] "Dictionary of Christian Antiquities."

stone, which was intended for the bishop at the time when the persecutions compelled the Christians to hold service there. The crudest kind of chair, set on the side where the Gospel was read, yet it testified to the bishop's authority. In the Mass said in primitive sanctuaries during the earliest ages, benches extended along the wall of the apse (whether in a catacomb or in a private house) from both sides of the cathedra where the bishop sat. Take note how the modern highly adorned bishop's throne is but the continuation of the selfsame idea. The episcopal chair, nowadays, is on the Gospel side of the altar in the cathedral, his episcopal church, to show that he holds authority in that see (*sedes*) over all the faithful of the diocese. "As our fathers did, so also do we" is the idea. Those who read the history of the early ages will be able to recognize dozens of like practices.

The relics of the saints are honored by the Church and are worthy of our veneration for these reasons:

1. For the fidelity they signify. The bodies of the saints were the especially engraced temples of the Holy Ghost; they were so near to God, and they gave all for Him. "If any man serve me," says our Lord, "him will my Father honor, and we will come and make our abode with him." Christ honors the saints; His Father honors them; His Holy Spirit honors them. Since this is so, then we should honor them.

2. For the blessings they bring. Relics have a quasi-sacramental virtue. "Virtue went forth from our Lord and healed people." Notice the account of this in Mark v, 25–34. Our Lord gives this power to many of His saints. Not only does He assure them of the resurrection of their bodies and of their future glory with Him, but before that resurrection the power of His spirit broods over the relics

of those whose deaths were so precious in His sight. He did this for His saints while still in the flesh, "And God wrought by the hand of Paul more than common miracles. So that even there were brought from his body to the sick, handkerchiefs and aprons, and the diseases departed from them, and the wicked spirits went out of them" (Acts xix, 11–12). Nowadays numerous miracles, wrought by application of relics, prove that the power of God's spirit lingers over these remains of saints and martyrs. What is this if not an honor God pays to His saints? Blessed are the dead who die in the Lord, blessed even in our behalf.

3. For a pledge of resurrection. They speak to us of the future destiny of matter in general, of the final glory of creation. The matter composing our bodies is good — the clay made by God's creative act. Death does away with it only for a time. It will come back. The dead shall rise again. That is why Catholics have such great reverence for the dead, for our cemeteries; why we so dislike the very idea of cremation. Surely, the bodies of the saints, their relics, which were so closely knit with their lives, their bodily purity and integrity, appeal strongly to our hearts.

Moreover relics remind us of the power of Christ to raise us from the dead. These bones, fragments of mortal clay even now endowed with miraculous powers, will have a glorious form one day. God will not suffer His holy ones to see corruption. So they remind us of the future resurrection and glorification of this poor body of our humiliation. "O grave, where is thy victory? O death, where is thy sting?" for we shall rise again, glorious and immortal.

In view of this teaching, therefore, it is not at all difficult to understand why the priest kisses the altar so often during Mass. We of the Catholic faith must never forget this lesson of the altar stone, must remember its meaning whenever we see the priest bend down to kiss it. Do you know anything else about altar stones? You know what they mean, but what about their use? It will be interesting to know that the priest must always have with him the altar stone in order to say Mass. Five things he can never dispense with: namely, altar stone, water, wine, chalice, and bread.

Here are a few more interesting things about the altar stone. During the World War our army chaplains carried in their altar kit a stone no bigger than both hands. They said Mass under trees, in trenches, in dugouts, in barns even, when the shells were flying thick and fast, but they always had an altar stone, sometimes resting on a board placed over a barrel or a big box. Take this leaf from the diary of a Catholic chaplain:

August 8th. There is little to record during the next couple of days except the discovery of a new cathedral and the happiness of daily Mass. This time I was not quite so well off, as I could not kneel upright, and my feet were in the water, which helped to keep the fires of devotion from growing too warm. When night fell I made my way to a new part of the line, which could not be approached in daylight, to bury an officer and some men.

Sunday, August 12, 1917. The following morning, though the colonel and other officers pressed me very much to remain with them, on the ground that I would be more comfortable, I felt I could do better work at the advanced dressingstation, or rather aidpost, and went and joined the doctor. The following night a shell burst at the entrance to the blockhouse, but this time exploded several boxes of rockets which had been left at the door. A mass of flame and smoke rushed into the dugout, severely burning some, and almost suffocating all, fifteen in number, You can imagine what I felt as I saw all my friends carried off to hospital, possibly to suffer ill effects for life. I was delighted to find a tiny ammunition store which I speedily converted into a chapel, building an altar with the boxes. I had to be both priest and acolyte, and, in a way, I was not sorry. I could not stand up, so I was able for once to offer the Holy Sacrifice on my knees.[1]

[1] *Dublin Review*, pp. 91-92, 1919; "Chaplains in the Great War."

THE ALTAR STONE

Again you have heard the expression "carrying one's sacristy in his saddlebags." The priest who has to ride across the plains to far-off missions carries all he needs in the saddle — vestments and all, strapped on the horse.

ALTARS AND PLACES OF SACRIFICE

a. Altar, Rome. b. Altar, fifth century. c. Rock Altar (Hebrew). d. Altar, Ravenna. e. Altar, Milan (835). f. Assyrian Altar. g. Phœnician Altar, Malta. h. Persian Fire-altars.

On the ocean, the priest says Mass with a box the size of the top of a desk as an altar. When opened, the top goes back and pasted upon it are the prayers which ordinarily are in frames on the altar. A board is laid over the empty box space upon which is placed an altar stone. Very likely some such arrangement was used on Columbus's ships, the *Niña, Pinta,* and *Santa Maria.* Mass was said on those ships, for there were priests aboard when Columbus crossed the ocean and discovered America in 1492. Long before that time, a Missa nautica, or dry Mass, used to be said at sea. A real Mass could not be said because of the rolling of the ship. When St. Louis of France (1226-1270) was on his way back from the Crusades, the divine office and Mass were said, and the Blessed Sacrament was reserved on his ship. The open-air military Mass originated with the armies of Castile and Aragon in the conflict with the Moslems. Militant priests of the great orders that were trying to defend Christendom from the Eastern hordes celebrated the field Mass with splendor, if campaign conditions permitted, on every Sunday. Interesting facts, surely, and things which every Catholic should know. Do we, as Catholics, take holy pride in these things? Or do we sit placidly by and say nothing about our religion to non-Catholics? If we are true to our love of the Mass, we should want to make such truths known. More than that, we should be anxious to find out new things about the Mass.

1. What priests were with Columbus when he discovered America? 2. Ask one of the Catholic chaplains how and where he said Mass when with the doughboys. 3. Can Mass be said anywhere else than in a church? Explain. 4. Where did the early missionaries in America say Mass? 5. What kind of altars do you like best? 6. Name and describe the appointments of the altar for Mass; for Benediction.

IV

THE INTROIT

The priest goes over to the missal, signs himself with the sign of the cross, and reads the Introit.

The first Roman Ordos describe the Mass as beginning at the Introit when the priest reached the altar. Having kissed the altar table, the priest goes to the right, opens the missal, and reads a short passage, called the Introit, the first words of the Mass proper. Originally this part was sung as the priest was entering the church and approaching the altar. To borrow a phrase, it was a priest's march. Imagine the priest walking toward the altar, and the people singing as he goes. That is the whole idea. *Introitus* = entering. In the old days the Introit was generally a Psalm sung as a fitting accompaniment of the solemn entrance of the celebrant into that part of the church where the altar stood. It was a means of solemnizing the minds of the people before the service began.

With this in view, Pope Celestine (A.D. 423) ordered that many Psalms be sung before Mass. So you see how much the early Christians must have used the Psalms. Indeed, the Book of Psalms was their only hymn book. Pope Celestine ordered Psalms to be sung at the Introit of the Mass, and Pope Gregory later arranged and compiled antiphons for the same. These antiphons, in their scope and workmanship, represent the finest art. Their main idea was to represent the great joy of the congregation at the coming of Christ. The Introit itself is designed, therefore, to bring back the advent of Christ to our mind.

The structure of the Introit consists mainly of scattered verses from the Psalms or detached fragments from the prophets. As a rule, passages from the Psalms and a short piece of prophecy were set together like mosaics to illustrate a truth, point a moral, or embody some special lesson of a feast. To the key words of the Scripture were often added other words with the idea of making the text more clear, or completing the lesson. This is done with perfect art. The idea was taken from Holy Writ and given more adequate expression in the voice of the Church. Examine some of the Introits and see for yourself. You will, no doubt, find each one of them a wonderfully beautiful, exquisitely wrought prayer. Take this one, for Christmas (Second Mass):

Lux fulgebit hodie super nos, quia natus est nobis Dominus, et vocabitur Admirabilis, Deus, Princeps pacis, Pater futuri sæculi, cujus regni non erit finis (Isaias ix).	A light shall shine upon us this day: for our Lord is born to us; and He shall be called Wonderful, God, the Prince of peace, the Father of the world to come; of whose reign there shall be no end (Isaias ix).
Dominus regnavit, decorem indutus est: indutus est Dominus fortitudinem, et præcinxit se (Psalms cii).	The Lord reigneth, He is clothed with majesty; the Lord is clothed with strength, wherewith He hath girded Himself (Psalms xcii).
Gloria Patri, etc. Lux fulgebit, etc.	Glory be to the Father, etc. A light shall shine, etc.

It will be seen that this gem of exquisite setting shows the part of a Psalm, and a fragment of Isaias' prophecy, clustering around the Gloria Patri and shedding their light upon the mystery of the word of God made flesh and dwelling among us. What could be more beautiful, more finely

THE INTROIT

wrought, more divinely artistic! A careful study of the Book of Psalms will give one a better grasp of these Introits.

There are stories of mere children of long ago who knew the Psalms, and joined spontaneously in their recitation. Take the case of the boy Columba destined to become the great light bearer to Britain.

> The little Columba was an apt pupil. It was his delight to accompany his master to the church, there to listen to the chanting of the Divine Office; and so keen of ear and quick of memory was the boy, that he had learnt some of the Psalms by heart before he could spell them out of the Psalter — the lesson-book of every young reader of his time. Cruithnechan, himself, was unaware of this until one day, when he took the child with him on a visit to a brother priest near Derry. The two clerics went together to church to recite the Divine Office, and Columba, as was his wont, knelt to pray before the altar. Now it came to pass that Cruithnechan lost his place, and was in great distress because he could not find it again. The Office came to a standstill, and the pause would have been a long one had not the boy's clear treble voice taken up the Psalm where the old man had halted, and chanted sweetly the alternate verses until the missing place was found.

If you have not already realized the importance of the Psalms, just study these points:

1. The Psalms should be very near and dear to us for very many reasons. They are used widely in the Mass. The Introit, Offertory, the Lavabo, and Communion furnish examples. Furthermore, fragments of them are found everywhere in the Eucharistic service, a verse here, a verse there; as in the Preface, Sanctus, etc. All of this shows how much use was made of the Psalms by the early Christians who learned them by heart, loved to cite them, sang them while at work, talked about their meaning, prayed with them. The Book of Psalms is for many reasons the very best textbook you can use.

2. Our Lord dearly loved the Psalms. He used to read them, as a little child, in the carpenter shop of Joseph. Doubtless, too, He sang little snatches of them, as you might hum a hymn. Can you not imagine Him talking them over with His blessed Mother? Then when He was twelve years old and went to the temple, for the Pasch: "Mary and Joseph found him in the temple, sitting in the midst of the doctors, hearing them and asking them questions. And all that heard him were astonished at his wisdom and his answers" (Luke ii, 46–47). Quite possibly He was discussing those Psalms which pointed to Himself as the Messiah, and yet the rabbis did not know Him. Undoubtedly the young Christ sang the beautiful Psalms which were part of that rite called the Passover, the great historical festival of the Jews. Year after year our Lord took part in this feast, "a living drama," in which were recalled the great facts of the national deliverance from Egyptian bondage.

3. The Gospels which our Lord preached are full of reference to David and the Psalms. Indeed our Lord was entirely familiar with those prayers and He quotes David time and again when speaking to the scribes and Pharisees as well as to His disciples. He sang those Psalms, too, in company with His disciples at the Last Supper which was in part the Pasch, in part the Mass. "And a hymn being said, they went out unto Mount Olivet" (Matthew xxvi, 30). The hymn thus sung was likely part of the great Paschal Hallel, or Hymn of Praise, consisting of six Psalms, cxii–cxvii. Lastly, on the cross our Lord recited the Psalms. In His greatest agony He cried out in the words of the Psalm, "*Eli, Eli, lamma sabacthani,*" that is, "My God, my God, why hast Thou forsaken me?" (Psalms xxi). In truth, this dreadful Psalm of dereliction may have been written for Christ Himself. It is typical of the life, suffer-

THE INTROIT 33

ings, and victory of Christ, and has been deemed a direct and exclusive prophecy of His Passion. We can piously picture our Saviour on the cross, murmuring this Psalm amid His awful sufferings, raising His voice betimes as He gasped the words in the Aramaic dialect He used, and exclaiming in the very expressions we are familiar with as the "seven last words of Christ on the cross." In point of fact, some of those words belong to Psalm xxi. (Nothing could prove more profitable than to take this Psalm and trace out verse by verse the direct reference to our Lord's life, sufferings, and death.) One can see how accurately the Psalmist portrayed just what came to pass when the Messias was put to death. Read the verses of this Psalm, and you may well believe that Christ Himself in silence continued the Psalm unto the end. Thus, thinking His thoughts, your soul will be united to His. Notice how the actual happenings parallel the words of Psalm xxi.

V. 1. "My God, my God, why hast Thou forsaken me?"
4. "But Thou (the Eternal Father) dwellest in the holy place."
7. "But I am a worm . . . outcast of the people" (Christ rejected by His own people).
8. "All they that saw me have laughed me to scorn" (the Jews and the soldiers at the foot of the cross).
12–14. Refers to the mob on Calvary heights.
15–16. The awful sufferings on the cross.
17. The nails in our Lord's limbs.
19. The soldiers quarreling over Christ's seamless garment.
23–32. The fruits of Christ's sufferings and death.

Pay more attention to the Psalms as you study the Mass. It is essential that you learn more about Christ and love Him. "This is eternal life that you know God the Father, and Jesus Christ whom He has sent." The Psalms will make you think. They were our Lord's textbook. He knew them by heart.

THE MASS

Through His life, even unto death, Christ used the Psalms. Could anything make them more precious in our eyes than that fact? Let us know them really and actively master some of them. That is just what the Church does in the Mass.

1. What are the Penitential Psalms? Why say them? 2. Do you know the difference between a Psalm and a Canticle? 3. Where else in the Mass do you find the Psalms used? 4. What is your favorite Psalm? Write a theme on it. 5. The greatest short story in the world is the Parable of the Prodigal Son. Which do you think the greatest song? Why? 6. Explain the difference between an ode, a psalm, a proverb, a parable, an epic, a hymn. 7. Name a good bookshelf for every Catholic student. 8. The priest reads many Psalms every day when he recites his breviary. Why?

V

KYRIE ELEISON

After the Introit, the priest returns to the middle of the altar, where with hands joined he recites aloud the Kyrie Eleison, a plea to God.

P.	Kyrie eleison	P.	Lord, have mercy
A.	Kyrie eleison	A.	Lord, have mercy
P.	Kyrie eleison	P.	Lord, have mercy
A.	Christe eleison	A.	Christ, have mercy
P.	Christe eleison	P.	Christ, have mercy
A.	Christe eleison	A.	Christ, have mercy
P.	Kyrie eleison	P.	Lord, have mercy
A.	Kyrie eleison	A.	Lord, have mercy
P.	Kyrie eleison	P.	Lord, have mercy

You will notice that Kyrie eleison is not Latin. Most of the language of the Mass is Latin; but you will find words of two other languages, Greek and Hebrew. These three are called "dead languages" because they are rarely used in these days.

Just as Latin, Greek, and Hebrew are little spoken, so to say, it may easily happen that in ages to come English, French, and German may become "dead languages" and others rise up in new civilizations to take their place. Yet the Mass will go on and Latin, Greek, and Hebrew will be in the Mass even till the end of time. Christ promised to protect His Church through all the ages, and the Mass will never be abandoned while men inhabit the earth.

Hebrew, Greek, and Latin were all spoken in Palestine when Christ lived there. His own native tongue was a

St. Matthew
A peculiar representation from a Mosaic of the fifth century

form of Hebrew (Aramaic). This was the language the Apostles spoke. When Peter, taken off his guard by the maidservant, denied Christ, he was himself betrayed by his Galilæan burr. Read about the incident in Matthew xxvi, 71-73.

Hebrew

"Matthew then composed the Logia (sayings of our Lord) in the Hebrew tongue, etc.," says Papias.

"Amen," "Hosannah," recall that Jesus was born of the Hebrew race.

"He shall be called a Nazarene" (Matthew ii, 23). Said of the Messias.

"Talita cuma" (talita = girl) (Mark v, 41). (Study that miracle!)

"Ephpheta." "Be opened" (Mark vii, 34). Said to the deaf man.

"Boanerges," which is, the Sons of Thunder (Mark iii, 17). Mark uses Aramaic expressions a number of times. See vii, 11, and xiv, 36.

"Cephas": "Thou art Peter, Cephas, and upon this rock I will build my church" (John i, 42; Matthew xvi, 18).

"Eli, Eli, lama sabacthani?" My God, My God, why hast Thou forsaken me? (Matthew xxvii, 46). Words of Christ on the cross.

Greek

St. John (xii, 20-23) tells how certain Greeks of Galilee came to Philip and asked that they might have a conversation with our Lord. And Jesus answered them. Just then He gave His last public utterance; it was on the Gentile question.

It is quite probable that our Lord spoke Greek, for there were many Greeks throughout His beloved Nazareth.

KYRIE ELEISON

Remember that the whole New Testament was written in Greek.

The language of the Roman Catholic Church continued to be Greek both in its literature and in its worship till the end of the second century. The writings of many early Popes and Christian teachers were in Greek; also you see early Greek inscriptions and drawings in the Catacombs.

All the first converts to Christianity spoke Greek, all the liturgies were originally in that language. No sooner was the faith brought to the West than the Mass was celebrated there — in Rome as well as in Palestine. The Greek language of the liturgy changed to Latin quite naturally as soon as the Greek language ceased to be the usual language of the Roman Christians. "By the second half of the third century the usual liturgical language at Rome seems to have been Latin, though fragments of Greek remained for many centuries. Latin is naturally terse, compared with the rhetorical abundance of Greek." It is not known exactly when Latin was adopted in the services at Rome, but the Church there had been founded more than a century and a half before it produced a single Latin writer. The first among ecclesiastical authors to use Latin was Pope St. Victor I (A.D. 191–203).

Latin

Pilate, who was the Roman governor of Judea during our Lord's ministry, sufferings, and death, ordered the sign put on the cross in three languages, Latin, Greek, and Hebrew.

"IESUS NAZARENI REX IUDEORUM."

"Jesus of Nazareth, King of the Jews!"

This is the "INRI" on our crucifix.

Latin, of course, is the language of the Church. The reason why Latin supplanted Greek in the greater part of the Western World is not hard to find. The spread of the Roman Empire, and the fact that its official language, Latin, was also the language of the see of Peter (Rome) show why the prayers and services of the Church became and remain Latin. Where Latin is not used for the Mass, a dead language still obtains, such as Syriac or Greek. They are used for fear that a new language might not catch and hold the true meaning of the Mass. Old languages preserve the ideas of words, like butterflies in amber. Once in the seventeenth century the missionaries to China appealed to Rome for permission to say Mass in the native language. The people found Latin extraordinarily difficult, utterly unlike their own in structure. The Church gave them permission to use Chinese; but insisted that the old classical Chinese, a dead language as changeless as Latin, be used instead of the ordinary speech of the people.

Listen to what a modern statesman has to say on this subject of using a dead tongue for the language of worship. "There is no Church," says Lloyd George, "that has made a surer and deeper search into human nature. Roman Catholics conduct their worship in the language of worship. Their Church utilizes every means of taking people beyond everyday interests; the language of commerce and of everyday occupation is left outside, and the people are taught the language of worship. That shows a shrewd, deep insight into the human mind."

Observe, finally, this Kyrie eleison which in Greek is said thus:

Kyrie eleison (3 times).	Lord (the Father), have mercy on us.
Christe eleison (3 times).	Christ (the Son), have mercy on us.
Kyrie eleison (3 times).	Lord (the Holy Ghost), have mercy on us.

These nine invocations have been said in the Mass for nearly 1500 years. In a very ancient book there is an account of how St. Cæsarius, Bishop of Arles, explains that in Rome and the churches of the East they said *Kyrie eleison* over several times "with much love and compunction." So we should say it, for this is a real prayer to be said for ourselves with much sorrow for our sins, and for others who may need God's mercy.

KYRIE ELEISON

1. What is mercy? How does it differ from piety, sympathy, condolence? 2. Name four instances in our Lord's life where He displayed singular mercy toward sinners. 3. In what languages did the Apostles preach the Gospel? 4. Can you show how the Latin language is peculiarly adapted to express the doctrines of the Church? 5. The Church is Catholic — that is, world-wide. From that fact, what would you argue as to the language employed by her? 6. The changes that have occurred in living languages, such as French, German, English, Italian, Polish, are deep and radical. How does that show the Church's wisdom?

VI

GLORIA IN EXCELSIS

Standing at the middle of the altar, the priest extends his hands, then joins them; and, slightly bowing, he says the Gloria in Excelsis.

This song of joy is sung or said in the Mass most of the time, except in Lent and Advent when the priest wears purple vestments. It is a translation from an old Greek hymn sung in the early centuries. There were, as you know, many hymns composed by the early Christians as far back as the first century. Most of them have been lost. A most interesting fragment of an early Christian hymn is found in St. Paul's Epistle to the Ephesians v, 14. It runs thus:

> Awake, thou that sleepest!
> Arise from the dead!
> Christ shall give to thee light.

Most of these early hymns were modeled on the Psalms written by David, the Psalter being the only public hymn book used. These in time were sung during the Eucharistic sacrifice and soon became an outstanding feature of the service. Pliny the Younger (A.D. 62–114) sent in an official report to Trajan telling the emperor that the Christians met and sang a hymn to Christ. The Roman authorities kept a sharp outlook on the early Christians. Observe how the Roman historian Tacitus (A.D. 53–117) published a nasty calumny about them, together with some information as to the spread of the Church. These are his words, and they are the earliest pagan reference to the infant Church: "This denomination had its origin from Christus, Who in the reign of Tiberius had been executed by the procurator, Pontius Pilate. The deadly superstition, though suppressed for a time, broke out again and spread not only through Judea, which was first to suffer from it, but through Rome also, the resort which draws to it all that is hideous and shameful." That will give you an idea of how the early Christians were misunderstood and persecuted by the pagans.

Meantime, as we have seen, the primitive Christians were going to Mass and praising God in words taken from the Psalms and Canticles of Holy Scripture. Later on these early chants were supplemented by hymns, original compositions based on the inspired Scriptures. Such was the Gloria in Excelsis, a sort of "private psalm" written in short verses which are very beautiful and full of exultant praise.

Gloria in excelsis Deo.
Et in terra pax hominibus bonæ voluntatis.
Laudamus te.
Benedicimus te.
Adoramus te.
Glorificamus te.
Gratias agimus tibi propter magnam gloriam tuam.
Domine Deus, Rex cœlestis, Deus Pater omnipotens.
Domine Fili unigenite, Jesu Christe.
Domine Deus, Agnus Dei, Filius Patris:
Qui tollis peccata mundi, miserere nobis.

Glory be to God on high.
And on earth peace to men of good will.
We praise Thee;
We bless Thee;
We adore Thee;
We glorify Thee.
We give Thee thanks for Thy great glory.
O Lord God, heavenly King, God the Father Almighty.
O Lord, the Only-begotten Son Jesus Christ;
O Lord God, Lamb of God, Son of the Father,
Who takest away the sins of the world, have mercy on us:

Qui tollis peccata mundi, suscipe deprecationem nostram.	Thou Who takest away the sins of the world, receive our prayer.
Qui sedes ad dexteram Patris, miserere nobis.	Thou Who sittest at the right hand of the Father, have mercy on us.
Quoniam tu solus sanctus.	For Thou only art holy:
Tu solus Dominus.	Thou only art the Lord:
Tu solus altissimus, Jesu Christe.	Thou only, O Jesus Christ,
Cum sancto Spiritu, in gloria Dei Patris. Amen.	With the Holy Ghost, are most high in the glory of the Father. Amen.

The first part of the hymn is found in St. Luke ii, 13–14, where he describes what happened on the first Christmas night. The first to sing these joyful words were the angels who announced to the shepherds the birth of Christ. So it was in the early dawn, on the hills outside Bethlehem, that those heavenly messengers announced to the shepherds that the Messias was born for Whom the Hebrews had been waiting a thousand years. Thus the first part of that hymn came from heaven.

The second part, beginning with "We praise Thee, we bless Thee; we adore Thee; we glorify Thee!" was added to the hymn by the early Fathers of the Church. In the life of a Greek virgin this was one of her early morning customs of praiseful prayer. Later on the whole hymn of the angels plus the extra-angelic prayer and praise were put in the Mass. It is a very joyful hymn and full of praise to God, and it is said with a spirit of joyous welcome to the Saviour soon to appear again on our altar in the holy sacrifice wherein He will come to us to be welcomed by the faithful attending Mass. It will soon be visitation time. It is in the Mass that Christ makes His periodic visitation to our hearts.

Young voices, clear and high; young hearts, lifted in prayer, these are what God wants. Let us, then, sing this

GLORIA IN EXCELSIS

song of praise, as we give our minds, our hearts, and our voices to welcome the coming Saviour. Speaking of our myriad-throated prayer, such as the Gloria in Excelsis, a stranger at our gates, Israel Zangwill, has said:

> There are two torrents that amaze me — the one is Niagara and the other the outpouring of reverent prayer falling perpetually in the Catholic Church. What with Masses and the Exposition of the Host, there is no day nor moment of the day in which the praises of God are not being sung somewhere — in noble churches, in dim crypts, and underground chapels, in cells and oratories. Niagara is indifferent to spectators, and so the ever-falling stream of prayer. As steadfastly and unremittingly as God sustains the universe, so steadfastly and unremittingly is He acknowledged, the human antiphony answering the divine strophe.

That is as it should be. There is every need of such public confession of God on the part of His creatures. "Let all peoples give thanks to Thee, O Lord!" Nor can public worship be more potent than in the Mass; for the Mass is Christ's own act, in which we are privileged to join, with our own praise, reverence, and homage. Here, then, it is very important that our lips as well as our heart should pay due praise "in the courts of the House of the Lord." If we do this, we cannot but feel the heroism and glory of our faith — that victory which alone can overcome the world.

1. Why is the Gloria omitted in Masses for the dead? 2. Point out how this hymn honors the Holy Trinity. 3. Have you learned to sing the hymn in the Gregorian form? 4. Do you know any "Glorias" written by Catholic composers?

GLORIA IN EXCELSIS DEO!

VII

DOMINUS VOBISCUM

*The priest kisses the altar, and, turning to the people, says:
"Dominus vobiscum," an ancient form of devout salutation.*

The spirit of joy pours forth from the Gloria to the next prayer. It is, as it were, contagious; it must spread itself. So after the Gloria in Excelsis the priest kisses the altar, then turns, faces the people, and opening his hands, says (or sings):

Dominus vobiscum.   The Lord be with you.

The altar boy (or the choir) replies in your name:

Et cum spiritu tuo.   And with thy spirit.

This is the way the early Christians saluted one another; and it is said to have been thus handed down by the Apostles. St. Paul, we know (Colossians iv, 18; II Thessalonians iii, 17–18), gives instructions in his letters to salute so and so. At the close of his epistles you find rich and full salutations at parting just as at meeting. In the East this is done to this day — the same idea. "In all things the Semites will proffer God's name whether for good or for evil." Customs remain the same for thousands of years; they do not change as in new countries. In Syria, to-day, when one goes by a field where men are working, or meets another wayfarer on the road, he salutes: "The Lord prosper you," or "Peace be to you"; and the answer is: "Blessed is he that cometh" or "The Lord be with your spirit."

Now the priest says this to you in order to pass on, so to say, our Lord's spirit to you. He does this eight times in the Mass. "May the Lord be with you," he says, because so long as you are in a state of grace you are really a part of our Lord. That is what is called the Mystical Body. Our Lord is the head, we are the members. Our Lord Himself uses another figure. "I am the vine; you the branches." See just what He meant by studying John xv, 1–10. Try to keep that picture well in mind. The Church is the vineyard, Christ the vine, and the congregation the branches.

When the priest says, with sincere desire, "Dominus vobiscum," he wants the Lord to be with you. He has just been speaking to the Lord, but now turns to you to say that he hopes that grace will be poured like the red life-giving sap from the vine into the branches. He wishes that our Lord's life will flow into your soul, and that thus, "we, being many, are one body in Christ, and every one members of one another" (Epistle to the Romans xii, 5). You should make it a point to say with all your heart: "Et cum spiritu tuo." You should also invoke the divine blessing on the priest. Thereby you want God to be with the priest, just as he wants God to be close to your heart. The priest is near to God's altar; you pray that he may have God's life more and more in him, for if the priest is full of the love of God, then he can lead the people nearer and nearer to Heaven.

You will notice that the priest when saying Dominus vobiscum extends his hands and opens his arms with reverence and affection to indicate the blessing is for all the people. In the early days of the Church when the priest greeted the people, all the faithful answered just as a choir does to-day. But now the altar boy answers; none the less you should say the same words inwardly from the fullness of your heart, for you thus really wish him the joy that the Lord may be with his spirit.

To make real your Dominus vobiscum, remember that it is not by our mind only but also by our actions that we are brought into contact with our Lord. It is not enough to say Dominus vobiscum, we must also translate it into action. Suit the action to the word. Set the example of what you teach. We should know exactly what the Dominus vobiscum demands of us. If put in practice, it achieves this: The Lord once with you, the Lord is on your side. Then you must stay with Him and do His will. Imagine standing at a companion's side, and yet playing or working against him. That is treachery. Speaking of this, our Lord said: "He who is not with me is against me." It is impossible to be neutral in this case.

All of us ought to be with Christ, on His side. Then He can praise our loyalty and say, "You are they who have continued with me." By heart and tongue should we cling to Christ. Until you do that you are not doing your full duty. Love of God is the thing that helps you to do right, for love of Him helps you to surmount all obstacles, face temptations, and even suffer persecutions.

Remember that the one way to be on God's side is to obey Him, and be alert in giving good example. Here is where good example comes in. "You are my friends, if you do the things I have commanded you" (John xv, 14), "For I have given you an example, that as I have done to you, so you do also" (John xiii, 15). Those are the words of our blessed Lord. Lay them as a foundation in your heart. Be awake to the daily need of being close to our Leader, following in His footsteps, giving good example. Now, good example is simply showing that we are in accord with the mind of Christ, giving all a sample of what we stand for in our conduct, showing everybody that we copy from our divine Master. "Let this mind be in you, which was also in Christ Jesus" (Philippians ii, 5). If we are kindred spirits with our Lord, then we can do good to others, always and everywhere. "In all things," says St. Paul, "shew thyself an example of good works (Titus ii, 7). Be thou an example in word, in conversation, in charity, in faith, in chastity" (I Timothy iv, 12).

We are nothing if we are not living up to the laws of God. You realize, of course, that conduct is three-fourths of life; also, that the world will take you for just what you are, and not what you ought to be. In fact, people will know and love you in the very measure that you are worth knowing, and worthy of being loved. Next to one's duty to God comes that duty of loving our neighbor as ourselves. Ninety per cent of converts to the Church come through the silent example of good Catholics. "Example," says Edmund Burke, "is the school of mankind, and they will learn at no other." Amazingly powerful, too, is the force of good example given by Catholic youth. Never forget that many will be ready to follow where you lead. In the world of to-day there is a vast field of work for boys and girls of real worth. Indeed the public look to our Catholic schools as power stations, and our pupils as dynamos of good conduct. Because our students are seen, heard, and studied by others, they are perhaps in the best position to do good by their living earnestness. Not only your parents and friends but the public have their eyes open and observe you in the world's crowded streets.

Nothing gives better evidence of the worth of Catholic education than the good example of Catholic school pupils. Undoubtedly they furnish the most potent proofs of what the Church stands for. It would be the greatest pity if any of our pupils were to fall short in this big thing at a time when the greatest display of high principle is needed in our dear land. Each must do his share to further the Catholic cause. Just before starting out in the morning let us ask ourselves a few questions: "Is my school better for my presence in it? My teachers deserve the best I have, do they get it? Am I living up to the standards of our school daily by giving good example?"

By doing that last, remember, you are offering to others help, encouragement, inspiration! In each day's school life you should lay up a treasure of good conduct and good example. "Grow great by good example and put on the dauntless spirit of resolution." To do that well one has to study the perfect model, Christ. One has also to cultivate a spirited, cheerful, honest temper. Besides, one has to be on guard against false imitation. Every school has at least two kinds of pupils, good and indifferent. All of them have their ideas, all set some sort of example. Everybody, too, has an inclination for imitation, but it makes all the difference in the world *whom* we imitate. Here is just where right principles come in. If you adhere to them, they will save you from imitating the evil you see about you. The whole purpose of the Catholic schools is to instill right principles and to impel youth to right conduct. And the ultimate standard by which we shall be judged, *Dominus vobiscum* or *dominus non vobiscum*, is our good works.

All will be well once good principles and practice are secured. School is a practice place, a training ground where you rub elbows with others and have every chance to show the best in you. Those who think that school is merely the place to have things put into your head are mistaken. It is the place where what is in you is brought out. Education = *educere*, to draw out. The best example comes when you are upstanding, forward looking, and stepping out determinedly and straightforwardly on the road of duty. You want to know what you ought to do? St. Paul tells you in these words: "Whatsoever things are true, whatsoever modest, whatsoever just, whatsoever holy, whatsoever lovely, whatsoever of good fame, if there be any virtue, any praise of discipline, think on these things" (Philippians iv, 8). These are the things for your thought and conduct. Fix your mind on what you have done along these lines and what you can do. School days are the best time to strengthen good habits in the stream of life; as a swimmer whose muscles grow strong the longer and harder he breasts the current. Keep the eyes of your soul on a high goal. The ancient Greeks had a word for man — *anthropos*. It was explained to mean "the looker-up"; that is, one who was not meant to crawl or to be like a beast, but upstanding and noble-minded all his life long. The thing, then, is to keep your soul free from evil, see to it that right principles are planted in your mind, and fear not to be honest and upright even in the presence of the ignoble.

A boy who gives good example is an athlete of Christ. Never is he afraid of the sneer or the curled lip. The aim of his life is to do things decently and according to Divine orders. Actions, he knows, speak louder than words. Manly and courageous, he has engaged himself to his divine Trainer to run a good race. Nothing daunted, he starts afresh every day, for he will not be a quitter. Steadfastly he follows along the narrow path of duty, resolutely keeping to what he knows to be the right way. On and on he goes. He has the spirit and the pluck to set the good pace and stick to it; he goes through what he starts, a good race; no matter how tough the strain, how hard the road. When he does this, others will be likely to follow. As a result, that sort of boy is bound to be the best kind of leader, thoroughly trustworthy.

A girl is no less a leader when she sets a good example to all round about her. She is in class to-day, perfectly dependable, and she will be the same to-morrow. When trying days come, she will prove reliable. The Catholic girl should keep her soul, like a bright, lovely candle, set in a precious candlestick. How needful this is in days like ours when so many growing girls are all for self-indulgence. It would be pathetic were our girls to copy such cheap models. Far be it from them to be lazy, peevish, languid, or listless, when duty looms large before them. "So let your light shine that all may see your good works and glorify your Father who is in heaven." If girls only realized their power for good example! And how humiliating the thought that

MARTYRDOM OF ST. BARBARA

some do disgrace their school and teachers by the bad example they set. A piece of advice which we would like to give to our grown-up girls is to remember that the virtue and goodness of to-morrow's citizens are in their hands. If Catholic girls, especially the older ones, fail to put aside vanity, envy, fear, and jealousy; if they do not make it their business to nip meanness in the bud and uproot the nasty weeds of suspicion which grow wild in the heart; if, in a single phrase, they do not give good example, who, then, will? To whom, pray, can we look later on to stem the tide of evil in this twentieth century? The hard logic of facts makes clear the need of Catholic girl apostleship. They say it is hard for a girl to be a leader, but the noblest leadership, the best example, can be given by girls. It is nonsense to say that you are bravely facing facts and doing your duty unless you are overcoming temptations and giving good example. "You are my friends," says our Lord, "if you do the things which I command you." And you know just what our blessed Lord wants.

As you say your Dominus vobiscum, remember that it calls for a big act — service. The real service, the real leadership, cannot be given unless we follow Him Who is the Way. For all of us it is vastly important to set good example. That, however, is no mere trifle. It requires the grace of God, will power, courage, perseverance. In undertaking this, your work in the world, keep in mind the four things that weaken and the four that strengthen the power of giving good example:

Laziness	Promptness
Irresolution	Firmness to do the right thing
False shame	Fearlessness in the face of criticism
Fear to do the right	Lasting courage of one's conviction

By the above tests pupils stand or fall. Or, as the Great Teacher once said, "By their fruits you shall know them." Very much effort should be spent towards equipping ourselves to give good example. We must learn better not only to do things that are right and refrain from doing things that are wrong, but also what we act for and why. What is right and what is wrong has been settled once for all by the teaching of Christ and His Church. They are the standard against which you can measure yourself. You owe them unflinching obedience. That is what St. Paul calls "your reasonable service," and St. Peter urges, "being ready always to satisfy every one that asketh you a reason of that hope which is in you" (I Peter iii, 15). Now as to results. Are you making your home, your school, your neighborhood better for your presence? You hear many people prate about action, action! Which is all very well. But action is worth little except it is right action. The world is always the worse for wrong action. "The unjust and oppressive, all those in fact who wrong others, are guilty not only of the evil they do, but also of the perversion of mind they cause in those whom they offend." High time to offset such hurt and work hard for righteousness. To put the matter in a nutshell, we need more Christian example to make this world a better place to live in. If you have the will to act right and look to your duty with practical eyes, then you will give good example; you will stand ready to do lasting service to all with whom you come in contact, service to your neighbor, service to your nation. That is what counts. What a day for that work!

1. Being Catholic Christians — that is, followers of Christ and His Church — what is expected of us in the way of good example? 2. Do you think you could name five vivid episodes in the New Testament where our Lord set for His disciples the most glorious example? 3. We

must not neglect to utilize to the full the example our blessed Lord left for us that we should follow in His footsteps. In view of this, give four instances of divine example needful for boys and girls of your time of life. 4. When the Jews were about to act ill, our Lord stayed their bad example. He not only taught them what was right, but showed them how to act. As illustrations of this, read John viii, 3–11; John ix, 2–41; Luke x, 25–37. Those cases are worth the notice of all. Which makes the strongest appeal to you? 5. The Pharisees, who were hypocrites, hated Jesus as soon as they found out that the people were losing confidence in them and going over to the Nazarene. "The chief priests therefore and the Pharisees gathered a council, and said, What do we? for this man does many miracles. . . . From that day therefore they devised to put Him to death." What is pharisaism? 6. Learn the origin of the following expressions, Good-by, Adieu, Godspeed, God's acre. Godsend. 7. "In our day," says a Catholic writer, "there are forces at work with conscious malice and invincible ignorance to undermine God's Church and assail His Vicegerent, the Pope. But there is one thing which diabolic opposition will not do, and cannot do. The Catholic Church is based on a rock and will always stand firm, and ultimately recover from to-day's assault of the evil one." Can you name some sworn foes of the Church to-day? Do you pray for the Pope? What prayer is often said in the Mass? Have you memorized it? 8. Do you know and say a prayer for the priest?

VIII

COLLECT

Immediately after the Dominus vobiscum the priest goes to the right of the altar, extends his hands, bows to the cross, and reads in the Missal the Collect, the Epistle, and the Gradual. While he says the Collect he holds his hands up as if in appeal; but for the others he rests his hands on the book.

The Collect always begins with *Oremus* (let us pray) because it is a prayer for everybody. We say it all together as brothers, members of the Communion of Saints; that is what it means to be Catholics.

The word *Collecta* means people gathered or assembled for worship. In the early Church those people said here several prayers, written usually by the Pope. Thus we have Collects composed by Leo the Great (Pope from 440–461) and Gelasius (Pope from 492–496). Many of the Collects used to-day even by Protestants were written by these and other Popes. They are exceedingly beautiful and of great antiquity. Indeed, they are perfect prayers. At the end of the Litany of the Saints you will find over half a dozen of them. They combine strength with sweetness; with them one is able to say much in saying little, to address the Most High in adoring awe, to utter man's need with profound pathos and with calm intensity, to insist on the absolute necessity of grace, the Fatherly tenderness of God, the might of the all-prevailing Name. They are never weak, never diluted, never ill-arranged, never a provocation to listlessness; they exhibit an exquisite skill of antithesis and a rhythmical harmony which the ear is loath to lose.

COLLECT

Observe how the Collect is said to God, the great God, the one God in Three Persons, and it generally ends: "Through our Lord Jesus Christ." We say "our Lord" because we are His family, members of the Household of the Faith. When we say this prayer, we feel the brotherhood of Christians; Christ, our Lord, is our Elder Brother; God is our Father. Through Christ we pray in the Collect for grace, mercy, and forgiveness.

The Collect accordingly consists of (1) an invocation to God; (2) the object desired by prayer; (3) a pleading of the merits of Christ, or in giving glory to Him.

After the prayers on the first two pages of your Catechism, there are no prayers in the world as beautiful as these Collects. It is easy to see why John Ruskin, though himself a non-Catholic, confessed, "all beautiful prayers are Catholic, all wise interpretations of the Bible Catholic." These Collects, being an achievement of spirituality as well as craftmanship, call for patient study on the part of all. No themes could be more worthy of thought and literary analysis. Try your mind at several of them. Take this for example:

Oremus:	Let us pray:
Da nobis, quæsumus omnipotens Deus: ut qui nova incarnati Verbi tui luce perfundimur; hoc in nostro resplendeat opere, quod per fidem fulget in mente.	Grant, we beseech Thee, almighty God, that filled with the new light of Thy incarnate word, what by Faith shineth in our minds, may show forth in our words.
Per eundem Dominum nostrum Jesum Christum filium tuum. Amen.	Through the same Jesus Christ, Thy Son, our Lord. Amen.

Amen is a Hebrew word which means "really and truly," "so be it," "I agree." When you say *Amen*, you are sealing the request, making the priest's prayer yours, and asking

God to count it as if you had said it. (Up to this point, three languages have been used in the Mass: Latin, Greek, and Hebrew.) This method of expressing concurrence in the prayer of another or in the truth of what another says is very old. The ancient Hebrews used that method frequently (Deuteronomy xxvii, 15). Our Lord often used one or two *Amens* for solemn emphasis (Matthew vi, 13; xxiii, 36).

Sometimes several Collects are said in the Mass: One of them is *Pro Papa*, for the Pope. This last should be studied if time permits. It is exceedingly beautiful in structure as in significance. Do you know where to find it in the Missal? Finding treasures of prayer is a very interesting, instructive, and profitable thing. The wisdom these prayers contain is "more precious than rubies."

Lastly, it may be noticed that the Collect, Epistle, Gradual, and Gospel are linked together in fine unity. They are like a sequence in music and present a beautiful harmony of prayer and thought. From a standpoint of structure and composition, what a perfect work of divinely inspired art the Mass is! Cardinal Newman had every reason in the world to write so beautifully of it: "To me nothing is so consoling, so piercing, so thrilling, so overcoming, as the Mass."

1. Make a literary and spiritual study of the exquisite Collect given in this chapter. If time allows, analyze others. 2. Do you know a Collect for the souls in purgatory, for peace of heart, for good conduct, for forgiveness of sins? 3. Up to this have you been able to tell, when hearing Mass, what is going on at each point? Can you truly say that your study thus far has uplifted and ennobled your outlook on life, and enkindled and renewed your courage in well doing? 4. Have you ever thought of inducing others to study the Mass? Do you give as Christmas or birthday presents such books as the Roman Missal, the New Testament, the "Imitation of Christ"? 5. The best definition of a friend is

this, from Cardinal Newman: "Give me for my friend one who will unite with me heart and hand; who will throw himself into my cause; who will take my part when I am attacked; and who wishes that others may love me as heartily as he." Are you that kind of friend toward our blessed Lord?

IX

EPISTLE

The Collect being said, the priest in an intelligible and clear voice reads the Epistle, holding the book so that the palms of his hands in some way touch the Missal.

After the Collect comes the Epistle. Like a silken thread drawn through cloth of gold, the prayer idea of the Collect runs through the Epistle and later on is found in the Gradual, even in the Gospel. But now for the Epistle, or, as it is sometimes called, the Lesson.

P. Carissime: Apparuit benignitas et humanitas Salvatoris nostri Dei: non ex operibus justitiæ, quæ fecimus nos, sed secundum suam misericordiam salvos nos fecit, per lavacrum regenerationis, et renovationis Spiritus sancti, quem effudit in nos abunde per Jesum Christum Salvatorem nostrum: ut justificati gratia ipsius, hæredes simus secundum spem vitæ æternæ: in Christo Jesu Domino nostro.

A. Deo gratias.

P. Dearly beloved, the goodness and kindness of God our Saviour hath appeared: not by the works of justice, which we have done, but according to His mercy He saved us, by the laver of regeneration, and renovation of the Holy Ghost, whom He hath poured forth upon us abundantly through Jesus Christ our Saviour; that, being justified by His grace, we may be heirs according to hope of life everlasting: in Christ Jesus our Lord.

A. Thanks be to God.

We ought to love the Lesson. In the Mass of the early Church, it was a very significant procedure. Then it was read by a deacon. He first imposed silence, just as a teacher would, by saying: "*Attendamus,* Let us attend and listen to the word of God." "Not," as St. Chrysostom observes, "as doing honor to the reader, but to Him Who speaks to all through the reader." And after the Lesson was read, the words: "Peace be to Thee" were said by the priest.

The Lesson or Lection, from *lectio*, reading, is a little piece of Holy Writ read to us. Sometimes it is taken from the Old Testament, but generally from the New Testament, especially from St. Paul's Epistles, and occasionally from St. Peter's, or one of the other Apostles. These Epistles were public communications written by the Apostles to their congregations, and sometimes to such individuals as Timothy, Titus, Philemon, the slave owner. They aimed at instructing, exhorting, guiding, correcting the early Christians. They are as necessary for us as for them;

SS. PAUL AND LAURENCE
(Catacomb at Naples.)

Paul bears a scrip (epistle) and Laurence a wreath (martyr's crown).

that is why the Church has us read just a bit of the Epistle. There is always some point, which if we read it as we ought, we will understand aright and profit greatly. Take, for example, the Epistle in last Sunday's Mass; look into it, and see what application is to be made of it. Then ask God for the grace to keep the Lesson in mind and put it into practice.

Every Catholic should have a New Testament. That book is the most valuable book in the world, because it contains the real teaching of our Lord. The Gospels in it tell us about the life and words of Christ, and the Epistles are the explanations of what our Lord said and meant, and what He wished all His followers to practice. Hence the importance of the Epistles; hence, too, the custom of the Church to have the Epistle read every day in every Mass all over the world. Which Epistle do you like best? Some are very tender and loving (St. John's); some very practical (St. Peter's, St. James'); some very deep, difficult, theological (St. Paul's). We repeat, the New Testament is the greatest book in the world. Therefore, we ought to study it, learn its lessons, be able to quote from it. St. Ignatius Loyola used to say that the only two worth-while books in the world are the Bible and the "Imitation of Christ." Let us try to understand that and cultivate a love for these two books and a habit of reading them.

During the reading of the Lesson the congregation sits down, after the custom of the ancients. They do not rise till the Gospel. While the priest is reading the Lesson from the Missal, let us read it in our prayer book. To understand the Lesson, we have to keep our minds concentrated on it. Like a mother, the Church comes to us with this Lesson and says: "Now I want you to take these words to heart, and keep them well in mind, for they will do you a world of good if you live up to them. They will keep you from losing faith. They will make you rise above the frivolities and worldliness you see on every side. They will show you how to be genuine Christians."

1. In inditing epistles what implements of writing were used by the Babylonians? by the Egyptians? by the Greeks? by the American Indians? 2. The Romans in a hurry used waxen tablets, *tabulæ*, upon which they wrote with an iron spike, *stilus*. This iron style was broad at the top and pointed below. When the writer made a mistake, he turned the style and with the broad end he erased what had been written. The wax was so soft that lines were thus easily wiped away, much as pencilings were sponged off the old-time school slate. Herein is the origin of the word "sincerity." To the ancient Romans a boy or girl *sine cera* was one who was not like the wax on the tablet; that is, soft, shifty, easily molded,

but firm, sound, steady, genuine, with strong dependable disposition. Of such a one Seneca says: *Bonum habebit sinceritatem suam.* Now what is your idea of sincerity? How do you know when you obey God sincerely? 3. St. Paul wrote many of his Epistles from prison, where he was chained by one arm to a keeper, a Roman soldier. One of those letters, the Epistle to the Ephesians, was very likely written on a strip of papyrus, about four feet in length. When rolled up into a scroll, the little bundle was no longer than ten inches. A trusted messenger would carry this letter to the congregation for whom it was written. Paul knew no fear. "For to me," he declares, "to live is Christ: and to die is gain" (Philippians i, 21). The prison letters of the Apostle are four in number: Colossians, Philemon, Ephesians, and Philippians. As you read them you can hear the clank of the chain upon the writer's arm. "I therefore," he writes, "a prisoner in the Lord beseech you that you walk worthy of the vocation in which you are called" (Ephesians iv, 1). Have you read those Epistles? If so, did you keep track of the prison idea? Suppose you read them once more with this in mind. They are intensely interesting; indeed other prison letters are very feeble efforts with very weak lessons alongside St. Paul's writings which were inspired by the Holy Ghost.

X

GRADUAL

The priest, remaining in the same position, reads the Gradual, with its versicle, two alleluias, and another verse, with an alleluia. A tract and sequence are read according to the time.

The Gradual follows the reading of the Lesson. This used to be done on the step of the *ambo* or pulpit from whence it takes its name — *gradus*, a step. It was recited on the lower step; only the Gospel could be recited on the top step. The Gradual is a sort of anthem or song woven of short texts taken from the Scriptures. As it continues the idea of the Lesson you can see it is a very pretty way to link the Epistle with the Gospel. Originally the Gradual consisted of a whole Psalm, but now it is only a few verses, epitomizing the Epistle. But these few verses are carved so exquisitely that they are little masterpieces, literary and spiritual.

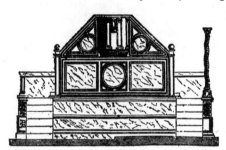

THE AMBO OF ST. LAURENCE AT ROME.

Two and even three existed in some churches; one was then used for the Gospel, one for the Epistle, and one for the reading of the Old Testament.

The Christmas Gradual in the Second Mass is very beautiful:

| Benedictus qui venit in nomine Domini: | Blessed be he that cometh in the name of the Lord! |

GRADUAL

Deus Dominus, et illuxit nobis.

A Domino factum est istud: et est mirabile in oculis nostris. Alleluia, alleluia.

Dominus regnavit, decorem induit: induit Dominus fortitudinem et præcinxit se virtute. Alleluia.

God is the Lord which hath showed us light.

This is the Lord's doing; and it is marvelous in our eyes. Alleluia, alleluia.

The Lord reigneth, He is clothed with majesty; the Lord is clothed with strength; wherewith He hath girded Himself. Alleluia.

(Psalms cxvii)

Here you find another Hebrew word: *Alleluia*, Praise the Lord. You know the first Christians, St. Peter, St. Paul, and the rest were all Jews. Before they were Christians, they were wont to meet on the Sabbath for their service in the synagogue. There they read the Old Testament in Hebrew. There, too, they sang the psalms and the prophecies just as the Jews do to-day in their synagogues. Read how our Lord went into the synagogue and evil Jews attempted to take His life. He read their own Hebrew prophecy about Himself, rebuked their unfaith, and told them the truth about themselves. (Luke iv, 16–30.) With that divine incident as a background you will be interested to know that archeologists have excavated around Nazareth and say they have found the very ruins of that synagogue where our Lord spoke.

It would be well to study here the sequence of thought contained in the Collect, Lesson, Gradual, Gospel of the Mass. Let us take the Second Mass on Christmas. If you are a Latin student, you will take pleasure in studying, translating, and interpreting the Latin text. Observe the connection of these parts, and be sure to trace the easy transition from one to the other.

All four parts show the same thought and prayer, indicating the completeness of this exceedingly beautiful liturgy. Observe the dramatic quality of this whole section of the Mass, the sustained loftiness of the Collect, the forceful message of the Epistle, the poetic beauty of the Gradual — all rising to the magnificent culmination of the Gospel. If you bestow truly spiritual interest in this part of the Mass, you will perceive its boundless beauties. Inspect the framework with its interwoven prayer, praise, and worship. Nothing slipshod, nothing overdone. Nowhere can you find such consummate art, such unity of design, such perfection of construction. As the ritual moves on you see the harmony of treatment; indeed, the method is like that of the divine Master Himself. So few words used, yet so much said that one feels the sweep of the infinite, one catches the spirit of the divine in it all.

If you bring to this study an inward eye, the eye of the spirit, you will be able to grasp its truth, and you will feel a deep spiritual sympathy born of true faith. You will follow better the thread of the engrossing petitions of the Mass. They will keep your soul spellbound.

All the chant (or words) between the Epistle and the Gospel have been called the Gradual; but this is not quite exact. In some Masses, after the Gradual comes the Tract, usually a Psalm or some fragment of the Scriptures, a sort of second Gradual, chanted straight through without a stop. This was done on the steps of the ambo or pulpit. For the Sundays of Lent, also on Mondays, Wednesdays, and Fridays of the same season — the official days of penance — you will find a Tract in the Mass.

Tacked on, as it were, to the Tract is a Sequence. At first this was a mere musical variation or addition to the Alleluia of the Gradual, but by degrees words crept in to be sung in the Mass. In time the few words grew into long poems. There were many of them, but now only a few remain. Every Latin student should translate and try to remember some of them. They are as follows:

For Easter Sunday: "Victimæ Paschali" (composed by a priest named Wipo about 1048).

For Pentecost: "Veni Sancte Spiritus" (written by Pope Innocent III about 1198).

For Corpus Christi: "Lauda Sion" (written by St. Thomas Aquinas about 1274).

At Requiems: "Dies Iræ" (composed by a Franciscan friar about 1250).

On Seven Dolors: "Stabat Mater" (written by a Franciscan friar in 1306).

There is no doubt that the above beautiful prayers (Sequences) were largely inspired by the bits of dramatic dialogue used in the Church as far back as the ninth century. They were called tropes, and were sung in this part of the Mass. These tropes were a minor drama within the great drama of the Mass. One feels how impressive they must have been amid the living silence of the worshipers who heard them. Thus on Easter Day the scene in Matthew xxviii, 1-6, was carried out in the following strikingly dramatic form:

The Celebrant (in a high voice): Quem quæritis in sepulchro?
The two clerics reply: Jesum Nazarenum crucifixum, O cœlicolæ.
Non est hic, surrexit sicut prædixerat.
Ite nuntiate quia surrexit de sepulchro.
Resurrexi!

This very old and very beautiful trope was composed by an Irish monk, Tutilo of St. Gaul's Abbey in Switzerland, back in the ninth century.[1] It is still to be had in a manu-

[1] Any investigator can go back much further and trace the activities of the Irish monks of early days with their gifts of faith and song. Sedulius, an Irishman (circa 400), was the author of the glorious Carmen Paschale. In that far-off time, the fifth century, he hinted at the Immaculate Conception of the Blessed Virgin. He is the earliest known writer to quote the tradition that our Lord after the Resurrection appeared first to the Virgin Mother.

script known as "St. Gaul's Ms. 484" and written before the year 940. Thus we learn from very ancient sources that the Church was the mother of the drama, and the sanctuary itself once served as a stage setting, the altar representing the sepulchre of Christ, while the priest and his assistants were the dramatis personæ: the priest, clad in a white garment, representing the angel, and the two clerics taking the place of the two Marys at the Sepulchre.[1] Even the rubrics tell just what is to be said and how the priest is to be garbed.

Is it any wonder, then, that the greatest authorities on this subject, like Gautier and Pollard, should admit that this quaint, sacred playlet, written by an Irish monk, is "the primal root of the future theater"? Upon Tutilo's Easter trope others were modeled, and in time there sprang from this germ the idea of the Easter play, the Christmas play, miracle plays, moralities, all these being the forerunners of the modern drama.

1. Name two peoples who attached immense importance to music in their schools. 2. Have you ever seen a miracle play? 3. Your school is an important agency for your education, but can you show how the following agencies help to make the boys and girls of to-day the men and women of to-morrow: Church, family life, trade, travel, theaters, newspapers, political and social institutions? 4. Write a theme showing that the Mass (as far as you have studied) is an educational influence of the highest order. 5. The highest aim of education is to make for the soul's immortal destiny. Can you explain this?

[1] "Irish Origin of the Easter Play," W. H. Grattan Flood, *Month*, April, 1923, p. 351.

XI

THE GOSPEL

Having read the Epistle and what follows, the priest leaves the Missal open and comes to the middle of the altar, where, raising his eyes to the cross, and immediately lowering them, he inclines profoundly, keeping his hands joined. During the time the altar boy is changing the Missal from the Epistle to the Gospel side the priest says " Munda cor meum," etc. These prayers being said, he stands erect, and goes, with hands joined, to the Gospel side where he reads the Gospel in a clear voice.

New life for old. The Gospel marks the end of the old law. Nearly all that has heretofore been done in the Mass corresponds to the Jewish service before our Lord's time. But when we come to the Gospel, the book is changed across to the Gospel side. This is to signify that with the Gospel came Christ, and a difference is thus marked. From now on we are in a new part of the Mass; the wholly Christian service, ushered in by the Gospel; the coming of Christ with the good news of our redemption. No longer does the Mass deal with the Old Dispensation, but with the New. There is a total change indicated by changing the book from one side of the altar to the other.

The Gospel is the clear and definite teaching of Jesus Christ. *All* the Gospel! Not what suits this or that little sect or denomination, but *all* the Gospel. So the Church insists. Our Lord declared that He had come down from heaven to give His soul a ransom for many. And after His death and resurrection and ascension His Apostles went forth teaching all nations to turn from evil ways and serve the one true and living God. They preached the commandments of love of God and of our neighbor; Our Lord's sermon on the Mount; the coming of a judgment; the death of Christ for the sins of mankind in accordance with the Scriptures of old. And they told the people how Christ had been buried, and had risen again from the dead, and would come hereafter to render to every man according to his works. And what they taught, they charged their disciples to teach. All that Jesus taught is to be found in the New Testament and in tradition. Of course, the Church has always, from the very beginning, acknowledged the twofold authority of the Written Word and the Unwritten Word. The Church dearly loves the Bible, the Word of God. Ever faithful to the request of her divine Founder, "Go and teach," she reads for us some part of the Gospel every day in the Mass.

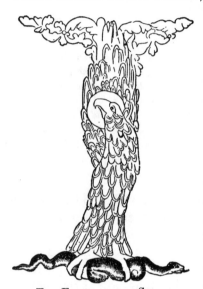

THE EAGLE OF THE SKIES.

The eagle represents Our Lord whose power over death was shown by His Resurrection.

Before the priest reads the Gospel, however, he stands with head bowed down before the middle of the altar and begs God to cleanse his heart and his lips, even as once the lips of Isaias were purified when an angel cleansed them in the temple:

THE GOSPEL

> And I said: Woe is me, because I have held my peace; because I am a man of unclean lips, and I dwell in the midst of a people that hath unclean lips, and I have seen with my eyes the King the Lord of Hosts.
>
> And one of the seraphims flew to me, and in his hand was a live coal, which he had taken with the tongs off the altar.
>
> And he touched my mouth, and said: Behold this hath touched thy lips, and thy iniquities shall be taken away, and thy sin shall be cleansed (Isaias vi, 5-7).

To say or hear the Gospel aright, one must be all the deeper in humility, all the stronger in faith, all the more earnest in seeking forgiveness. So with bent head the priest prays:

Munda cor meum ac labia mea, omnipotens Deus, qui labia Isaiæ prophetæ calculo mundasti ignito: ita me tua grata miseratione dignare mundare, ut sanctum Evangelium tuum digne valeam nuntiare. Per Christum Dominum nostrum. Amen.	Cleanse my heart and my lips, O Almighty God, who didst cleanse the lips of the prophet Isaias with a burning coal; and vouchsafe through Thy gracious mercy, so to purify me that I may worthily proclaim Thy holy Gospel. Through Christ Our Lord, Amen.
Dominus sit in corde meo et in labiis meis, ut digne et competenter annuntiem Evangelium suum. Amen.	The Lord be in my heart and on my lips that I may worthily and fittingly proclaim His holy Gospel. Amen.

Then going to the Gospel side, he says:

P. Dominus vobiscum.	P. The Lord be with you.
A. Et cum spiritu tuo.	A. And with thy spirit.
P. Sequentia sancti evangelii secundum N.	P. The continuation of the holy Gospel according to N.
A. Gloria tibi, Domine.	A. Glory be to Thee, O Lord.

If you are near the altar, you may notice that the priest makes a triple cross — one on his forehead, one on his lips, one on his breast. This is a prayer that the holy Gospel may be first in our minds, that we may *know* about our Lord, and understand and believe all his Gospel teaches. "Let this mind be in you, which was also in Christ Jesus" (Philippians ii, 5).

The cross on our lips means that we must be able to *speak* the words of the Gospel. It is our duty to spread this good news. The world sadly needs the Gospel to-day. "Open, O Lord, my lips, and my tongue shall announce Thy praise."

The cross on the breast means the life of Christ should be *lived* in one's heart. If it is there, it will mean that you love Him. If you love Him, you will not be able to love anything low or mean or wrong. You will avoid sin, sloth, selfishness. "If you love me," He says, "you will keep my commandments and I will come and abide with you, will stay in your heart." And if you truly love Him, you will really want to receive His words at the Gospel, and Himself in Holy Communion. No one can be saved without love of God. But God is never unjust, never commands impossibilities. He helps us to love Him by grace, which lifts us above our nature, brings us nearer to God. Let us pray God that each Gospel we hear read may find us not only attentive hearers, but alert doers of the word.

As for the Gospel itself only a few lines, of course, are read (or sung), yet they give us a complete message, good tidings. How keen we should be to hear that good news and to prize every word of it; for the Gospel is the message of redemption in Jesus Christ which was preached by our Lord Himself and His disciples. In the Gospel Christ speaks directly to each one of us. The words of our Lord are the most precious things in this world. The pictures, parables, examples He shows us should be the visions ever next our heart. They tell us of His love, mercy, gentleness, patience, longsuffer-

THE GOSPEL

ing, charity, etc. The miracles He wrought, every action as well as every word, have their special meaning. What good tidings are conveyed in the Gospel of the Second Mass on Christmas!

In illo tempore: Pastores loquebantur ad invicem: Transeamus usque Bethlehem, et videamus hoc verbum, quod factum est, quod Dominus ostendit nobis. Et venerunt festinantes; et invenerunt Mariam, et Joseph, et infantem positum in præsepio. Videntes autem cognoverunt de verbo, quod dictum erat illis de puero hoc. Et omnes qui audierunt mirati sunt: et de his, quæ dicta erant a pastoribus ad ipsos. Maria autem conservabat omnia verba hæc, conferens in corde suo. Et reversi sunt pastores glorificantes, et laudantes Deum in omnibus, quæ audierant, et viderant, sicut dictum est ad illos.

A. Laus tibi, Christi.

At that time, the shepherds said to one another: Let us go over to Bethlehem, and let us see this word that is come to pass, which the Lord hath showed to us. And they came with haste; and they found Mary and Joseph, and the Infant lying in a manger. And seeing, they understood about the word that had been spoken to them concerning this child. And all that heard wondered; and at those things that were told them by the shepherds. But Mary kept all those words, pondering them in her heart. And the shepherds returned, glorifying and praising God; for all the things they had heard and seen, as it was told unto them (Luke ii, 15–20).

A. Praise be to Thee, O Christ.

The Gospel ended, the priest raises the Missal with both hands and inclines a little, while kissing it where he signed it in the beginning, saying at the same time, in a low voice:

Per evangelica dicta deleantur nostra delicta.

By the words of the Gospel may our sins be blotted out.

If you read your Missal in daily Mass, you find one beautiful message following another. That way of hearing Mass is the best and surest. You bring home to your heart vision after vision. And messages, too, the most precious in this world. Every one of them will help you onward and upward. Each points out for us the road to go by, the way to walk in. There is something more. Have you tested your powers of observation when reading these Gospels? Ask yourself, What do I know of the Gospels, what one do I really love? Better still, meditate on them! Take this Gospel quoted above as an experiment. It is the story of Christmas night, with its stars and its song, and its angel words about the sweetness of peace and who shall have that peace. The poet Milton, meditating on this Gospel, represents our Lady as telling the Child Jesus:

> At Thy Nativity, a glorious choir
> Of Angels, in the fields of Bethlehem, sung
> To shepherds watching at their folds by night,
> And told them the Messias now was born,
> Where they might see Him; and to Thee they came.

What do you see in this Gospel? Do you stop to think how many hundreds of years the Church has been saying those words to her children? She wants all to know the good tidings which Jesus Christ brought from His Father. Hence her eternal anxiety to have us hear "the gospel of the glory of the blessed God," which hath been committed to her trust.

There is a Gospel assigned to be read every Sunday and Holy Day. The Church wants us, week in and week out, year after year, to come back again upon those scenes in our Lord's life, so that, knowing them better, we may love Him more dearly. That is why the Gospel is read both in Latin and in English. Only the Catholic Church has retained every line of the Gospel. Our Church teaches the truths that is in Christ Jesus, all the truth, and nothing but the truth. Catholic means *universal*. It means the exact

THE GOSPEL

opposite of a sect. The Catholic Church is the religion of the whole Gospel. It is not merely our religion; it is the religion of Jesus Christ. Dwell long on the following passage:

> I like the Roman Catholic Church because it stands so immovable in its allegiance to Jesus Christ, as very God. None of its leaders ever question the Divinity of Jesus. I like it because it believes in the religious training of its children, and, at great sacrifice of time and money, gives it. I like it because it stands for the purity of home life and the sanctity of the marriage vows. Thank God for that Church's strong and clear protest against the cheap divorce-mills that disgrace our American civilization. I honor it for its defense of the Bible. I especially thank God for the stand that Church takes in this land against anarchy on the one hand and an impossible Socialism on the other. I go to sleep every night with a firmer feeling of security because we have in this city the Roman Catholic Church.

Such is the tribute that a voice from without the fold pays to the sanctity and uncompromising fearlessness of the Catholic Church. It is a quotation from a sermon by a Methodist clergyman recently read at a meeting of the Catholic Federation in Seattle.

At the end of the Gospel, the priest kisses the book. In olden days there was a special Gospel book, rolls of the Gospel beautifully inscribed. After the Gospel was read the book was carefully placed in the case or casket by an acolyte who had brought it into the church. Nowadays when the Gospel is read the server says:

> Laus tibi, Christi! | Praise be to thee, O Christ!

What a field is the Gospel, from Bethlehem to Calvary, and what a harvest of truth it yields! The average Catholic high school student should make it his religious business to learn about the land which Jesus loved. A pity, that it should be a *terra incognita!* How much do *you* know, say, about the surroundings in which Christ lived as a boy, at your age? Did you ever take the time to find out? Of the early life of our Lord amid the surroundings of Nazareth, a scholar writes:

Nazareth is usually represented as a secluded and an obscure village. Many writers on the life of our Lord have emphasized this, holding it proved by the silence of the Gospels concerning His childhood and youth. But the value of a vision of the Holy Land is that it fills the silences of the Holy Book, and from it we receive a very different idea of the early life of our Lord from the one generally current among us.

Full and rich was the present life on which the eyes of the boy Jesus looked out. Across Esdraelon, opposite to Nazareth, there emerged from the Samarian hills the road from Jerusalem, thronged annually with pilgrims, and the road from Egypt with its merchants going up and down. The Midianite caravans could be watched for miles coming up from the fords of Jordan; and, as we have seen, the caravans from Damascus wound round the foot of the hill on which Nazareth stands. Or if the village boys climbed the northern edge of their hollow home, there was another road within sight, where the companies were still more brilliant — the highway between Acre and the Decapolis, along which legions marched, and princes swept with their retinues, and all sorts of travellers from all countries went to and fro. The Roman ranks, the Roman eagles, the wealth of noblemen's litters and equipages cannot have been strange to the eyes of the boys of Nazareth, especially after their twelfth year, when they went up to Jerusalem, or visited with their fathers famous Rabbis, who came down from Jerusalem, peripatetic among the provinces. Nor can it have been the eye only which was stirred. For all the rumour of the Empire entered Palestine close to Nazareth — the news from Rome, about the Emperor's health, about the changing influence of the great statesmen, about the prospects at court of Herod, or of the Jews; about Cæsar's last order concerning the tribute, or whether the policy of the Procurator would be sustained. Many Galilean families must have had relatives in Rome; Jews would come back to this countryside to tell of the life of the world's capital. Moreover, the scandals of the Herods buzzed up and down these roads; pedlars carried them, and the peripatetic Rabbis would moralise upon them. The customs, too, of the neighbouring Gentiles — their loose living, their sensuous worship, their absorption in business, the hopelessness of the inscriptions on their tombs, multitudes of which were readable (as some are still) on the roads round Galilee — all this would furnish endless talk in Nazareth, both among men and boys.[1]

While we are on the subject of the Gospel it might be well to ask ourselves a few pertinent questions. Do we know Christ and follow His teachings? It is the knowledge and conduct that counts. Of all the hours in the day how few are given over to actual study and schooling! Consider how much time is spent inside the school, and outside. And where and how do we spend our extra time? These questions count. Truly what we need is the correct answer to each one. We also need to think well on these answers with a view to self-improvement.

Let us see what we are doing with our days. Out of every day, you spend say, 16 hours at home, in sleep, meals, study, and duties; $2\frac{1}{2}$ hours in class if averaged for the whole year, counting vacations, Saturdays, and Sundays; then $5\frac{1}{2}$ hours are left over and above. It will be seen that the school claims but few of your hours. All the time you are away from school your education is going on. In other words, you are learning here and there, thinking on this thing or that, receiving certain impressions, growing in knowledge or experience of some sort. So, in or out of school, your ideas, thoughts, conduct are moving either in right ways or wrong; they make you or they mar you. Think, then, what those many hours may mean for your future. Your success here and hereafter depends on using aright all the hours you have at hand. In the fine days of boyhood, in the radiant years of girlhood, is the best time to make your mind as full and rich as possible. This you can do in and out of school.

[1] G. A. Smith, "Historical Geography of the Holy Land," pp. 432–433; London, Hodder & Stoughton, 1904.

The real point here is how to make best use of your day. Make out a plan for yourself. Talk it over with your teacher. A teacher's work is to help you to think for yourself, and set you going the right way. But, remember, Christ is the Way, the true Way without which there is no going. "For I have given you an example, that as I have done to you, so you do also" (John xiii, 15). Just calculate what a small fraction of actual time you give to our Lord. Summed up, is it even one hour? "Could you not watch one hour with me?" Now the Mass plus a visit to the Blessed Sacrament after school or in the evening would make up just that hour which Christ has a right to expect from His friends. Nothing is so helpful to Catholic students as daily Mass and a daily visit to the Blessed Sacrament. It is a sad thing for any of us to let even one day go by without visiting our Lord. St. Thomas Aquinas used to sit and pray before the Blessed Sacrament whenever he was in need of light and inspiration. And he got just those things. St. Thomas, remember, was "the strongest and most virile intellect which European blood has given to the world." He remembered everything that he read so that his mind was a huge library. More than that, he could say the greatest grace he ever had, sanctifying grace excepted, was that of having understood everything that he ever read. He knew the whole New Testament by heart. Better still, he put its words into practice.

1. In what languages were the Gospels originally written? Explain. 2. Who are the synoptists and why are they so called? 3. Which is your favorite Gospel? Give your reasons. 4. Tell what you know about St. Matthew, St. Mark, St. Luke, St. John. 5. Do the Gospels tell all that Our Lord said and did? What do you mean by tradition? 6. Each Gospel-writer sets out to tell about special features and teachings of Our Lord's life. Can you explain? 7. Every one of us has a need of studying the Gospel. Is there any hint of this need, in the Mass?

XII

CREDO

At the middle of the altar, extending, elevating, and joining his hands, the priest says the Nicene Creed. When he comes to the words, " and was incarnate," he kneels down, and continues kneeling to the words, "was made man." As he says the last words of the prayer, he makes the sign of the cross. At the word "Amen," he places his hands on the altar.

The Creed marks the end of the Mass of the Catechumens, or the first part of the Holy Sacrifice.[1] In the olden days just before it was said all who were not baptized Christians had to leave the church. St. Ambrose gives us an inkling of life in those days in a letter he sent to his sister, Marcellina. Written during the Arian troubles of 385–386, when soldiers were sent to break up the services in his church, the letter runs thus:

The next day (it was a Sunday) after the lessons and the tract, having dismissed the Catechumens, I explained the Creed (*symbolum tradebam*) to some of the Competents (people about to be baptized) in the baptistry of the basilica. There I was told suddenly that they had sent soldiers to the Portiana basilica. But I remained at my place, and began to say Mass. While I offer, I hear that a certain Castulus has been seized by the people.

This summary of the chief truths of the Christian faith, which St. Ambrose was teaching his converts, was nothing more than the Creed. There were many names by which it was known: *Symbolum, Regula fidei, Credo*, etc. This same St. Ambrose could boast that the Church of Rome had always preserved undefiled the symbol of the Apostles, that is, the Creed.

[1] See Appendix, Mass of the Catechumens.

The Nicene Creed

Credo in unum Deum, Patrem omnipotentem, factorem cœli et terræ, visibilium omnium, et invisibilum. Et in unum Dominum Jesum Christum, Filium Dei unigenitum: et ex Patre natum ante omnia sæcula; Deum de Deo, lumen de lumine, Deum verum de Deo vero; genitum, non factum, consubstantialem Patri; per quem omnia facta sunt. Qui propter nos homines, et propter nostram salutem, descendit de cœlis (hic genuflectitur). Et incarnatus est de Spiritu sancto ex Maria Virgine; ET HOMO FACTUS EST. Crucifixus etiam pro nobis: sub Pontio Pilato passus, et sepultus est. Et resurrexit tertia die, secundum Scripturas. Et ascendit in cœlum, sedet ad dexteram Patris. Et iterum venturus est cum gloria judicare vivos et mortuos: cujus regni non erit finis. Et in Spiritum sanctum Dominum et vivificantem, qui ex Patre Filioque procedit. Qui cum Patre et Filio simul adoratur et conglorificatur; qui locutus est per Prophetas. Et unam, sanctam, catholicam et apostolicam Ecclesiam. Confiteor unum baptisma in remissionem peccatorum. Et exspecto resurrectionem mortuorum, et vitam venturi sæculi. Amen.

I believe in one God, the Father almighty, maker of heaven and earth, and of all things visible and invisible. And in one Lord Jesus Christ, the only-begotten Son of God, born of the Father before all ages; God of God, light of light, true God of true God; begotten not made; consubstantial with the Father, by whom all things were made. Who for us men, and for our salvation, came down from heaven (here all kneel); and was incarnate by the Holy Ghost, of the Virgin Mary; AND WAS MADE MAN. He was crucified also for us, suffered under Pontius Pilate, and was buried. And the third day he rose again according to the scriptures; and ascended into heaven. He sitteth at the right hand of the Father; and he shall come again with glory to judge the living and the dead; and his kingdom shall have no end. And in the Holy Ghost, the Lord and giver of life, who proceedeth from the Father and the Son, who together with the Father and the Son is adored and glorified; who spoke by the prophets. And one holy catholic and apostolic church. I confess one baptism for the remission of sins. And I await the resurrection of the dead, and the life of the world to come. Amen.

CREDO

The Gospel gives us a glimmering perception of Christ. The Credo cries out our recognition of Him; nay, our absolute faith in Him. "I believe, O Lord." The priest, raising his hands to heaven, recites the Credo. "The word 'I' comes before the word 'God.' The believer comes first, but he is soon dwarfed by his beliefs, swallowed in the creative whirlwind and the trumpets of the Resurrection."

The Creed is a summary of the chief truths which Christ taught; saying it is a confession of our Christian faith. Our Lord Himself, when He told the Apostles to teach and baptize all nations in the name of the Father and of the Son and of the Holy Ghost, expected such an avowal on the part of the baptized Christian. "He who shall confess me before men him will I confess before my Father Who is in heaven; but whosoever shall deny me, etc." So His followers were glad to confess Him before all men, "before many witnesses." At the Last Supper, our Lord in His farewell discourse to the Apostles told them just what to believe and why. Read St. John xvii. This is a touching, poignantly beautiful prayer and merits close study.

Since the Master was soon to send His disciples forth to all nations it was needful that they make sure of His teachings — their creed. Else how could they be "the salt of the earth, the light of the world"? Evidently our Lord took time to teach the disciples and have them understand. It is interesting and instructive to observe what was said and done at the Last Supper when Christ gave the Apostles His final instructions. Read the entire story in the New Testament. For a better understanding of the background of your creed note what came to pass. What our Lord said and did was as follows:

Teaching and Example	Matthew	Mark	Luke	John
Instruction on last point of the creed: Life Everlasting			xxii, 14–18	
Washing of the Apostles' feet (humility) . . .				xiii, 4–6
Rebuke to Peter for his lack of understanding . . .				xiii, 7–12
Warning sounded for Judas	xxvi, 21–25	xiv, 18–21	xxii, 21–23	xiii, 21–30
Further instruction on the need of service . . .				xiii, 20
Humility so necessary, and perseverance			xxii, 24–30	
Consecration and Holy Communion	xxvi, 26–29	xiv, 22–25	xxii, 19–20	
Judas went out into the night				xiii, 31
The farewell discourse . .				xiv, xvi
Christ's prayer for His disciples				xvii

Education, somebody has said, consists largely in putting heart into people. In other words, encouragement. That is just what our Lord did at the Last Supper. Anybody can see how much time He took to instruct the Apostles in the new faith and to get them ready for their First Communion. No men had greater need for light, faith, strength, than they. Hence they received instructions, rebukes, encouragements, prayers, Holy Communion, then more instruction. This teaching of the disciples about their faith, their work in the world, their membership in the one Church must have taken a long time. That is why the Mass also takes some time. It is not done and over with in a minute. It has many prayers, acts of faith, spiritual encouragements.

So when you say the Credo, think of our Lord Himself giving you those wondrous truths, more valuable than gold and rubies. Your souls will be open to His gaze in the Mass just like the Apostles' were when they were gathered at the first Mass. And your souls are precious in God's sight. His words should be more precious than ever in these days when so many have lost them. The great want of the world to-day is reflection on the teachings of Jesus. Proud and pampered freethinkers do not want to listen to His words, do not care to submit to the yoke of Christ and defend His truth. But we do.

Remember the Mass is the renewal of that same Last Supper which we have just been following. Yet, sad to say, those truths which Christ revealed to His disciples and which He told them to teach were bound to be twisted by men of ill will. Heresies came with their misty, indistinct ideas, truth mixed with error. They did much damage to the faithful who were sometimes led into error — for error has its agents, and its noise is heard everywhere. Then the Church teachers met in Nicæa, in General Council, in the year 325, and formulated a statement of the Christian faith — all that Christ has taught. That is why it is called the Nicene Creed. In it the things Christ revealed stand forth like a grand cathedral, every part of which is divine truth firmly knit together and built up into a spiritual edifice of faith.

And now, centuries afterward, we who are gathered together at the Mass, say this same Nicene Creed. We profess our belief in all that Christ has taught: "That the love wherewith the Father hath loved Him may be in us, and He in us." One body, one faith, one baptism, one belief — in Jesus Christ. That is the Church. The congregation of all those who profess the faith of Christ, partake of the same sacraments, and are governed by the vicegerent of Jesus Christ. The vital difference between Catholics and

Protestants is that Roman Catholics believe all that Christ has taught, whereas Protestants believe just about what they feel like; for they have been estranged from Christ's Church and His Sacraments. Catholics in this century witness the truth of what Christ says, just as the Apostles did, just as Catholic Christians for the past 1900 years have done. We believe the same truths that the Apostles taught, taking them from the lips of their Master. These are the same truths for which the confessors and martyrs died. It were well to consider those martyrs, for they are the Church's heroes and heroines and should be our models.

But before we consider the Christian martyrs, who died for the Apostles' Creed, let us look back into Old Testament times. Even before the coming of Christ, there were men and women whose faith in God was a wonderful thing. Of these St. Paul speaks in Hebrews xi, which you should read. "The Power of Faith" would be a good title for that chapter. Notice the enumeration of the trials, tortures, sufferings those early saints (for they were saints) underwent for the cause of God, for their *Credo*.

> Who by faith conquered kingdoms, wrought justice, obtained promises, stopped the mouths of lions. Quenched the violence of fire, escaped the edge of the sword, recovered strength from weakness, became valiant in battle, put to flight the armies of foreigners. . . . And others had trial of mockeries and stripes, moreover also of bands and prisons. They were stoned, they were cut asunder, they were tempted, they were put to death by the sword, they wandered about in sheep-skins, in goat-skins, being in want, distressed, afflicted. Of whom the world was not worthy; wandering in deserts, in mountains and in dens, and in caves of the earth (Hebrews xi, 33–38).

And all this suffering by those who had not "received the promise," that is, who lived before the Incarnation, before Jesus came upon earth. Yet they believed, and departed

CREDO

this life in the true faith of God's holy name. When finally our Lord did come, died, and rose from the dead, He descended into limbo to free those souls of the just.

The Christians having better promises and a better covenant, the teaching of Christ, did not fall behind those martyrs of the Old Law. Indeed, thousands of them gave up their lives for the sake of Christ, saying their Credo, with faith unconquerable.

Martyr means, essentially, a witness for some dogma or practice of God's church. In popular parlance, any one who sacrifices his life or even any persistent sufferer is called a martyr; we speak of our martyred Presidents, Lincoln, Garfield, and McKinley. *Martyrem non facit pœna, sed causa.* "It is not the pain and penalty he suffers which makes the martyr, but the cause," says St. Augustine. Before the Church calls any sufferer a martyr, her chief care is to inquire into his *cause*. Why did the persecutor put him to death?

If he died for the sake of Christ, if he was put to death because he would not deny his Master, or any of Christ's teachings, then he was a real martyr. Our Lord prepared His followers for such trials, and He told them that He would give them strength and courage and patience to become martyrs, were that what He wanted of them. Luke xxi, 9–19, tells just what our Lord said to them and to every real martyr. Notice what graces He promises them: courage, outspokenness, "a mouth and wisdom," patience and perseverance, that is, eternal security. It was not long ere the words of Christ came true. There were many martyrs. Of the twelve Apostles, all save St. John shed their blood for the sake of Christ.

The first martyr was St. Stephen. Read the account of his martyrdom in Acts vi, 5 — vii, 60. Of the two hundred

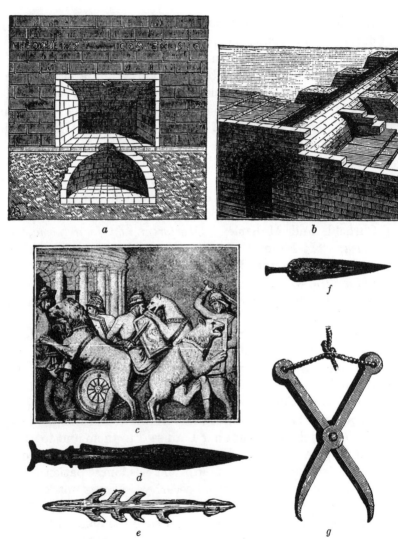

SCENES AND IMPLEMENTS CONNECTED WITH THE TRIALS OF CHRISTIAN MARTYRS

a. Prison at Rome.   *b.* Cloaca Maxima at Rome.   *c.* Trials of early martyrs.
d. Roman sword.   *e.* Spiculum or barbed arrowhead.   *f.* Short sword.
g. Forfex or shears.

thirty-four Popes who preceded Pius XI, eighty-eight have been canonized or beatified. The first fifty-six Pontiffs form an unbroken succession of saints, of whom thirty-three were martyrs. St. Denis, the twenty-sixth Pope, who died A.D. 272, was the first Sovereign Pontiff who was not called upon to shed his blood for the faith, but his five immediate successors laid down their lives for their faith. From the earliest days, from Stephen's time down to our own day, there have been countless martyrs, boys and girls, men and women, who have died rather than deny our Lord.

THE COLOSSEUM (FLAVIAN AMPHITHEATER)

Picture to yourself for a moment those unconquerable athletes of Christianity. They are dragged before tribunals, cast as food to wild beasts, stretched over burning coals; flames consume them, their members are rent asunder with hooks of iron, their flesh is torn into bits and falls from their bodies in shreds. Nothing frightens them, they know not fear, they jeer at their sufferings; they smile in the midst of torments. Their bodies are torn and maimed, the steel furrows and lays open the flesh of their limbs, and still they bless God, thank their executioners, and sing canticles of joy. Jesus Christ lives in them, suffers with them, and fills them with His own divine strength.

Read the accounts of such martyrs as Tarsicius, Agnes in Rome; Sir Thomas More, Oliver Plunkett in England; Father Jogues, René Goupil in America.

Try to think, when Credo time comes, what a host they make, those martyrs for the Catholic faith and for the Mass.

> Ah, see the fair chivalry come, the companions of Christ!
> White Horsemen, who ride on white horses, the Knights of God!
> They for their Lord and their Lover sacrificed
> All, save the sweetness of treading, where He first trod![1]

Writing about the myriad martyrs for the Mass, especially those who suffered for their faith in modern times, Canon Barry says:

'In the constitution of the Church of Scotland which was drawn up under Knox's influence' — I am quoting J. A. Froude — 'to say Mass or to hear it was made a capital crime, under the authority of the text, "The idolater shall die the death."' By English law many priests were executed with unspeakable barbarity as traitors, the sole evidence against them being the fact of their having said Mass; and this law continued in force beyond the time of Bishop Talbot, who was brought up for trial at the Old Bailey. When we bear in mind the commands of St. Paul to his Corinthian converts, the evidence of Pliny and St. Justin Martyr, with all that we learn from the paintings in the Catacombs, illustrating the Roman Liturgy as it was actually celebrated by St. Peter's successors, we may judge how fierce was the hatred of the powers of darkness against the Holy Sacrifice which, by their human instruments, they strove to utterly take away. But there is no counsel against the Almighty. At that very time when the Mass appeared to be doomed, it was crossing the Atlantic, establishing itself in Mexico and Quito, winning a future which has planted it all over the Americas.

When we in America stand up and say the Creed — the same faith for which so many died — we should feel proud

[1] Lionel Johnson, "Te Martyrum Candidatus."

of those witnesses (Wisdom iii, 1–8). They are surely in heaven, and we should pray to them to make our faith firm; that is, to obtain for us the grace always to believe and never to forget about our faith, to be ready and willing to die rather than deny what Christ taught.

In the middle of the Creed, you bow your head because the Creed tells of Jesus being born, and you bend your knee, as the Magi and the Shepherds did, to worship Him. For if He had not been born, there would be no Creed, no martyrs, no Catholic Church, and no hope of heaven in the life to come.

1. Let the Latin class translate the Nicene Creed in their Mass book. 2. In what everyday ways can Catholics betray their faith? 3. How can they imitate, though remotely, the Confessors and the Martyrs? Do Catholics in bigoted sections have many opportunities to confess their faith? Do you? 4. Study Lionel Johnson's poem: "Te Martyrum Candidatus."

PART TWO

XIII

THE OFFERTORY

The priest kisses the altar, and turning to the people, says "Dominus vobiscum"; then with hands joined he reads the Offertory. That done, he takes the veil off the chalice, places the chalice outside the corporal, and presently offers the host upon the paten. Later the chalice, containing wine in it, is offered.

The second part of the Mass begins with:

P. Dominus vobiscum	P. The Lord be with you.
A. Et cum spiritu tuo.	A. And with thy spirit.

Then the Offertory anthem:

P. Deus firmavit orbem terræ qui non commovebitur, parata sedes tua, Deus ex tunc, a sæculo tu es.	P. God hath established the world which shall not be moved. Thy throne is prepared from of old: Thou art from everlasting. (Psalms cxii, 1–3)

St. Augustine tells how in his day the people sang hymns from the Book of Psalms before the oblation. This hymn was called the "Offertorium, or the 'Offertory,' sung during the offering." Again, the *Ordo Romanus* of A.D. 800 says that after the Creed, the bishop salutes the people, saying, "The Lord be with you." After that he says, "Let us pray." Then the Offertorium is sung, with verses. While these verses were being sung the people drew near to the altar, presented their gifts, bread and wine (*oblations*), to the deacon. No longer is this done, for the wine is in a cruet and the host is on the paten which the priest unveils after reciting the offertory anthem. However, let us not forget what was done in very early days.

It must be clear by this time that we have reached the second stage of the Mass. A Dominus vobiscum opens this part, just as it does the third and fourth stages of the Holy Sacrifice. The first part began with the Sign of the Cross, which, after all, is a Dominus vobiscum in gesture. Now the sacrificial action is really begun. The Offertory marks the beginning of the *Missa Fidelium*, the more sacred mysteries, at which in the early Church only Christians were permitted to attend. The more important part of the Mass is now begun. We are approaching the real sacrifice.

ABEL OFFERING UP A LAMB
Here is represented one of the first sacrifices.

It will not do to forget that in the olden days sacrifices were offered to God on stone altars, and later in the temple. "I will bring them into my holy mount, and will make them joyful in my house of prayer; their holocausts and their victims shall please me upon my altar, for my house shall be called the house of prayer for all nations" (Isaias lvi, 7). Let us go back in spirit to earliest days and study the sacrifices of Abel, Abraham, and Melchisedech. There is much useful, vital instruction in these episodes in the lives of the great men of old. These three and their dutiful sacrifices have a special mention later on in the most sacred part of the Mass.

Abel, the second son of Adam and Eve, was a herdsman by occupation, and he offered God a more excellent sacrifice than Cain. A picture of the pastoral life is given in Gene-

THE OFFERTORY

sis, and you see Abel's spirit of true piety which was expressed in giving God his best; that is, the firstlings of his flock, and of these the fattest portions. "Abel was a shepherd, and Cain a husbandman. And it came to pass after many days that Cain offered, of the fruits of the earth, gifts to the Lord. Abel also offered of the firstlings of his flock, and of their fat: and the Lord had respect to Abel, and to his offerings. But to Cain and his offerings He had no respect: and Cain was exceedingly angry, and his countenance fell" (Genesis iv, 2–5).

In the New Testament our divine Lord Himself speaks of Abel whose "just blood hath been shed upon the earth" (Matthew xxiii, 35). Abel was the first martyr, a hero for his faith in God.

Abraham's sacrifice is familiar to all. When Isaac was grown to be a lad, God tried Abraham's faith by ordering him to sacrifice his only son. Abraham did not hesitate. The boy was brought three days' journey, the altar was prepared, and the sword was raised to slay the victim when a voice from heaven was heard. God wished not a hair of Isaac's head to suffer. What He wanted was proof of the patriarch's absolute trust in Him, his readiness to give up what was most precious in his eyes. "Abraham lifted up his eyes and saw behind his back a ram amongst the briars sticking fast by the horns, which he took and offered for a holocaust instead of his son" (Genesis xxii, 13). Whereupon the holy covenant between God and Abraham was ratified anew.

The last scene of a sacrifice for our present study is in the promised land. Abraham was not long on the soil of Hebron when a war broke out in his immediate neighborhood. In the strife his nephew Lot was captured and carried away. Abraham no sooner learned of this than he armed his men, pursued the enemy, and recovered Lot, the other prisoners, and much booty. It was a great victory after a long pursuit. After thus defeating Chodorlahomor and his Babylonian allies, Abraham on his return was met by the priest of the most high God, who blessed him and received tithes from him of the spoil of war. Melchisedech was an ancient priest, who ruled in Salem. The name Salem (old site of Jerusalem) is found in the Tel-el-Amarna tablets, B.C. 1400. "Melchisedech, the king of Salem, bringing forth bread and wine, blessed Abraham and said: Blessed be Abraham, by the most high God, who created heaven and earth. And blessed be the most high God by whose protection the enemies of God are in thy hand" (Genesis xiv).

AMPHORÆ

Early Christians, coming to Mass, brought offerings of wine for the Holy Sacrifice.

In these three studies, Abel, Abraham, Melchisedech, there is provided for you a proof of the early sacrificial acts the whole trend of which was to prepare the world for the Mass. We must follow the current of the ideas of sacrifice down to the Great Sacrifice. The sacrifice of the Mass was foreshadowed by Melchisedech's offering of bread and wine, was foretold by the prophet Malachias (i, 11), and was instituted as a sacrifice by our divine Lord Himself.

A sacrifice is an act of divine worship which consists in destroying, wholly or partially, a sensible substance, and then offering it to God in acknowledgment of His sovereign dominion over all things. The plan given below will make sure your grasp of a difficult subject. You will recognize

THE OFFERTORY

easily the point to which those ancient sacrifices were divinely intended to lead.

THE ESSENCE OF SACRIFICE
In the Old Law

I Offering and Destruction	II Object	III Priest	IV Purpose
Sacrifice means offering, killing, eating. The sacrifices of the Old Law were both bloody and unbloody. The bloody sacrifices consisted chiefly of lambs, oxen, and goats. The unbloody ones were flour, oil, wine, etc.	Bread and wine, or sheep and oxen, or first fruits and firstlings.	Chosen among men for purposes of reconciliation. In the Old Law one family was set aside exclusively for this honor.	A. The acknowledgment of God as the sovereign Lord of all things. B. Sacrifice presupposes sin, the need of reconciliation with God, or atonement.

In the Mass

I	II	III	IV
Christ offers Himself and we partake of the Victim from off the altar of sacrifice.	Bread and wine become the body and blood of Christ by the words of consecration.	Christ is the great High Priest. "Thou are a priest forever according to the order of Melchisedech."	Christ offers Himself for the whole world. "He Who is high as eternity, Whose arms stretch through infinity is lifted up on the cross for the sins of the whole world."

The Church has defined that the Mass is a real, true, sacrifice, one with the blood-stained immolation of Christ on Calvary. The only difference between the Mass and Calvary is that on Calvary Christ's blood was really shed,

96 THE MASS

whereas in the Mass the real shedding is represented by the twofold consecration which sacramentally, though not really, separates body and blood. No one has better expressed what the Mass is than Blessed Peter Canisius, S. J., in his famous Catechism: "The Sacrifice of the Mass is really the holy and living *representation* and at the same time the unbloody and efficacious oblation of the Lord's Passion and that blood-stained sacrifice which was offered for us on the Cross."

The real sacrificial act is not yet, for it is bread and wine that are now offered, and not the body and blood of Christ. "The oblation is not only the act of offering, but at the same time the bread and wine offered" (St. Justin). Here and now the offerer is the priest, with the congregation. By observing what goes on at the altar one can see that the priest uncovers the chalice, and takes up a little plate of gold or silver called the paten (*patena*, a flat dish). On this is the bread, the host. He holds up the paten with the host on it, and says a prayer in which he tells God he is offering it: for his own sins and failings, for all those present, for all faithful Christians, living and dead, that all may have health for life everlasting.

GREEK OBLATE   COPTIC OBLATE
It was an ancient custom to impress the oblates with a cross.

| Suscipe, Sancte Pater, omnipotens, æterne Deus, hanc immaculatam hostiam, quam ego, indignus famulus tuus, offero tibi Deo meo vivo et vero, pro innumerabilibus peccatis, et offensioni- | Accept, O Holy Father, Almighty, Everlasting God, this stainless host, which I, Thine unworthy servant, offer unto Thee, my God, living and true, for mine innumerable sins, offenses, and |

THE OFFERTORY

bus, et negligentiis meis, et pro omnibus circumstantibus; sed et pro omnibus fidelibus Christianis vivis atque defunctis, ut mihi et illis proficiat ad salutem in vitam æternam. Amen.

negligences, and for all here present; as also for all faithful Christians, both living and dead, that it may be profitable for my own and for their salvation unto life eternal. Amen.

This offering breathes the very spirit of St. Paul's lines: "For every high priest taken from among men, is ordained for men in the things that appertain to God, that he may offer up gifts and sacrifices for sins: Who can have compassion on them that are ignorant and that err: because he himself also is compassed with infirmity. And therefore

FOUR VERY EARLY CHALICES

The first two of the above chalices came from the basilica of Monza and date from the seventh century. The third is an eighth century chalice in the convent at Kremsmunster in Austria. The last, found at Gourdon in France, is one of the earliest known, going back beyond the sixth century.

he ought, as for the people, so also for himself, to offer for sins" (Hebrews v, 1). At the Last Supper, our Lord took bread. Later on He changed it into His precious body. So here in the Mass bread is used: the bread is a gift of God, and we offer it back to Him. "Gifts," says Loyola, "are the utterances of love, valued for the love they betoken." In place of those gifts Christ is going to give Himself, in the consecration of the Mass.

Having offered the bread, the priest takes the chalice, and goes to the epistle side of the altar, where he pours into the cup some wine and a few drops of water. It was Pope Alexander I (117-138 A.D.) who ordered that in the Mass wine should be mixed with water because of the water and blood which issued from the heart of Jesus on the cross. Study John xix, 33-35. Quite clear, then, must be the beautiful prayer with which the priest accompanies the pouring of water and wine into the chalice:

Deus, qui humanæ substantiæ dignitatem mirabiliter condidisti, et mirabilius reformasti: da nobis per hujus aquæ et vini mysterium, ejus divinitatis esse consortes, qui humanitatis nostræ fieri dignatus est particeps, Jesus Christus Filius tuus Dominus noster; qui tecum vivit et regnat, in unitate Spiritus Sancti, Deus, per omnia sæcula sæculorum. Amen.	O God, Who in creating human nature didst wonderfully dignify it, and still more wonderfully reform it; grant that by the mystery of this water and wine, we may be made partakers of His divine nature, Who vouchsafed to become partaker of our human nature; namely, Jesus Christ, our Lord, Thy son, Who with Thee, in unity with the Holy Ghost, liveth and reigneth, God, world without end. Amen.

The prayer itself tells you why the priest mixes water with wine. First, the Sacred Heart spent its last drop of blood and water for our salvation. "Thus, O my lovely Redeemer, your death has been the sacrifice which You wished to offer to obtain my pardon" (St. Alphonsus Liguori). Next, the mystical union of the water and wine is a symbol of our Lord Himself. He was Man and God. He had two natures, the human and the divine, so closely joined, like the water and wine, that nothing could divide them. The wine shows our Lord's divine nature joined with water, His human nature.

It will help to think about yourself and Christ as the water mingled with the wine in the chalice so that it cannot be seen. The rich, sweet wine stands for Christ. The

THE OFFERTORY

poor, pale, tasteless water stands for us. Let not this lesson be lost. When the water is mixed with the wine, it shows how we must be made one with Christ. They are so closely mingled now that no one could possibly separate them. Nothing can separate us from Christ but mortal sin. Suffer death rather than that.

The priest next takes the chalice and returns to the middle of the altar, where he raises it on high as he did the host. Be sure to learn the prayer the priest says when he lifts up the chalice and offers it to God. "*We* offer," he says. Again, a little later, he asks: "Brethren, pray that *my* sacrifice and *yours* may be acceptable to God, the Father Almighty" (Orate Fratres). So you see the people unite with the priest in offering the sacrifice of the Mass. Be sure to keep that well in mind. The importance of the people's part in the Mass is also shown by the fact that some one else must be present before the priest can say Mass; they must both join in the sacrifice. The offerers of the bread and wine are priest and people: "We" is the word used, not "I."

Offerimus tibi, Domine, calicem salutaris, tuam deprecantes clementiam: ut in conspectu divinæ Majestatis tuæ, pro nostra et totius mundi salute cum odore suavitatis ascendat. Amen.	We offer unto Thee, O Lord, the chalice of salvation, beseeching Thy clemency that, in the sight of Thy divine Majesty, it may ascend with the odor of sweetness, for our salvation, and for that of the whole world. Amen.

"We offer unto Thee, O Lord, the chalice of salvation." It is the chalice of our salvation, for soon the precious blood will be there. But now let us mention in our prayer, not only ourselves but our parents, our friends, our future. Thus we offer to God a mingled cup containing ourselves, all we love, our desires, and the manifold mysteries of life.

We can be sure to trust them all to Him, whose consecration will turn them into the life-giving blood.

The chalice speaks to us of the fullness of divine love. In it will soon be the very outpouring of the Sacred Heart. The cup is an apt symbol of the sacred blood, "that wine which maketh glad the heart of a man." The chalice, or cup, used by our Lord at the Last Supper is no longer to be found. This Holy Grail has been the object of search for centuries. Possibly you may gain some idea of what it was like from the crude chalices depicted on the walls or vaults of the Catacombs. Very old traditions tell of cups made of gold, silver, bronze, onyx, even blue glass. From references, woodcuts, inscriptions, and the like we know that cups of the chalice type have been in use in the Mass.

With the wine in the chalice and the bread on the corporal, the oblations are now prepared, even offered. But that is not enough. Conduct and motive must enter into every offering. In order that our sacrifice may be acceptable to God our hearts must be right. That truth underlies all acceptable sacrifice. Recognizing it, the Church recites two short prayers. One for a right heart; the other for the special blessing of the Holy Spirit. The first has the whole spirit of the oblation — a spirit of humility with a contrite heart. It is there in less than a dozen words. The only way a sacrifice will be acceptable to Almighty God is through a contrite and humble heart. Those versed in sacred history can show you how God wants the right spirit before anything else. The case of Cain and Abel bore that out. And all through the ages it is so recognized by the righteous. In the sixth century B.C. Baruch minced no words about it:

> I have put upon me the sackcloth of supplication and I will cry to the Most High in my days.

THE OFFERTORY

Thus saith the Lord: Bow down your shoulder and your neck. The soul that is sorrowful for the greatness of the evil she hath done, and goeth bowed down and feeble . . . giveth glory and justice to Thee, O Lord (Baruch iv, 20; ii, 18–21).

You may remember also what another prophet, Daniel, declared:

As in holocausts of rams and bullocks, and as in thousands of fat lambs; so let our sacrifice be made in Thy sight this day, that it may please Thee. That we may find Thy mercy . . . in a contrite and humble spirit let us be accepted (Daniel iii, 39–40).

The test of a worthy person is to have a humble heart and a contrite spirit. On, on, this truth moved through the ages till it found perfect expression in Jesus Christ. He who did no guile, who was the spotless all-holy Lamb of God, came to offer on Calvary the sacrifice of a troubled spirit, a broken and contrite heart. As God revealed to us in the beginning, as His prophets have told us, as His divine Son has shown us, it is necessary to practice heartfelt contrition.

Having briefly considered this truth, we have now to see wherein it applies to us in the Mass. There, all have need of sorrow and a sense of sinfulness. That does not necessarily demand tearing our hair or going about in sackcloth and ashes. It does call, however, for humility, sincerity, and genuine repentance. The only road to heaven is that of repentance. And repentance is what He wants who alone sees the heart. "The wickedness of sinners shall be brought to nought: and thou shalt direct the just: the searcher of hearts and reins is God" (Psalms vii, 10). Evidently nothing is more necessary than sincere repentance, based upon true self-knowledge which is humility. St. Teresa once asked our Lord why of all virtues He loved humility best. "Because," He replied, "I love truth."

The saints were everywhere humble. They had a great sense of sinfulness, a desire of self-abasement and mortification, a longing to make satisfaction for sins. They humiliated themselves because they wanted to be just; they were pleasing to God because they were just. Would you expect God to love you and hear your prayer if you were vain, proud, self-sufficient? If we want to have our part in the Mass duly recognized by God, then let us approach this sacrifice in the right spirit. Humility and contrition are needed. It will never do to hold our heads high and pose as if before a lying mirror. To try and make ourselves out what we are not is folly. God will say to us what we would say to any deceiver in similar circumstances. We should therefore purify ourselves before God by a sincere detestation of all sin and a deep desire for purity of heart. Only thus, in a spirit of humility and a contrite heart, may we present ourselves and our sacrifice to God.

Since each of us should do interiorly as well as exteriorly what is represented by the words and action of this prayer, let us, with bent head, blush inwardly for our sins, while from the bottom of our heart we pray with the celebrant, who with bowed head recites

| In spiritu humilitatis, et in animo contrito suscipiamur a te, Domine; et sic fiat sacrificium nostrum in conspectu tuo hodie, ut placeat tibi, Domine Deus. | Accept us, O Lord, in the spirit of humility and contrition of heart; and grant that the sacrifice we offer this day in Thy sight may be pleasing to Thee, O Lord God. |

Thus begging that our oblation be acceptable, that our hearts may be so changed that we may be made worthy of being offered to God along with Jesus Christ, we go on with the priest to beg God to change the bread and wine into the body and blood of our Lord by the power of the Holy Spirit. Then comes, softly and sweetly and plead-

THE OFFERTORY

ingly, the beautiful invocation to the Holy Ghost to bless, by virtue of the cross of Christ, the sacrifice we have fully prepared.

| Veni, sanctificator, omnipotens, æterne Deus, (*benedicit oblata, prosequendo*) et bene ✠ dic hoc sacrificium tuo sancto nomini præparatum. | Come, O Almighty and Eternal God, the Sanctifier, (*he blesses the offerings*) and bless ✠ this sacrifice prepared for the glory of Thy holy name. |

In these complete prayers the whole act of offertory is summed up. We shall have occasion to note again and again in the Mass similar appeals for help and blessing. But now with this spirit of humility and this sincere prayer we may well have an unshaken confidence that God's Holy Spirit will bless our offering and hear the prayers which we have addressed to Him.

1. How much water does the priest pour into the chalice? Why? 2. Suppose there is no wine at hand, could the priest then say Mass? 3. You do not drink of the chalice in Holy Communion; do you then receive the blood of Christ? Explain. 4. There was a time when the faithful received Communion under both forms. Why the change to the present custom? 5. Of what materials were chalices made, down through the ages? Look up the splendid article "Chalice," in the "Catholic Encyclopedia." 6. Expand the following lesson from St. Chrysostom: "The table was not of silver, the chalice was not of gold in which Christ gave His blood to His disciples to drink, and yet everything was precious and truly fit to inspire awe."

ASSYRIAN SACRIFICES

No matter how far one goes back into history, he will find men offering sacrifice to God.

XIV

LAVABO

The sign of the cross is made over the oblation, and the priest, with hands joined, goes to the epistle side of the altar. Outside the edge of the altar he washes the thumb and forefinger of both hands, and then dries them, reciting at the same time the Psalm, Lavabo.

Near the time of the great mystery occurs the Lavabo, a second ceremony of purification. Looking back over the first part of the Mass, you can recall how the Confiteor was recited. That was to purify ourselves, to make our heart clean, by a sincere detestation of every kind of sin. Nothing could be more important than that your heart be crystal clear, filled with sunlight, cleansed and adorned for the coming of Christ. The washing of the hands means just that. We want our Lord to "wash us yet more from our iniquity and cleanse us from our sins" (Psalms 1, 4). Not once but often should we make the effort to purify ourselves. Here, then, in the second part of the Mass is the washing of hands — an important external act expressing the cleansing of the soul from every stain.

If you take the point of view of the East, you will readily understand this action of the Mass. Water signified purity; "washing the hands," a figure taken from the practice of the priests, was declarative of cleanliness. In Eastern lands the dust and sand blown by the winds make washing a frequent process. There are many lavations. Especially was this practice of washing connected with the services of the temple in Jerusalem. There were lavers, big bronze bowls, before the tabernacle in which the priests washed their hands and feet before offering sacrifice (Exodus xxx, 18–21). When a leper was brought back to health, running water was required to be used. Or again, there was the washing of hands, as a protestation of innocence. If a murder was committed in ancient Israel and the murderer was unknown, the elders met for the Oath of Purgation. "And all the elders of that city that are next to the slain man, shall wash their hands over the heifer that is beheaded in the valley. And they shall answer and say, Our hands have not shed this blood, neither have our eyes seen it."

GLASS CYLIX

This vase, with Peter and Paul in gold leaf, was probably employed for liturgical purposes.

You can read the old law in Deuteronomy xxi, 1–8. Speaking for God, the prophet Ezechiel declared: "And I will pour upon you clean water, and you shall be cleansed from all your filthiness, and I will cleanse you from all your idols. And I will give you a new heart, and put a new spirit within you: and I will take away the stony heart out of your flesh, and will give you a heart of flesh. And I will put my spirit in the midst of you; and I will cause you to walk in my commandments, and to keep my judgments, and do them" (Ezechiel xxxvi, 25–27).

Enough has been said to show that water in the Old Law symbolizes the means of moral cleansing. It was the same in the New. Of the baptismal cleansing of the soul, Christ said: "Unless a man be born again of water and the Holy Ghost" . . . (John iii, 5). Observe, too, how beautifully St. Paul speaks of Christ's love for His Church: "he delivered himself up for it, that he might sanctify it, cleansing it by the laver of water in the word of life: That he might present it to himself a glorious church, not having spot or wrinkle, or any such thing; but that it should be holy, and without blemish" (Ephesians v, 25–27).

Surely you can see why the act of washing has a place in the Mass. It is indicative of innocence, of an ardent desire to meet our Lord with a clean conscience, with a pure soul. Each one should strive to secure interiorly what is symbolized by the external action of the priest. Our Lord is presently to present us to His Heavenly Father. Obviously, therefore, a pure state of soul is what we need; otherwise how are we going to "draw near with a true heart in fullness of faith, having our hearts sprinkled from an evil conscience, and our bodies washed with clean water" (Hebrews x, 22).

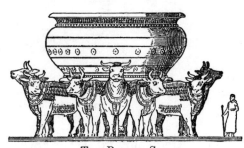

THE BRAZEN SEA
This enormous bowl was used for washings before sacrifices.

The Lavabo signifies that we should be free from every defilement of sin. It is par excellence the psalm of Innocence. By it both priest and people beg God for freedom from sin. The priest stands before God's altar, in close relation to Jesus Christ. The people are to be partakers in the sacrifice. Their inmost nature should turn toward God and to Him only. They should be guileless. Each should say: "I carry my soul in my hands, and wash it and see that it is clean, ready to offer to the Eternal Father a pure and wholesome sacrifice of my very self." That

LAVABO

wish, that hope, that prayer finds fitting expression in the words, acts, and movements of the Lavabo. Outside the edge of the altar, the priest washes and dries his fingers, reciting, even as he cleanses and dries them, the Psalm:

Lavabo inter innocentes manus meas: et circumdabo altare tuum, Domine.	I will wash my hands among the innocent: and will compass Thine altar, O Lord.
Ut audiam vocem laudis: et enarrem universa mirabilia tua.	That I may hear the voice of Thy praise: and tell of all Thy wondrous works.
Domine, dilexi decorem domus tuæ, et locum habitationis gloriæ tuæ.	I have loved, O Lord, the beauty of Thy house: and the place where Thy glory dwelleth.
Ne perdas cum impiis, Deus, animam meam: et cum viris sanguinum vitam meam.	Take not away my soul, O God, with the wicked: nor my life with men of blood.
In quorum manibus iniquitates sunt: dextera eorum repleta est muneribus.	In whose hands are iniquities: their right hand is filled with gifts.
Ego autem in innocentia mea ingressus sum: redime me et miserere mei.	But as for me, I have walked in my innocence: redeem me, and have mercy on me.
Pes meus stetit in directo: in ecclesiis benedicam te, Domine.	My foot hath stood in the direct way: in the churches I will bless Thee, O Lord.
Gloria Patri, etc.	Glory be to the Father, etc.

Such, then, is the exquisite prayer of the washing of hands. The rapid review, given above, of the use and significance of washings makes sufficiently clear the meaning of this psalm. But there is still more worth knowing about this subject. A rich historical background sets off the beautiful ceremony of the Lavabo. We have seen how scrupulously careful the Jews were in their many washings, and how concerned they were with cleanliness when they went to religious worship. It will help to see other instances of this; they will shed more light on the Mass.

Amongst God's servants of old, David did not dare go to the sacred festival because he was not clean at that time. Jeremiah was "restrained" probably by uncleanness, and could not go into the temple (Jeremias xxxvi, 5). Isaias quailed at the consciousness of his unworthiness, at the thought that he had dared to cross the threshold of the temple. Then said he: "Woe is me, because I am a man of unclean lips, and I dwell in the midst of a people that hath' unclean lips, and I have seen with my eyes the King, the Lord of Hosts."

WASHING OF HANDS IN THE EAST
The host laves the hands of his guest.

Similarly, in New Testament times, when our Lord came, the custom of washing frequently, especially before meals, was still in vogue. This is referred to in the account of the marriage feast of Cana. There were six stone water pots for the water of purification, which our Lord later turned into wine (John ii, 6).

On the occasion when our Lord entered the house of Simon, the Pharisee, the host did not give Him water to bathe His feet. According to the usages of the East, it was customary for the master of the house, when receiving guests, to provide them with water to wash their feet. Usually this feet-washing took place before a banquet and its absence on this occasion was remarked by Christ. But Mary Magdalen poured precious ointment on our Lord's feet, and He took occasion to chide the Pharisee while He praised the faith of the repentant sinner (Luke vii, 44).

At the Last Supper, our Lord Himself rose and washed the feet of His disciples in order to teach them humility. "I am among you as he that serveth" (John xiii, 1–17). It was the function of a slave to wash the feet of the guests. That is why St. Peter grew indignant and protested, but the divine Master gently rebuked him. "If I wash thee not, thou shalt have no part with me" (John xiii, 8–10). This is plainly a parable of things spiritual. Our Lord tells Peter how humble he must be, if he would have the spirit of Christ; he must follow not his own way but the way of his divine Master; by staying close to Christ in love, humility, and obedience the disciple's earthly thoughts will be spiritualized, his earthly aims elevated, and pardon secured for his shortcomings and sins.

All this happened, remember, at the Last Supper, where the first Mass was said. The Church never forgets even a single detail or lesson coming from that holiest of evenings, which meant so much for us and for our salvation. Accordingly in every Mass there is a washing, not of the feet, but of the hands. It symbolizes the need of forgiveness of sins by repentance and prayer. Having voiced our repentance in the Confiteor, we now pray in the Lavabo for the complete forgiveness of sins which Christ alone can effect in our souls. How careful should we be to pray, all of us, for we have need of divine help.

The Lavabo is said when the priest washes his hands over the little basin and the server hands him a towel. Outward appearance here has inward significance. The washing of the hands is to show how pure and clean should be the hands and heart of the priest when he comes to consecrate and receive the Blessed Sacrament. In view of this the priest says the prayer of the psalmist who of old stood on God's side and compassed His altar, who wished always to wash his hands in innocence and sought to give thanks to God in His house. A few moments ago, the priest begged that the oblation be accepted by God, and he offered it in a spirit of humility and with a contrite heart; but now, above all things, he wants to be innocent; he wishes to wash his hands in innocence, aware all the time that he is moving about in God's presence. Soon he will be offering Christ Himself. How important, therefore, to walk in His truth — to lead a good life; how necessary that "the heavens hold firm the walls of his innocence, keep unshaken that temple, his soul, that he may stand and offer a worthy sacrifice."

What the priest asks for in this psalm-prayer, we also need. Unfortunately, we are apt to stray from the right path. The fact is that once we let ourselves drift there is a spontaneous tendency to sin. Directly we find ourselves in that path it is time to set ourselves straight with our conscience. Christ "is not only the object of our worship, He is also the voice of conscience, and, more than that, He is our judge, He is the umpire of our eternal destiny." Here, in the Mass we are going to offer ourselves — body, soul, mind, life, all that we are — to God. Just as Jesus will offer Himself in the hands of the priest, so He will let us offer ourselves with Him. What a privilege! Yet we must make ourselves worthy of being presented to God, worthy to be an "acceptable people." To purify ourselves from errors or faults by a deep sincere act of contrition is a condition of hearing Mass well. Then we can pray: "Have mercy on me, O Lord, that I may serve Thee in all innocence: This I can do only by a great trust in Thy power and mercy. Keep my feet in the right way, and allow me in choir to praise Thee always with Thy saints." Only with a pure heart can one join truly in with the voice of thanksgiving and proclaim all God's wondrous works, especially the work of redemption. That is what we are here at Mass to do. We can be thanking our Lord in our inmost soul that He once offered Himself on the cross to save us and now lets the same sacrifice take place before our eyes so that we may be there and may each receive for our souls some of the great grace He pours out at this solemn moment. Naturally, if our hearts are clean, we shall be full of gratitude, we shall proclaim our loyalty to Christ, in the very words of this Psalm.

Voicing the spirit of the Psalm, we choose God in preference to sinners. We love the altar and the house of God better than worldly things. "One day in thy house is better than a thousand in the tents of sinners." There is more still. There is the promise always to observe a certain line of conduct in fidelity to the teachings of our childhood.

> I have sat not with the council of *vanity*.
> Neither will I go in with the doers of *unjust things*.
> I have hated the assembly of the *malignant*.
> And with the *wicked* I will not sit.   (Psalms xxv, 4–5)

Mark well the four points — danger points for youth: vanity, unjust things, things malignant, things that are wicked. They are one and all pitfalls to be avoided. At no time have young people been in greater need of timely warning. Especially those of high-school age; for from fourteen to eighteen, they are interiorly subjected to heavy strain and temptation; they are in sore need of cultivating habits of courage, self-command, and circumspection. Devotion and self-rule are worth more than all the information or culture in the world. No education is worth while except it generates devotion and self-rule. John Ruskin used to decry a certain type of so-called education "as little better than a training in impudence." Certainly Catholic education is not that, for Catholic education is devotion and self-rule or nothing. This is emphatically the time for all to learn and practice these two big things, devotion and self-rule.

It is also the time for hammering into our soul salutary warnings concerning vanity, unjust things, the malignant, and the wicked. Those are the very things that all of us must shun, for they are traps which catch many souls. To deal with them is to go into danger, to be tempted the more. Hence we ask God: "Take not away my soul with the wicked, nor my life with the bloody men; in whose hands are iniquities; their right hand is filled with gifts." Catholic boys and girls need to be on guard to-day against suchlike, so suddenly they find themselves in an evil social environment. Sinners and sin are everywhere. They always have some tempting bait to offer to youth. Look sometime into a show window and see the array of hooks, baits, flies, frogs, etc., for fishing displayed there. In life Satan sets an array of baits for souls simple enough to let him play them like fish, and we are silly enough to fancy we are having our own way, not his. These baits are clearly pointed out by the psalmist. Make careful note of them.

Without virtue and good, steady habits we are apt to become vain and conceited. Vanity always is unreal, hollow, bad. The subjects for vanity are good looks, talent, small successes, and the like. They are all right until we put too much stock in them, and are content with our own judgment of ourselves instead of referring everything to God. Vanity is contemptible because it is untruthful and selfish. Vain boys and girls do not want to put their feet in the right way. They think they know more than their parents and teachers and priests. They will not listen to the counsels of their elders. Their conceit would vanish if they only knew how much they will think of it after they have battled with life and eaten the dust of humility. "Nothing is so aggravating as the peculiarly worldly wisdom of a girl of fifteen, and nothing so transient. It is only one of the endless and constantly varying forms of mimicry." Both girls and boys are liable to vanity. Once they get the sin into their soul they pride themselves on what they are, and possess, forgetful of how little it is at most. They are greedy of admiration, seek those who will flatter them, and shun those who restrain them. No longer are they innocent, amiable, and well behaved; they are willful, spiteful, bound to have their own way; and they are bitterly disappointed when no notice is taken of their claim to admiration. They like to be well dressed, but have no care for their soul. They become lazy, dreamy, utterly selfish, and they spoil their young lives at the very start. If vanity is allowed to grow by itself, it may and does lead into great danger and sin, for vanity permits good advice to pass over its head, and quickly tires of right doing. Be yourself. Ape no vanities. Have a fine scorn for petty pretense at position and undue power. "What thou art," says Thomas à Kempis, "that thou art; nor canst thou be anything save what God sees thee to be." That is worth remembering.

Never stoop to do unjust things. Stake your life daily in the venture of honesty. "Justice," says Shakespeare, "is the king-becoming virtue." Whoever can be said to take his chance when he ought, not when he can; who shows fair play and good faith; who prefers a difficult deed to an easy one; and scorns the temptation to excuse himself if he fails; such a one is a true Christian sportsman, since he does no injustice either to others or to himself. Be just, then, even in the face of gibes, flouts, and jeers.

A girl of sixteen in a trolley car was passed by when the conductor was collecting fares. "A nickel's as good to me as to him," she said to her companion, forgetting that the first rule of the game of life is fair play and fair pay. That act of hers may have been the beginning of sneak thieving. Dissimulation, dishonesty, artifice — how they spoil our "young and rose-lipped cherubim, so that the boy is no longer as glorious, or the girl as fair, as they were once."

That which is virtually bent upon harm or evil is called malignant. You may have had, or seen, at one time an infected finger. It is ugly, and painful. A tiny germ did that, because it was malignant. Now sin is the germ that poisons the soul far more than any microbe could poison the body. Keep that in mind. If boys and girls were influenced only by the good, free from contact with bad influence, it would be an easy matter to keep from sin. But our age is one where sin has its easy way with youth; its net may be drawn around souls ever so early to render them helpless captives to vanity and human respect. Besides, an evil world is ever ready to steal in with its poisoned precepts, and may change all that is attractive into something that is very undesirable. Take, for example, swearing. How readily some boys swear! There is nothing courageous about that. Any thug or rowdy can do, and does, just that. It requires no brains, no study. And it never does, or will, indicate courage. "Such is the natural reverence of every pagan American Indian for the name of God, that they have no swear words in their own language." And yet you sometimes hear Catholic boys take the Lord's name in vain! Evil communications corrupt good manners. No doubt young minds are pliable and elastic, and easily, alas! too easily accommodate themselves to any one they meet. Girls have a natural love of color, rhythm, and ornament. They sometimes foolishly put themselves in danger through these things. Never were they in greater need of safeguards than nowadays. In your youthful inexperience you may fall in with evil unless you are guided by advice, good example, Catholic tradition. There are so many insidious vices at large, on the streets, in the temper of the times, in slang, in songs, in newspaper reports and stories. Invariably they infect the soul of the girl and boy who are not on their guard. Contact with such influences renders both girls and boys restless, pleasure mad, unsteady in character. Too often does Satan with steady, long-skilled hand draw about them a web of evil as difficult to break through as the steel meshes of a coat of armor. No wonder weariness and sadness cloud young temperaments in the very freshness of their time, when their lives should run safe and sweet. How many young people are blasé, dissatisfied with everything! They behave like overgrown children anxious only to have their way, and their whims provoke effects quite scandalous. What will become of them if they act thus even before they have found life? We must keep in mind the greatest of all truths — "that moral good is the highest good, and moral evil the deepest evil."

Those who have been brought up in ignorance of the polluting fashions of the world come at a critical time to high school. If by God's mercy they reach the age of fifteen without knowing much of wickedness, without having an idea of evil, their eyes open to these things soon enough. It is time, boys and girls, to look things straight in the face; it is also quite time for you to think, if only in view of saving your soul. Be strong: watch and pray. Too often you may feel a rising in your mind against discipline and restraint kindly imposed upon you. This is unworthy of Catholic youth. You do not understand that your ignorance of sin is a glory, you do not yet know how beautiful a thing is your integrity. It is just at this time you are so open to attacks. Bad books, bad plays, bad companions may readily furnish the near occasions of sin, and you may easily forget that the flames you wish to touch will certainly burn your fingers. Knowledge may easily be received from those who are wicked. Easily may your minds be tainted and your sweet innocent youth spoiled.

Having learned what these dangers are, the duty before us is to avoid them. Undoubtedly then our task is to make a clean way for ourselves through all these foes. The Lavabo warns us against them; sins that soil and profane the house of worship (both our soul and the Church) and make it a den of thieves. Therefore, they are to be eliminated; we are to wash ourselves clean of them as we would cleanse our hands of filth. Free our soul from what is foul. Every sin, every moral irregularity, prints a stain upon the soul. They are blots which should be entirely cleansed from the soul, so that it can say: "In simple and pure soul I come to You, dear Lord." That is the lesson of the Lavabo.

1. What is a credence table? Look up the origin of the word "credentarius" as it was understood in the Middle Ages. During Mass what do you expect to see on the credence table? Could you not provide certain linens and embroider them for use in the Mass? Let your sewing class consult with the pastor on that matter. 2. What is the spirit of

this verse: "Domine, dilexi decorem Domus Tuae et locum habitationis gloriæ tuæ"? What is the best practical application of that text for boys and girls of high-school age? 3. On what occasion did our Lord say: "Go, wash in the pool of Siloe"? Why? What else can you say as to Christ's remarkable procedure in that case?

POOL OF SILOE

XV

SUSCIPE SANCTA TRINITAS

Arriving at the middle of the altar, after the Lavabo, the priest stands erect, raises his eyes to the cross, and immediately lowers them again. Then, as he inclines moderately, he recites the Suscipe, or offering to the Holy Trinity. The great silence has already fallen and the sacrifice proceeds.

The bread and wine have been blessed; done also is the washing of hands which will soon bear the Son of God. The preliminaries of the sacrifice would seem to be complete; but not yet. Like children, we still insist on offering our gifts; not only once but many times. Love gives and gives and gives. "Take these gifts, dear God," it would utter again and again. That is the spirit of the Suscipe sancta Trinitas. The priest has returned to the middle of the altar and there he shall stay till the end of the Mass, before God's stone of sacrifice, Golgotha. Watch what he does. For one moment his eyes are raised to the cross, then lowered. With head bowed in humility he makes the offering of the gifts to the Holy Trinity.

Suscipe, sancta Trinitas, hanc oblationem quam tibi offerimus ob memoriam Passionis, Resurrectionis, et Ascensionis Jesu Christi Domini nostri: et in honorem beatæ Mariæ semper Virginis, et beati Joannis Baptistæ, et sanctorum Apostolorum Petri et Pauli, et istorum, et omnium sanctorum; ut illis proficiat ad honorem	Receive, O Holy Trinity, this oblation which we make Thee, in memory of the Passion, Resurrection, and Ascension of our Lord Jesus Christ and in honor of blessed Mary ever virgin, of blessed John the Baptist, of the holy Apostles Peter and Paul, and of all the saints: that it may be available to their honor and to our salva-

SUSCIPE SANCTA TRINITAS

nobis autem ad salutem; et illi pro nobis intercedere dignentur in cœlis, quorum memoriam agimus in terris. Per eundem Christum Dominum nostrum. Amen.

tion: and may they vouchsafe to intercede for us in heaven, whose memory we celebrate on earth. Through the same Christ our Lord. Amen.

The whole offering is summed up in this exquisite prayer. There was a time when the Suscipe used to be said privately. The prayer met with such approval that by 1570 it was entered in all the Roman missals. In this prayer heaven and earth draw nearer than ever. God and His creatures are united once more upon the height of Calvary. For as you say the Suscipe you offer those gifts to the Holy Trinity; you call upon Mary, the angels, and the saints, heirs to the graces flowing from Calvary; you summon the whole Church — in heaven, in purgatory, on earth — to commemorate the mysteries of the Passion, Resurrection, and Ascension. What solemn vistas open out for eyes of faith! What could be a more fitting prelude to the solemn part of the Mass just beginning. Soon, very soon, will He come Whose holy act will be to the honor and glory of all the angels and saints, and to our own salvation.

With the altar set for the sacrifice, the great silence of the Mass has begun. All the way from the Offertory to the Communion there is but little audible prayer. The reason for this is not far to seek. The priest is copying the conduct of Christ on the cross. The Mass, remember, is a divine drama with a wealth of meaning, fraught with graces and helps for the soul; wherefore the eyes of the whole Catholic world should be upon it, as it is acted and will be acted on the stage of the altar even till the end of time. Its whole trend is meant to exhibit the acts and scenes on Calvary. To this end movements and words are aimed: even the tones the priest uses are never scattered, never meaningless. One of the most intensely dramatic features of the Mass is the silence. It used to be very deep when the curtain was drawn across so as to shut out the priest and the altar from view.

You will find something very attractive in a study of the great silence of the Mass. If you could cultivate appreciation of its deep significance, sensitiveness to the appeal of steady prayer, readiness for the very keen and thrilling religious perceptions that can be evoked, you would begin to realize the great beauty of this profound silence. Especially profitable will it be, if our boys and girls grasp the real background of our Lord's passion and death as narrated in the Gospels, and see how the Church keeps faithful to the silence of Christ.

Our Lord on the cross said seven last words before He yielded His spirit into the hands of His Eternal Father. The nailing to the cross took place at nine o'clock (Mark xv, 25, it was the third hour). About this time our Lord gave forth three utterances. From midday to three o'clock in the afternoon, usually the brightest part of the day, there was darkness. Besides the testimony of the three evangelists, early Christian writers speak of this eclipse, and appeal to heathen testimony to support the truth. During the three hours of darkness our Lord was silent. And after six hours on the cross He cried out words which point to the deep struggle going on in His soul. The order of the Seven Words, as they are called, is:

Before the Darkness

I. The prayer of Christ for His enemies (Luke xxiii, 34).
II. The promise to the penitent robber (Matthew xxvii, 44; Luke xxiii, 43).
III. The charge to Mary and St. John (John xix, 26).

SUSCIPE SANCTA TRINITAS 121

At the Close of the Darkness
IV. The cry of distress to the Heavenly Father (Matthew xxvii, 46).

Just Before His Death
V. The exclamation: "I thirst" (John xix, 28).
VI. "It is consummated" (John xix, 30).
VII. The final commendation of His spirit to God (Luke xxiii, 46).

Seven times the gr at silence on Calvary's cross was broken. Having noted this fact, notice how seven times, too, the great silence of the Mass is broken. Ever bearing in mind the events of our Lord's passion, the Church in a divinely dramatic remembrance observes the spaces of silence from the Offertory to the Communion. Athrob with silent prayer, the action and movement of the Mass go on in a drama of overwhelming majesty. And the stillness is broken but *seven times*, when the priest raises his voice in certain prayers. The vocal parts in the Canon of the Mass are: 1. Orate Fratres. 2. Preface. 3. Nobis quoque peccatoribus. 4. Pater Noster. 5. Pax Domini. 6. Agnus Dei. 7. Domine non sum dignus.

The Mass is the best place to learn the value of silence. Lucky for us if we can learn the lesson of silence early in life. A growing number of girls and boys as they go on and up through the high school master the habit of thoughtful, meditative silence over their prayer book when at Mass. If we will hear Christ in our heart, we must place ourselves apart. That is why going to Mass mornings day after day makes us better Catholics, better characters. Mass sets our hearts thinking aright, lets in light on ourselves, stirs us to duty toward our neighbor — all this while uniting us more closely to Christ. Nothing is more useful than silence. In silence and hope shall your strength be. Did you ever know that the American cent of 1787 bore the motto

THE MASS

"Mind Your Business"? Be not like the indiscreet person who talks for talk's sake, who knows not how to make conversation without prying into what is none of his business. Of such, a great writer says: "As the inquisitive, in my opinion, are such merely from a vacancy in their own imaginations, there is nothing, methinks, so dangerous as to communicate secrets to them; for the same temper of inquiry makes them as impertinently communicative." Silence is a valuable discipline. See how our Lord practiced voluntary silence on the cross. "Dumb as a lamb before His shearers, and He opened not His mouth." In the Mass, from the cross, He speaks to us in silence. There may we learn these vital truths. "Solitude is the mother country of the strong, silence is their prayer." "Solitude is the audience chamber of God." Never talk or whisper unnecessarily during the Holy Sacrifice.

St. Mark
This evangelist is usually shown with a lion.

1. Give two instances in the life of our Lord where He practiced divine silence. 2. Solitude is a rich green pasture or a closed garden, where the soul can cultivate its higher will, its better self, so as to make it take root, grow, bud, and flower into a higher life. Explain this truth. What is a retreat? Does your high school have an annual retreat? 3. Can you tell the values of a spiritual retreat? 4. What example did our Lord set in this matter? 5. Describing the desert, one who had lived there for many years says: "Men seek gold, solitude, forgetfulness. Some wander for the love of wandering. Others seek to hide from the world. Criminals are driven to the desert. Besides those, all travelers crossing the desert talk of its enchantments. They all have different reasons. Loneliness, peace, silence, beauty, wonder, sublimity — a thousand reasons! Indeed, they are all proofs of the call of the desert. But those men do not go deep enough. . . . The traveler gazes out

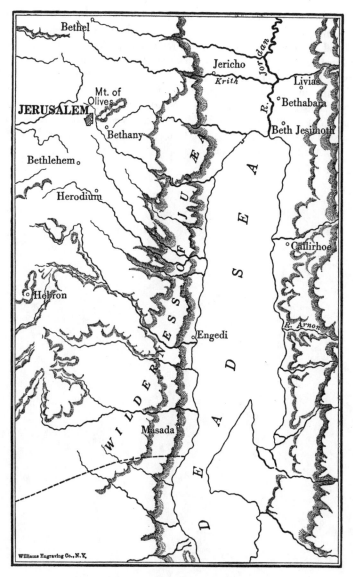

THE WILDERNESS OF JUDÆA

across the desert. The waste land stretched there, vast and illimitable, the same as all the innumerable times he had gazed. Solemn and gray and old, indifferent to man, yet strengthening through its passionless fidelity to its own task." This, about the Great American Desert, where men go to live, sleep on the ground, seek peace amid the silence and solitude, and infinite vistas; where they feel their remoteness from petty things, and commune with God. Nearly nineteen hundred years ago there lived a famous solitary in Palestine. Who was he? How many years did he spend in the desert? Can you describe that desert? 6. Who was St. Anthony of the Desert?

XVI

ORATE FRATRES

The priest bends, kisses the altar, as if to salute Jesus Christ. Next, he turns round and greets the people with "Orate Fratres," asking the prayers of the congregation that the sacrifice they are offering may be pleasing to Almighty God.

Very soon we shall reach the Canon. It is only a step from here. Every moment brings us nearer to the more solemn part of the sacrifice, now that the oblations are on the altar and the washing of hands performed. The first break in the great silence occurs at the Orate Fratres. This prayer is a fresh devotional addition introduced during the Middle Ages. That was back in the ages of faith. It was then a new invitation to pray, a special request for the prayers of the people; another "Orate" added to the many "Oremus" pleas heard in the Mass. One big lesson we are learning is this: the nearer the moment of the sacrifice approaches the greater should be our prayer and recollection.

"Pray that your sacrifice and mine may be acceptable." "Yours and mine," says the priest. As in peace or war we all stand together for our dear land; so in the Mass we are all as one. All are one in Christ, who once prayed: "Holy Father, keep them in thy name whom thou hast given me, that they may be one as we also are. . . . That they all may be one, as thou, Father, in me, and I in thee; that they also may be one in us" (John xvii, 11, 21). The Mass does just this, for in it, as on the cross, Christ draws all to Him and the Father keeps us in His holy name. Shortly that sacrifice will be in progress. Of this you know that the people are co-offerers with the celebrant. What is done for them in the Mass is somehow done *of* and *by* them through Jesus Christ. Therefore their intercession must be mutual. "My sacrifice and your sacrifice," says the priest. Yes, it is our sacrifice. And remember it is to be made with a contrite and humble heart. God will never despise any offering made in that spirit.

P. Orate, fratres, ut meum ac vestrum sacrificium acceptabile fiat apud Deum Patrem omnipotentem.	*P.* Brethren, pray that my sacrifice and yours may be acceptable to God, the Father Almighty.
A. Suscipiat Dominus sacrificium de manibus tuis, ad laudem et gloriam nominis sui, ad utilitatem quoque nostram, totiusque Ecclesiæ suæ sanctæ.	*A.* May the Lord receive the sacrifice from thy hands, to the praise and glory of His name, to our benefit, and to that of all His holy Church.

The Orate Fratres is like a leave-taking prayer. This said, the priest faces the altar, and does not turn to the people again until after the sacrifice is consummated, at the Communion. From now on he turns his face steadfastly toward God and the holy sacrifice he is about to offer. It is as if he were entering into solitude, face to face only with God, occupied entirely with the great mystery about to be performed. Most of us have felt the sense of awe or have at least thought of the holy silence in this part of the Mass. If we give this deeper study, we shall become more intelligent Catholics. We will not fail to note much that it signifies, for it is a "silence, speaking of prayer." In the past, besides silence, there was also seclusion in the sacrifice. Early altars used to be covered with a canopy, supported by columns, and known as the ciborium. As this covering was much like the flower cup of the Egyptian water lily, it must have looked very graceful and beautiful.

From the roof of the ciborium veils of rich stuff were suspended, like window curtains on a rod, so that it was easy to draw them tight or leave them open as the need might be. A good idea of an ancient altar with ciborium and veils drawn can be formed from the mosaic found in the Church of St. George in Thessalonica.

This representation dates back as far as A.D. 500; indeed it may be much earlier. What a pity that we have not more pictures of the early altars. However, enough evidence is on hand to show just what happened in the Mass. As to the custom of drawing the veils at the more solemn part of the sacrifice, St. Paulinus of Nola (354–431) is thought to speak of it in these lines:

CIBORIUM, WITH VEILS DRAWN

Mosaic in the Church of St. George at Thessalonica

| Divinum veneranda tegunt lataria fœdus, | Veiled are the holy altars For the pledge divine. |
| Compositisque sacra cum cruce martyribus. | Hush! the white-robed Martyrs gather Round the Cross sublime. |

So runs the dim, beautiful reference, like distant music, in the Mass. Clearer, however, is the testimony of St. Chrysostom, a contemporary of St. Paulinus. This great Greek Father of the Church tells how in his day (347–407) the veils were drawn in the Mass so as to conceal the priest offering the sacrifice, nor were they withdrawn till after the Consecration. So the service went on, as it were, within a secret citadel. In view of this ancient practice it is easy to understand why, even to this day, the priest never turns to the people during the next part of the Mass.

The ciborium with veiled altar dates back quite early. But go back centuries beyond that time. Go back ages before Christ came. As you read the Old Testament, you find this very interesting circumstance. In the Old Law, the High Priest, ministering at the sanctuary, entered the Holy of Holies. The veil of the temple hid him from the people. "And the veils shall be hanged on with rings, and within it thou shalt put the ark of the testament" (Exodus xxvi, 33). That veil was rent when our Lord died (Matthew xxvii, 51). Which meant that Christ had made the real atonement insuring for us a free access to God. His sacrifice did away forever with the old sacrifices. Nowhere is this made so clear as in the ninth chapter of the Epistle to the Hebrews. The new sacrifice is one in which "Jesus is entered for us, made a high priest forever according to the order of Melchisedech" (Hebrews vi, 20).

HIGH PRIEST
Clad in the robes of his sacred office.

Now our Lord will soon come upon the altar, our High Priest, but He will allow the visible oblation to be made by the hands of his priest. Accordingly the priest enters, as it were, into the Holy of Holies. Very soon he is to consecrate and offer in a visible manner the body and blood of Jesus Christ under the form and appearance of bread and wine. What he has requested as a last word, so to say, is that the people pray earnestly that the sacrifice may fulfill three ends. There is no better time, then, to pray earnestly that this Mass may be: (1) to the praise and glory of God; (2) to our own profit; and (3) to the benefit of all His holy Church.

(1) "To praise God is to confess that God is good." That is why the psalmist sang: "Praise the Lord for he is good: for his mercy endureth forever." Read Psalm cxxxv and you will grasp the whole idea of praise. You will never find a lyric more beautiful than that one. It is instinct with praise, brimful of esteem and regard for the goodness of God. In this connection, note three kinds of praise: (1) the praise of love; (2) the praise of thanksgiving; and (3) the praise of admiration.

God is good in Himself, hence the praise of love. To love God is to do His will. Naturally we want to please those we love. More than that, we become what we love — and to love God is to become Godlike! To be Godlike copies of our Master, reflections of His likeness, this is nothing more or less than praise. Now, imitation is a very sincere form of praiseful affection. And Christ says that we are His disciples if we do the things that He commands. The Mass gives us the highest opportunity for praise, the praise of sincere service.

God is good to us, so we praise Him with the praise of thanksgiving. "Praiseful prayer, prayerful praise." Says the psalmist: "Sing ye to the Lord a new song, his praise is in the assembly of the saints." But the Mass will soon be the assembly of the saints joined with Christ on the altar offering up the sacrifice of praise to the Heavenly Father as the psalmist did:

> Like the tones of a harp are thy commandments, O Lord,
> When I am walking in the ways of life.

God is good in all His works, hence the praise of admiration. That is what Psalm ciii gives. "Whatever else God may have intended in creation, He must have intended this, to make a show of His own excellence outside Himself. He can only create upon the model of Himself." So it happens that "The heavens shew forth the glory of God, and the firmament declareth the works of his hands" (Psalms xviii).

Not the heavens only but the earth declares God's glory. The oceans declare His immensity. The deserts speak of His eternity. The fertile earth tells of His providence. The flowers of the field proclaim His beauty. Indeed, nature is a ladder upon which reason can climb from earth to heaven. "God may be adored in the curve of falling waters, may be praised in the veining of a flower." Who says that we are not near God when we pray to Him in the woods, on the water, when we are surrounded by all His beautiful creation? We praise by reason. Reason shows us how God can be known from His creation — and therefore becomingly praised. Repeatedly this truth is made clear in Holy Writ. "For," says St. Paul, "the invisible things of him, from the creation of the world, are clearly seen, being understood by the things that are made; his eternal power also, and divinity" (Romans i, 20).

Praise, then, of this threefold character is to be offered to

God in acknowledgment of His sovereign dominion over all creatures.

(2) The sacrifice of the Mass is to our own profit. Praise, as we have seen, is one end for which we offer up the sacrifice. There are many others. When our Lord came on earth to live here, and, at the age of thirty-three, to give up His life, this was all for us and for our salvation. "I am come," He said, "that you may have life and have it more abundantly." Now the Mass is the continuation of Christ's self-giving for us; that is, for our benefit. That is precisely what is conferred upon us in the holy sacrifice. The Mass will draw down upon our heads the dew of God's grace — light, power, truth. The Mass also obtains for us pardon of sin and the spiritual strength to rise, go forward, and do the will of God. Hence one may say that the Mass is the greatest gift on this earth. Those who hear it aright come away vastly richer in soul and better able to do their work in the world. Those who neglect Mass lose their love of Christ and for His holy laws. How can such people ever respect the law of the land if in their hearts they have no love for God? The real blame for the present carelessness of many young folks and for the evil doing of older people rests with irreligion. They do not love Christ, they do not go to church, they do not keep the Commandments. The world was happier when people — all the people — loved Christ, went to Mass, kept the Commandments. To-day the Mass makes better Catholics and better Catholics make better homes. Better homes make better citizens, better government, better conditions — peace, good will, prosperity — all of which contribute to happiness. Note how good practicing Catholics are the best citizens, the most law-abiding; observe that the Catholic Church does for her children just what Abraham Lincoln wanted done everywhere

in our dear land. She implants in their hearts true reverence, not only for the law of God but for the laws of our land.

(3) The sacrifice of the Mass is offered for the benefit of the whole Church — the congregation of all those who profess the faith of Christ. They are all the flock of Christ. If you turn to the history of any nation under heaven, you can see how the Church from age to age had to fight against the forces of evil. "Fear not, little flock," our Lord has assured us. And He makes good His promise by coming to us in the Mass. That "endless repetition of His sacrifice from sunrise to sunset, on the altars of the Church, to the end of the world" is for all, for His Church. The Real Presence is to bring us to Himself, to keep us fresh and alive and vibrant with His spirit — that we should be in Him and He in us. In the Mass, "the personality of Christ, which is the pivot of Christianity, has become not only a center and source of grace for His whole Church, but a means of grace" — of mystical contact of millions of souls with the great sacrifice.

Looking backward on the history of the world, since Christ came on earth, one can see how Catholics, true to the spirit of Christ, have done their share for the world's betterment. Our Lord in the Mass gives them grace, light, power to do His work among men. Now, our Lord has for you a work to do in the world. To fail in that would be a sin. The Church of which you are a member has in every age a big work to do. Its most important work at the present time is the solution of the social question. Study your Church history to see how well your Holy Mother did her work in the past ages. In the beginning the Church suffered the martyrdom of her children; after that she addressed herself to the work of the sanctification of the people; then she took up the defense and definition of her doctrines;

the development of the monastic life; the transformation of the barbarian invaders; the elaboration of Christian art and literature; the adaptation of science to the teachings of the faith; the marvelous devotion to all kinds of charity; and to-day her task will be the solving of the great social question which is now agitating society. "The past half century has been a momentous one for the Catholic Church by reason of the great changes in conditions encountered in many parts of the world. There have been steady gains and successes where she has been let alone, and corresponding losses and defeats where the civil authorities had the wish and the power to interfere." A bird's-eye view of the Church's career in this world will give you the reason why we pray so fervently in this part of the Mass that Christ will give His whole Church grace and strength to extend His kingdom on earth.

1. What idea did our Lord give His disciples concerning how their work in this world would be received? 2. It is an open secret that certain organizations are behind the attempt to prosecute Catholics and their schools in one way or another. Do you know them? 3. What is the cornerstone of the Catholic Church in America? 4. Do you know anything about the trials of the Holy Father these days? 5. What do you consider the five greatest evils at large to-day? 6. If we are going to eliminate prejudice in our community, how must we strike at its roots?

XVII

SECRETA

After the Orate Fratres, the priest with outstretched hands recites the secret prayers. Before concluding the last prayer, he joins his hands, then disjoins them, places the right on the altar, and with the left turns the pages of the Missal to the Preface.

Having asked for the prayers of the people, the priest goes on to say the Secrets. The word "Secreta" gives us the clew to the meaning of this part of the Mass. No one fails to sense the quiet, the stillness of the sacrifice. More than ever does one feel the holy hush of the Mass. We should give to the Mass deeper attention than we devote to anything in the outside world. All our attention. Not a fraction of it, but all of it, given freely and undivided. Hallowed moments, surely, these are. And all of the incidents — prayers and petitions, movements and ceremonies — are closely related. Not one is insignificant. Follow them in their sequence and to their climax in the mystical tragedy of Calvary — the Consecration and Communion. Had we the vision of an archangel, that were not broad enough to embrace the wondrous mystery in its fullness. Nevertheless with eyes of faith we can follow the course of the Holy Sacrifice.

Turning to the altar after the Orate Fratres, the priest prays in a voice so low as to be heard only by himself. To this prayer (or prayers) was given the name *Secreta*. The priest begs God to make him worthy, clean of heart, for he

SECRETA

is now at the threshold of the more solemn part of the service. Moreover he begs God to accept the oblations for the most holy use to which they will be put at the Consecration. Hence, the Secreta is called the prayer *super oblata*. Over the bread and wine the priest in a low voice prays (Second Mass of Christmas):

Munera nostra quæsumus Domine, nativitatis hodiernæ mysteriis apta proveniant, et pacem nobis semper infundant: ut sicut homo genitus idem refulsit et Deus, sic nobis hæc terrena substantia conferat quod divinum est. Per eundum Dominum nostrum Jesum, Christum, filium tuum, qui tecum vivit et regnat in unitate Spiritus Sancti, Deus, per omnia sæcula Sæculorum.	May our offerings, we beseech Thee, O Lord, be in keeping with the mysteries of the day's nativity, and ever infuse into us peace, that as He Who was born man shone also as God, so this earthly substance may bestow upon us what is divine. Through the same Jesus Christ, Thy Son, our Lord, Who liveth and reigneth with Thee in the unity of the Holy Ghost, God, world without end.

This is a true offertory prayer in which God is asked to accept our gifts and give us in return His grace. But why, you may ask, say the prayer silently? "The silence of the priest designates the hiding place of Christ. The priest says some things secretly because at the time of the Passion of Christ, His disciples did not confess Christ but secretly."

Further reason for this silence is to remind the people that they should be exceedingly attentive and exhibit the deepest respect, insomuch as now the priest is entering into the holiest part of the Mass. The memorial of Christ's passion is about to be celebrated, so our hearts should be filled with awe and reverence. Even the low voice of the priest is charged with mystery. Besides "all that which is most grand and august takes place in silence. The operation of the Holy Ghost, which changes the bread and wine into the Body and Blood of Jesus Christ, is not perceived by the senses; the Word is there, but He is silent. The sacred humanity is there, but it is always under the veil of bread and wine. The divine Saviour takes a real body on the altar, He offers Himself, He prays, He sacrifices Himself, and still nothing is seen or heard by the faithful. Is there anything more reasonable than that during these holy mysteries the Church should express by a profound and religious silence the admirations he has for her God, Who thus secretly works them?"

Speaking further of this truth, a Catholic writer says:

So few realize the beauty of silence, the ineffable loveliness of the perfection of quiet, the sense of distance from the fret and fume of things that do not matter — the solemnity of the nearness of the divine kingdom on earth. There are three silences: the silence of God, the silence of our churches, and the silence of our own souls, and we can enter all these silences and come out refreshed and strengthened. The silence of God in nature, in His heavens, the sun, the moon, the stars, all silent and beautiful, yet strong in their power. His silence in His grace — in the workings of His creatures, in His flowers and trees and mountains; the perennial quiet, for the blossoms falling, the curfew calling, the birds singing are but the little foil for the supreme quiet. The storms and floods are the pent-up forces of Nature's power, and evince her latent energy in spite of the sweetness of quiet — like a man who dreams and writes, puts down his pen and fights.

The silence of the church! What speaks more appealingly than the exquisite quiet, the stillness of the very breathing, near the Tabernacle of silence, where souls can meet their Lord; the loneliness and yet the awe-inspiring, mystic silence of the soul at prayer, the ineffable atmosphere of God's home on earth, the balm and solace, the sense of profound awe and yet sweetness unimpaired, of any church of God where He dwells with the children of men.

The silence of the soul! Tortures unexpressed can take place unknown and unheard in a soul; storms of temptation, like sweeping blasts, can search and sway the soul; and outpourings of grace and gentle inspirations of the Holy Spirit, victories unknown and defeats unimagined, all exist in the silence of the soul. Is it not a precious thing, silence —

"silence deep as death." We do so need it in the present day: not the silence of hypocrisy and lying, not the muffled concealment of evil unsuspected, but the voluntary silence of depths of thought, and that going apart from the crowd and the hum, and dwelling, not in the temple made of hands, as poor Tutankhamen, but the temple of God, our souls. Pain and sorrow we all bear, heavily pressing and wearily bending sometimes, but there is always the rest for the sad in the silence of the soul, for He can turn our sadness into joy if His peace is there, than which nothing greatly matters nor is there worth to be found in all the peerless alabaster and golden glory of the ancient world.[1]

Too many of us find the above lesson hard. Yet it is just what we need. Mass-time is the time to shut out the noisy world. Silent, then, in our deepest worship, the still small voice of conscience can be heard like "the whisper of a gentle breeze," and our mute plea will go straight to Him "to whom all hearts are opened, all desires known, and from whom no secrets are hid."

1. When Job was afflicted by God, his three friends condoled with him in silence. "And they sat with him on the ground seven days and seven nights, and no man spoke to him a word: for they saw that his grief was very great" (Job ii, 13). Who was Job? Can you explain this long silence? 2. Recall two occasions when our Lord maintained divine silence. 3. It used to be said playfully of John Henry Newman in Oxford that "when he opened his mouth it looked as if it never could shut, and when he shut his mouth it looked as if it never could open." What is the difference between a person who is silent, and one who is taciturn, and one who is canny? Of the three, which do you prefer?

ANGELS

[1] Edith Pearson in *Catholic Times*, March 24, 1923.

XVIII

THE PREFACE

As soon as the priest has ended the Secreta, he raises his voice in the "Per omnia sæcula sæculorum" to let the people know that the Preface is about to begin. In a High Mass this part is sung.

The silence is broken for a second time when the priest says in a clear voice the "lifting up" prayers. These comprise the Dialogue and the Preface, the later a solemn prayer offered by the priest in the name of the whole congregation.

The Dialogue is an invitation to pray, "to lift up one's heart." It may fittingly be considered as one of the foundation stones of primitive liturgy. Authors such as St. Cyprian, St. Cyril, St. Augustine, back in the third and fourth centuries, allude to it. And it always preceded the Preface proper. We ought to join in this, for St. Peter, the first Pope, says to all of us: "Be you also as living stones built up, a spiritual house, a holy priesthood, to offer up spiritual sacrifices, acceptable to God by Jesus Christ" (I Peter ii, 5). Be sure we help in this offering, as the priest prays to God.

P. Per omnia sæcula sæculorum.	*P.* For ever and ever.
A. Amen.	*A.* Amen.
P. Dominus vobiscum.	*P.* The Lord be with you.
A. Et cum spiritu tuo.	*A.* And with thy spirit.
P. Sursum corda.	*P.* Lift up your hearts.
A. Habemus ad Dominum.	*A.* We have lifted them up to the Lord.
P. Gratias agamus Domino Deo nostro.	*P.* Let us give thanks to the Lord our God.
A. **Dignum et justum est.**	*P.* It is meet and just.

"It seems to me," says Kenelm Digby, "that there is something so very solemn and majestic in the very sound of these words used by the Church, the sense of which is perfectly understood by the most simple Catholic who hears them, while they are never heard but when the soul is occupied with heaven, with truth, with love, with God — something so greatly affecting in the thought that it was with these same words the saints of the Church, during so many generations of men, gave utterance to their faith; there is something in all this so strongly appealing to the heart, and even to the judgment, that I can hardly conceive how any man who has a heart and judgment, who is sus-

ANCIENT SIGN OF WELCOME
The Romans carried these tesselæ wherever they went.

ceptible of the sublime, could ever hear the *Per omnia sæcula sæculorum*, or the *Vere dignum et justum est*, without an elevation."

This lifting up of our hearts, this giving of thanks, and these glorious affirmations of the Dialogue are very needful nowadays. There are many people around us who forget God, never think of Him, set their hearts, not toward heaven, but elsewhere. They have their hearts down on the ground; they are of the earth, earthly. Beg of God the grace not to be like that, but to have your heart lifted up. Pray for those poor, bewildered creatures who know not how to turn to God and heaven for help, who have no faith, as we have.

Sursum corda! Love heaven, not earth. Set your heart

on the things above. It is imperative to lay aside all things of earth and look steadfastly to God.

> To thee have I lifted up my eyes, who dwellest in heaven.
> Behold as the eyes of servants are on the hands of their masters,
> So are our eyes unto the Lord our God, until he have mercy on us.
>
> (Psalms cxxii)

If we expect Him who is enthroned in the heavens to be gracious to us, it is unseemly to let our eyes wander everywhere, to give thought to persons, pretty dresses, the choir in the Church, or those who may be in the choir. All such ideas are out of place, where motives and actions should correspond to the sacred occasion. How the servants in a house wait upon the mistress, and respond to her every beck and nod with most eager attention! Will it do if no longing gaze goes forth from us to our Lord, if we have no thought of His coming? Rather recall your dear Lord. Here and now, above all times and places, it is right to think of Him, to give thanks to Him, to look for His coming (in the Consecration) with upward glances of waiting faith. Pray then, thus: "Turn away mine eyes that they may not behold vanity; open Thou them, and I will consider Thy wondrous things." Only with hearts single, and attention undivided can we dwell on Christ's message. To do otherwise is to be mindless of Christ's message, to let His grace go out in darkness, to miss our privilege of communion with His angels and saints.

The Preface is a very ancient, stately prayer, undeniably one of the most beautiful in the liturgy; beautiful in style, rhythm, and cadence. It leads up to the Canon, the most important part of the Mass. Originally it was counted as a part of the Canon, and its keynote, one of thanksgiving, is the keynote of the whole Canon which is one long prayer

— the Eucharistic, or thanksgiving prayer. It is a prelude of praise and thanks, richer than any melody, ushering in the acts preliminary to the approaching sacrifice. There are thirteen different forms of the Eucharistic Preface in the present Roman Missal. At one time the number was much greater. "Besides these Eucharistic Prefaces," writes Dom Cambrol, "there is a certain number of others for great liturgical functions, such as ordinations, the blessing of the paschal candle and of the palms, of a font, the dedication of a church, etc. These Prefaces, like those of the Mass, are generally connected with a prayer, or rather, prologue, which introduces and leads up to the Preface." In the Mass Preface there is an air of expectant attention together with ready praise. In this way one is prepared for a better understanding of what is to come. Following is the order of the Preface:

1. The priest repeats the invocation he has given to the people to return thanks to God. "Yes," he says, "it is truly meet and just, right and salutary, that we should always and in all places give thanks to Thee, O holy Lord, Father Almighty, eternal God." Always, indeed, and in all places!

As has been well said: "In these days of ours when the age spirit sees all things in man, instead of in God; when it refuses to look beyond the visible scene and exalts man's ever changing self into a present deity; when governments are grasping with an absolutism that is quite pagan; it is most necessary that we should daily, standing in this maelstrom of moral evil and political chaos, raise our hearts and our hands to Him, Who alone is High and Holy, the Absolute Sovereign, that inhabiteth Eternity."

2. Then the priest enumerates some of the blessings for which we are so grateful.

3. Upon that, he appeals to Christ, our Lord, Son of God, "through Whom the angels praise Thy majesty, the dominations worship it, the powers are in awe. The heavens and the heavenly hosts, and the blessed seraphim join together in celebrating their joy."

4. The priest ends the Preface with: "Holy, holy, holy!" the voice of the angelic choir ushering in the most solemn part of the Mass.

Witness this beautiful Preface:

Vere dignum et justum est, æquum et salutare, nos tibi semper et ubique gratias agere, Domine sancte, Pater omnipotens, æterne Deus: Qui cum unigenito Filio tuo, et Spiritu sancto, unus es Deus, unus es Dominus: non in unius singularitate personæ, sed in unius Trinitate substantiæ. Quod enim de tua gloria, revelante te, credimus, hoc de Filio tuo, hoc de Spiritu sancto, sine differentia discretionis sentimus. Ut in confessione veræ sempiternæque Deitatis, et in Personis proprietas, et in essentia unitas, et in majestate adoretur æqualitas. Quem laudant angeli atque archangeli, cherubim quoque ac seraphim, qui non cessant clamare quotidie, una voce dicentes:

Sanctus, sanctus, sanctus, Dominus Deus Sabaoth. Pleni sunt cœli et terra gloria tua: Hosanna in

It is truly meet and just, right and profitable unto salvation, that we should at all times and in all places give thanks unto Thee, O Holy Lord, Father Almighty, Eternal God: Who, with Thine only-begotten Son and the Holy Ghost, art one God, one Lord; not in the oneness of a single person, but in the Trinity of one substance. For what we believe of Thy glory, as Thou hast revealed it, that we believe of Thy Son, and that of the Holy Ghost, without any difference or inequality. So that in the confession of the true and eternal Deity, we adore a distinction in persons, a unity in the essence, and an equality in the majesty; which the angels and archangels, the cherubim, and likewise the seraphim, praise, and cease not daily to cry out with united voice, saying:

Holy, holy, holy, Lord God of Hosts. Heaven and earth are full of Thy glory. Hosanna in the

THE PREFACE

excelsis. Benedictus qui venit in nomine Domini: Hosanna in excelsis.

highest. Blessed is he who cometh in the name of the Lord. Hosanna in the highest.

A glance at any one of the Prefaces will reveal a high, holy atmosphere and give us a keener awareness of our immortal destiny. What a privilege to be a sharer in this prayer, in this destiny. You are no longer a stranger, but a domestic of God. The Preface keeps us up in the atmosphere of the angels

> An ampler ether, a diviner air,
> And fields invested with purpureal gleams;

and this air of heaven sweeps the soul pure and clean.

These are sublime moments for the soul, inspiriting flashes of our heaven-home, spacious and universal and eternal. We ought often to think of that place where joy and praise and possession are for ever and ever. "If you be risen with Christ," says St. Paul, "seek the things that are above, where Christ is sitting at the right hand of God. Mind the things that are above, not the things that are upon the earth" (Colossians iii, 1–2). With Christ you rise to a life spiritual and divine — the life that the Mass stirs in you more strongly. That life of Christ hidden in God is hidden from the eyes of men. But you can live that life in Him by grace; later on it will be in glory in eternity. "Let your life be hidden with Christ in God," now and for the rest of the Mass.

The Preface enables us to do just that. By a deliberate effort we seek security from distractions; we hide, as it were, from all creatures in the heart of Christ. Thus to hear Mass is to be of one mind with the Church. Plainly, it is now the hour to think only of our Lord who will soon come on our altar. We must have no more thoughts of bodily things, or of time, or of the people about us; rather do we focus our mind on the altar and raise our hearts heavenward, winging our whole thought above the things of earth, so that without being wearied, we may go on to participate in His life, earn His grace with which our soul will be greatly filled.

"Through Whom the angels praise Thy majesty." The holy angels know and honor that life of Christ, hidden in the heart of God. We can safely say now that we are reaching nearer and nearer to that life in the Mass. To that end

ANNOUNCING ANGELS
(From a Fifth Century mosaic in San Vitale, Ravenna.)
Angels are God's messengers to mankind. Even mankind's messengers to God, for they bear the prayers of the just before the throne of God.

we must be in tune with what is happening; we must enter this part of the Mass in the right spirit. If so, you will find the rest of the Mass like heaven — our home and refuge. The Mass is an open door to the celestial kingdom. At the Preface we are in reality in closer union with the angels in heaven, as we offer thanks and praise to our hidden Christ, on whom our life hinges and our eternal welfare depends. From now on "our conversation is in heaven; from whence also we look for the Saviour, our Lord Jesus Christ, who will reform the body of our lowness, made like to the body of his glory, according to the operation whereby also he is able to subdue all things unto himself" (Philippians iii, 20–21).

THE PREFACE

1. Many times in the Old and New Dispensations there have been angelic visitations to our earth. Are you able to recall instances? 2. In our Lord's life how many recorded times did the angels appear to Him? 3. Not all are able or called to serve in the sanctuary. Suppose, however, the altar boy was absent from Mass, could a girl serve Mass? 4. Do you consistently practice a devotion to your Guardian Angel? 5. Do you know by heart the Dialogue in the Mass? Is your choir familiar with the Gregorian responses?

XIX

THE SANCTUS

At the Sanctus, the priest joins his hands and inclines moderately. The bell is rung thrice. At the words "Benedictus qui venit," the priest stands erect, and makes the sign of the cross on himself; and at the words "Hosanna in excelsis" he joins his hands.

On hearing the bell ring, there is a stir of expectancy. Everybody kneels, as the priest recites the Sanctus, the prayer which divides the Preface from the Canon. Notice the naturalness of it all. It is as if a big crowd were awaiting the appearance of an important visitor or speaker. Somebody says, "He is coming," then you hear exclamations, the crowd is athrob with life, voicing its far-off welcome. With just that dramatic fidelity, the faithful are awaiting the coming of our Saviour. As the Sanctus bell is rung, hope rises to joy, the joy of anticipation. A drama of expectancy begins to unfold until the Consecration — "that awful event which is the scope and the interpretation of every part of the solemnity." There is the looking forward to Him whose blessed feet are already treading the eternal hills on the way to our altar. Even now the contemplation of this is stirring worship in loving hearts. The people are expecting Him every minute, because it is certain that Christ is coming. An active, energetic force runs through the whole congregation, as they say with the priest:

Sanctus, sanctus, sanctus, Dominus Deus Sabaoth. Pleni sunt cœli et terra gloria tua: Hosanna in	Holy, holy, holy, Lord God of Hosts. Heaven and earth are full of Thy glory. Hosanna in the

THE SANCTUS

excelsis. Benedictus qui venit in nomine Domini: Hosanna in excelsis.

highest. Blessed is he who cometh in the name of the Lord. Hosanna in the highest.

This Sanctus is a glad cry of praise to the majesty of God. A God-announcing prayer, it is composed of pæans of joy from the Old and New Testaments. It rings with the song of angels, is brilliant with the light of an unseen world, is swept with the air from the plains of heaven. No wonder we kneel down and worship as we repeat those high, holy words. Dante gives us the true spirit of the Sanctus prayer when he says: "As of their will Thine angels make sacrifices to Thee, singing Hosanna, so may men make of theirs" (Purgatory xxi, 20). We say, "Lord God of Hosts," for our Saviour is the chief of the heavenly hosts, the captain of our salvation, the head of the militant Church of which we on earth are members.

CHRIST'S ENTRY INTO JERUSALEM
The right hand of our Lord is raised in blessing.

On the night Christ was born, a multitude of that heavenly host, angels who surround the throne of God, was heard by the shepherds on the hills of Bethlehem. They sang a song of praise like the Sanctus: "Glory to God in the highest" (Luke ii, 14). This song of the angels at Christ's birth upheld the dignity, the divine nature of the Child who was to redeem the world.

A marvelous series of events in sacred history is summoned before us by the Sanctus, Sanctus, Sanctus!

When Isaias entered the temple one day, God gave him a glance into the invisible world. Isaias wrote the traces of the impression of this ecstasy. "I saw the Lord sitting upon a throne high and elevated: and His train (the skirts of His royal robe) filled the temple. Upon it stood the seraphims: the one had six wings, and the other had six wings: with two they covered his face, and with two they covered his feet, and with two they flew. And they cried one to another, and said: Holy, holy, holy, the Lord God of hosts, all the earth is full of his glory" (Isaias vi, 1–3).

Isaias perceived what the divine glory is, and he recounts for us the seraphic Sanctus. The three holies hint of the Holy Trinity. This antiphonal song of the seraphim shows that endless worship is their blessed occupation; it also shows dimly the coming of a Redeemer, at Whose advent earth will be filled with God's glory.

SERAPHIM
An artist's idea of angelic beings in Isaias' vision.

When the Redeemer did come, and rode into Jerusalem from Mount Olive, the people with great enthusiasm hailed Him as the Messias; they strewed palm branches in the way, and the children shouted gladly as they ran along before Jesus:

"Blessed is he that cometh in the name of the Lord: Hosanna in the highest." Mark xi, 1–10.

Hosanna is another Hebrew word used in the Mass; so is *sabaoth*, which means *armies, hosts, regiments*. When the Jews cried *Hosanna*, they used it as a congratulatory expression and applied it in its highest sense to the Messias.

THE SANCTUS

Notice how the Jews spread their garments before the Messias, an extraordinary token of respect such as was paid to kings and great conquerors. *Hosanna in the highest* means *may our Hosanna be ratified in heaven.* *Hosanna* is an exclamation of praise meaning *Save now, Give Thy salvation. Glory and honor to the Son of David* it seems to say. And that was their way of giving welcome to Christ. Well may it be ours also.

After our Lord went back to heaven St. John saw the vision and heard the anthem of the seraphim (Apocalypse iv) sung by the six-winged living creatures round about God's throne. In the midst of his trials, temptations, banishments the beloved disciple was encouraged by the vision and support of Christ. God is seen on His heavenly throne, surrounded by representatives of the angelic creation and of the Church. These beings ceaselessly watch Him, praise Him, are alert to do His divine will, are for ever and ever bent on worshiping Him. "And the four living creatures had each of them six wings; and round about and within they are full of eyes. And they rested not day and night, saying: Holy, holy, holy, Lord God Almighty, who was, and who is, and who is to come" (Apocalypse iv, 8).

These living creatures "have been perpetuated in Christian usage, and the descriptions given of them in Holy Scripture have been embodied (those of the cherubim or "four living creatures," first, and somewhat later those of the seraphim) in Christian art from the fifth century onwards. They were regarded as the spirits of love and of knowledge respectively."

Notice now that the Lord of heaven and earth is on His way to visit us, accompanied by His heavenly host. And because Jesus is coming to us in our church, we join with the seraphim and the true worshipers of old; and we use the selfsame greeting that they used. It is called the Trisagion, or Thrice-holy. Holy, holy, holy! The Church calls it the Sanctus. And we use it to hail the conqueror of sin, Christ our Lord. Youths and maidens, old men and boys, big and little, rich and poor — a myriad-throated multitude. We say it because we, too, want to do God's will on earth as the angels do it in heaven. With eyes of faith, we see God's presence over all the earth, and earth paying homage to God. It is our turn to do the honors now. For Christ is coming. The Captain of our Salvation is about to draw near. Soon He will be on our altar. Faithful to Him, we wish we could escort Him with tears and praise, with alms and embraces. "That we may worthily praise Thee." Nevertheless we can greet Him with silent prayers. Ere He comes our glad hearts cry out: "Welcome, Jesus, blessed art Thou Who comest in the Name of the Lord. Holy, holy, holy! Lord God of Hosts!"

It is during this part of the Mass that we should bestir ourselves to better preparation. Let us make sure that our minds and hearts are fixed on earnest prayer. About 1300 there lived a great mystic and scholar, St. Gertrude. As a mere child she went to live near a Benedictine convent, and later became a nun. She passed from innocence to sanctity and was privileged with one vision after another. In one of her visions this is the account of what happened:

<small>One day at chapel, she heard supernaturally sung, the words, "*Sanctus, sanctus, sanctus.*" The Son of God leaning towards her like a sweet lover, and giving to her soul the softest kiss, said to her at the second *sanctus*, "In this *sanctus* addressed to My person, receive with this kiss all the sanctity of My divinity and of My humanity, and let it be to thee a sufficient preparation for approaching the communion table." And the next following Sunday, while she was thanking God for this favor, behold the Son of God, more beauteous than a thousand of angels, takes her in his arms as if He were proud of her, and presents her to God the Father,</small>

THE SANCTUS

in that perfection of sanctity with which He had dowered her. And the Father took such delight in this soul thus presented by His only Son, that, as if unable longer to restrain Himself, He gave her, and the Holy Ghost gave her also, the sanctity attributed to each by His own Sanctus — and thus she remained endowed with the plenary fullness of the blessing of sanctity bestowed on her by Omnipotence, by Wisdom, and by Love.[1]

In reiterating our welcome *sanctus, sanctus, sanctus!* to the Saviour soon to come among us, we may well pray for clearer vision, for higher aims, for wider vistas of faith. For "this is the victory which overcometh the world, our faith" (I John v, 4). Further, "without faith it is impossible to please God" (Hebrews xi, 6).

1. When the sanctus bell rings what should devout Catholics do? 2. St. John in his Apocalypse tells us the names of the nine choirs of angels. Have you read all about his vision? 3. The Apocalypse was written partly to relate the happenings to the Christians during the reigns of Nero and Domitian. St. John shows the power of Satan in the world, ever renewing his attack against the people of God. And he sees how in the end God shall overthrow Satan and all his forces of evil. Have you read that book?

[1] "Revelations of St. Gertrude."

PART THREE

XX

CANON

Now comes the Canon. One long prayer, ending at the "Lord's Prayer," it is sometimes called the Action — a great action, great in its dignity, beauty and beneficence, the greatest action that can be on earth. The word *agere* bears in classical writers the special sense of performing a sacrificial act; hence the word *actio* was applied to that which was regarded as the essential portion of the Eucharistic sacrifice. The sacred drama, acted in this portion of the liturgy, is in places a real representation, an actual repetition of the divine acts at the Last Supper.

The Church, for our sake, dramatizes the tragedy of Calvary. She does this with a genius beyond that of the greatest dramatists of the earth. Indeed, God's holy spirit guides her. To the essential first Mass — the Offertory, Consecration, and Communion — she has added; age after age, she has built up, piece by piece, an absorbing liturgy, a magnificent soul-drama, heavenly inspired in its details. Those sacred functions are worthy of our closest attention. What our own mental imagery, our language, and expression never could convey, the Church conveys in the noblest utterance. She surrounds the holy sacrifice with the most expressive acts and forms. She uses lights, vestments, incense, attractive ceremonies. Acts and movements reveal mysteries. Sounds and words become signs of holy hidden things. Two worlds, the seen and the unseen, become linked together in this divine drama.

Nowhere is this drama of Calvary so actually realized as in the Actio or Canon. This is the very heart of the Mass. It extends to the "Lord's Prayer," contains the words of Consecration, and in its form is fixed and invariable. Indeed, the word "Canon" designates the standard by which anything is tried. In this sense it was used with regard to the Mass very early. St. Clement, in his first epistle to the Corinthians, desires the brethren "not to transgress the set rule (canon) of their services." "It well behooves us," he urges, "to take care that looking into the depths of the divine knowledge, we do all things in order, whatsoever Our Lord has commanded to be done, not rashly and disorderly, but at certain determinate times and hours. And therefore He (that is, Christ, our Lord) has ordained by His supreme will and authority both where and by what persons they are to be performed; that so all things being piously done unto all well-pleasing, they may be acceptable with Him." Isn't it wonderful that this letter from an early Pope, who was St. Peter's disciple and likely served the Mass of the first vicar of Christ, should come down to us? More than anything else these words of St. Clement remind us to keep our thoughts on our Lord, our eyes on His service, our hearts ready to reap the graces. These He is even now showering upon us in the Mass.

BISHOP ORDAINING A PRIEST
(From a MS of Henry II's time.)

CANON

Now that we have reached the most solemn part of the Mass, it is important to have a clear idea of its structure. No one can study attentively the Canon and examine its motives and purposes without lasting profit. Every line of it is instinct with hope and love, saturated with the supernatural, full of that vital faith which makes us Christians, coheirs of Christ, and members of His mystical body.

Not so many ages ago a double Canon was recognized: the Canon of the Consecration and the Canon of the Communion. For us, however, it will help to take them together in order to hold fast to the idea of the sacrificial act. On this plan we divide the double Canon into fifteen parts. There are six including the Consecration, six including the Pater Noster, and three including the Communion. These parts are often known by their first words.

The plan here is to show you the third part of the Mass with the double Canon in perspective. Thus you may be enabled the better to perform the greatest of all your spiritual duties, that of hearing Mass well.

St. Peter

St. Peter is usually represented with keys.

It is both important and desirable that Catholics should get a good view of the order of the Mass. This requires close attention. The problem will be to trace each part and keep in mind just what is meant by it, just as in harmonized music you would study the varying parts and see how they are bound together by their common relation to the melody. The parts of the Mass combine into a perfect harmony of praise, thanksgiving, expiation, and prayer. These four ends of all sacrifice find place here in the heart of the Mass. Our Lord has willed that in the Mass we should stand under His cross and see Him with eyes of faith as He offers His sacrifice to His Heavenly Father. Follow each part, therefore, and note the ends for which the holy sacrifice is offered. Then your prayer will be directed as incense in God's sight, and the lifting up of your heart will be as a worthy sacrifice.

THE CRUCIFIXION *Boyermans*

XXI

TE IGITUR

The priest, after finishing the Preface, places his right hand on the altar, and with his left turns to the Canon; he then joins his hands before his breast, and extends and elevates them somewhat; he raises his eyes to the cross, and immediately lowers them devoutly, joining his hands; then, with hands on the edge of the altar, and profoundly inclined, he begins the Canon.

The Canon, the heart of the Mass, opens. The mystery of Calvary will presently be renewed. We are now on the way to Golgotha.

Immediately following the Sanctus the priest turns a page of the Missal and a full-length crucifixion may be seen. He raises his hands toward the crucifix over the tabernacle, makes a profound inclination, kisses the altar, and proceeds with the prayer. Once the custom was to bend over the Missal and kiss the first word of the Canon: Te. The T represented a cross — the *crux commissa* or Tau cross. One should remember that the cross is in evidence very much, from now on, because in the Mass Christ dies mystically. "The word of the cross to them that are saved, that is, to us, is the power of God" (I Corinthians i, 18). Here, near the approach to the cross, we are on our way to find love, truth, wisdom, sacrifice — all that speaks of the true life and enduring peace.

Te igitur, clementissime Pater, per Jesum Christum Filium tuum Dominum nostrum supplices roga-	Wherefore, O most merciful Father, we humbly pray and beseech thee, through Jesus Christ

mus ac petimus (*osculatur altare*), uti accepta habeas, et benedicas (*jungit manus, deinde signat ter super oblata*), hæc ✠ dona, hæc ✠ munera, hæc ✠ sancta sacrificia illibata (*extensis manibus prosequitur*): in primis quæ tibi offerimus pro Ecclesia tua sancta catholica; quam pacificare, custodire, adunare, et regere digneris toto orbe terrarum, una cum famulo tuo Papa nostro N. et Antistite nostro N. et omnibus orthodoxis, atque catholicæ et apostolicæ fidei cultoribus.

thy Son, our Lord (*he kisses the altar*), that thou wouldst vouchsafe to receive and bless (*he joins his hands together, and then makes the sign of the cross thrice over the offerings*) these ✠ gifts, these ✠ offerings, these ✠ holy and unblemished sacrifices (*he extends his hands and continues*), which in the first place we offer thee for thy holy Catholic Church, that it may please thee to grant her peace: as also to protect, unite, and govern her throughout the world, together with thy servant N., our Pope N., our bishop, as also all orthodox believers and professors of the catholic and apostolic faith.

A moment ago at the Sanctus we were enjoying the fellowship of joy and praise at Christ's near approach. Now we are united once more in the prayer, not of praise, but of intercession to the Heavenly Father for the Church. But why for the Church? Because she has to battle with the world in her work of clinging fast to the will of Christ, of preserving and explaining His teachings and saving them from being twisted by false teachers. All through the ages false philosophies, backed up by the gates of hell, have fought consistently against the teachings of Christ. They have taken the most sacred ideas of the Gospel and used them in the interest of slavery, tyranny, of treason to truth. Against them the Church is ever at war, and she has Christ's word for it that her foes shall never prevail against her. "Holy Father, keep them in thy name whom thou hast given me; that they may be one, as we also are. I have given them thy word and the world hath hated them, because they are

TE IGITUR

not of the world; as I also am not of the world" (John xvii, 11, 14). The Church is only an extension of Christ's life and words; and we must keep His cross in mind, live and conform to His teachings if we would be true Catholics. The Te Igitur is a prayer that we may prevail against Satan.

With swift sweep the priest's hand makes a cross thrice over the Oblation. Just now out of the depths of his heart he is praying, pleading to the Giver of all, the Almighty Father through Jesus Christ, our Lord, to accept and bless these ✠ gifts, these ✠ offerings, these ✠ holy, undefiled sacrifices, which we offer. "We," he says, not "I." Catholicity is a social religion, a mystical body. "If Christians are to live together," says Cardinal Newman, "they will pray together; and united prayer is necessarily of an intercessory character, as being offered for each other, and for the whole, and for self as one of the whole. Intercession becomes a token of the existence of a Church catholic." Nowhere is that prayer of intercession more marked than in the Mass; and God will not, cannot, be deaf to us when we so importune Him in behalf of our friends in their necessities, in behalf of the Christian world, in behalf of the whole Church. This is the universalism of our prayer.

The keynote of this prayer is catholic. Let us see if we understand this. The Church is neither Italian nor English nor American; neither primitive nor medieval nor modern. She is more than all these. She is not behind the times, not before the times, but she is all round the times, since she is Catholic, world-wide, age-old, destined to teach all nations and embrace all truth. "Rome is the lighthouse on the rocks of time."

In the Te Igitur, therefore, you pray for the holy Catholic Church on earth, and you ask God to pacify, protect, unify, and govern it together with His servant, the Pope, and our bishop and all faithful worshipers. Our intercession is for the world and the Church on earth. Never was need of that prayer greater than to-day when the Church has bitter enemies arrayed against her. In every land, alas! are to be found bigots who try to undermine her influence, who teach their children hideous grudges, and seek to extend their envy and hate from generation to generation. The real blame for much of the world's present unhappiness rests with such foes of the true Church.

Our Lord told His followers to look for this. "Blessed are ye when they shall revile you, and persecute you, and speak all that is evil against you, untruly, for my sake" (Matthew v, 11). Peace and the sword are for the Church, whose greatest peace of mind is attainable amid the most strenuous warfare against evil, in the determined apostleship of love in this world, still dark and cold. The Church must ever be the bitter opponent of evil and sin, and that is why she is hated and vilified.

A very large number of people are opposed to the Catholic Church even in our own America. They are easily misled. For them also should we pray, that God may dispel their bigotry. In Europe there are two camps to-day — the Catholic and those opposed to the Faith one way or another. "To the first camp, the Catholic, belong by far the greater number: the greater part of the French, of the twenty million dispersed Irish people, of the Spanish, of the Italians: the people of all the upper Danube valley and of much of the Hungarian plain; and many Germans of the Rhine valley. On the other side are the directing minds of Great Britain, of the northern Germanies and of Scandinavia, all the dispersed millions of the Jewish nation, and lastly, it still includes a majority of the organized academic world in every country." What need, then, that the

TE IGITUR 163

Church should be united in charity, safely guided by orthodox, consistent teachers, and ably administered by her hierarchy? For that we now pray.

1. Do you know just what our blessed Lord told His followers concerning the opposition they would meet with and what He would do for them? Read Matthew x, 16–19. 2. "As to bigotry, if that vulgar giant is dead, its ghost rules on, and now and then stalks forth in the land unashamed. It scares only the timid and half-hearted." Just what is bigotry? What, do you think, are the influences that make people bigots? 3. Give the name of the Pope, the Apostolic Delegate, your archbishop, your bishop. 4. Have you on your fingers' ends the Catholic statistics of the United States? How many archbishops, bishops, priests, religious communities; how many Catholics, all in all? How many Catholic seminaries, universities, colleges, high schools, parish schools?

XXII

MEMENTO

During the Memento for the Living, the priest slowly raises and joins his hands, holding them at the top of his breast. While in this attitude of prayer, the names are expressed of all those for whom he intends specially to pray. This done, the priest disjoins his hands, lowering them as before, and continues the Commemoration.

Catholicism has nothing to do with narrowness or prejudice. "Go ye therefore and teach all" — and pray for all. We pray for all men. That is our Catholic way. What do our Lord's words imply save this duty? And the Mass sets the example for us, in the Memento, Domine, by reminding us to pray for our own, those of the household of the faith, and thus our charity will impel us to pray for all men. As to the spiritual significance of this prayer, any one can see that at a glance. It is a prayerful memento. We hope that you will make it with all your mind and heart. Not merely for yourself but for all who need help must this prayer be offered.

Thoughtfulness is a wonderful thing. The Church holds in deep remembrance all her children — all, to the ends of the earth. Every day finds her mind dwelling on them, so dear to her. Indeed, she is memory itself, in sacred robe, with lips of prayer, making her plea at God's altar.

Thousands of her children are not so thoughtful. They forget too often even their own. This may amount to sheer ingratitude, so the Church constantly reminds us of the other members of the household of the faith and urges us

MEMENTO

to pray for them. *Ne obliviscaris*, she cautions her children. Do not forget. Wise, holy Mother, with her intuitive knowledge of forgetful human nature, and her anxiety to bring her children into close intimacy with one another for prayer and mutual helpfulness. No one can read attentively the prayers of the Canon of the Mass without realizing both the thoughtfulness of our holy Mother and the tremendous value of her remembrance. Here is another shining instance of her mother heart where all are kept in eternal remembrance.

The priest at the altar is mindful of those present, and even of the absent ones. He utters a prayer of petition for them, for all the faithful living. He enlists the power of the Heavenly Father on behalf of them, one and all, the prayer being public and official, fruitful in good for all.

Very appropriately the priest and the people pray:

Memento, Domine, famulorum famularumque tuarum, N. et N. Et omnium circumstantium, quorum tibi fides cognita est, et nota devotio: pro quibus tibi offerimus, vel qui tibi offerunt hoc sacrificium laudis, pro se, suisque omnibus, pro redemptione animarum suarum, pro spe salutis et incolumitatis suæ; tibique reddunt vota sua æterno Deo, vivo et vero.	Be mindful, O Lord, of Thy servants, men and women, N. and N. And of all here present, whose faith and devotion are known to Thee; for whom we offer, or who offer up to Thee, this sacrifice of praise for themselves and all pertaining to them, for the redemption of their souls, for the hope of their salvation and well-being, and who pay their vows unto Thee, the eternal God, living and true.

Our Lord, at the Last Supper, did the same thing when He said the prayer for His disciples: "I pray for them: I pray not for the world, but for them whom thou hast given me: because they are thine . . . Holy Father, keep them in thy name whom thou hast given me; that they may be one as we also are. . . . Sanctify them in truth. . . . And not for them only do I pray, but for them also who through their word shall believe in me; That they all may be one, as thou, Father, in me, and I in thee; that they also may be one in us" (John xvii). Not only then did Jesus pray for those present, but for the absent also; His mind goes out to all who through the disciples' teaching shall be brought to the true faith, the believers in every country and in every age. The Church never has ceased to continue that prayer. It is the same in the Mass as when Christ said it at the first Mass, or as St. Paul in the same spirit wrote from his prison cell. "Therefore we also cease not to pray for you and to beg that you may be filled with the knowledge of his will; . . . that you may walk worthy of God in all things pleasing" (Colossians i, 9–10). This is the idea of the *salus* or health which in its final condition means *heaven*.

In the Te Igitur the Church prayed for all her children, the holy Catholic Church. Now while commemorating all the living she prays specially for all who are present at the holy sacrifice, "whose faith and devotion are known to Thee" and who by being there enjoy special graces. But her prayers are not limited merely to those present. There is nothing narrow about the heart of our holy Mother. All the living faithful have a place in her great heart and she is anxious that God will do great things for all her children, absent as well as present. You can see all this in the Mass where Christ's spirit is over all and above all.

It is interesting to note here the mention of living persons, of special benefactors to the Church. In the beginning this special mention was made of those who had furnished the bread and wine for the oblation; their names were inscribed on the diptych, or two-leaved tablet, and were read aloud; or the diptych was simply laid on the altar, after the oblation of the bread and wine, and before the Consecration. As time went on the names were added of those who held civil and spiritual authority among the faithful. Finally the prayer embraced all who were true members of the household of the faith. If a person lost the faith or fell into heresy, his name was removed from the *diptycha vivorum*. Thus we find St. Augustine threatening, in case of certain conduct: Delebo eum de tabula — "I will remove his name from the diptych." Of such diptychs we have pictures, a few dating from the fifth century. One of these is a beautifully engraved folding tablet with cornucopia ornamentation. To be sure there has been much modification of the earlier method of using the diptych. No longer is a tablet or book used; instead we have the fixed form of prayer called the Commemoration of the Living.

AN ANCIENT DIPTYCH

The general fruits of the Mass, remember, belong to all the faithful who are not separated from Catholic unity. Te igitur — *petimus* — *Imprimus pro ecclesia tua sancta Catholica*. Then the special fruits belong to those for whom the sacrifice is specially offered, either from a title of justice or charity, or from some other motive, as the Mass is instituted for the benefit of men, and should particularly benefit those for whom it is by name offered by the priest, and for whom he intends specially to pray: *Pro quibus tibi offerimus, vel qui tibi offerunt hoc sacrificium laudis.*

1. What do you understand by broad-mindedness? Give the Christian ideal of neighborliness as our Lord explained it in the Gospel. 2. Do you make it a practice to pray for all poor sinners; for those who have none to pray for them; for pagans, infidels, apostates, and bigots? Of course you ought to pray after the example Christ set for you when He hung on the cross. 3. Does it ever occur to you to pray for the many poor, overworked, and underschooled boys and girls in America who have not your opportunities? "While traveling nearly four thousand miles in the past few weeks," says Harold Cary, "I have seen seven-year-old boys and girls who work regularly ten hours a day on their hands and knees in New Jersey; fourteen-year-olds in Pennsylvania coal-mine breakers; boys and girls in New England cotton mills, in Wisconsin factories, in New York tenements."[1] In the face of this, don't you think you ought to pray God to enlighten our legislators?

[1] *Collier's National Weekly*, July 28, 1923, p. 10.

XXIII

COMMUNICANTES

With hands outstretched, the priest proceeds with the Communicantes. At the name "Maria," he inclines his head to the Missal; at "Jesu Christi," toward the cross. And at the close of the prayer "Per eundem" he joins his hands.

In the light of what we have gained already from our study of the Mass, it should be easy to grasp the meaning of the Communicantes. One thing is clear about this part of the Mass. In it we are coming into close touch with Heaven. *Communicantes* means getting into communication with the saints in glory.

To eyes of faith, a divine spectacle presents itself as the liturgy rises steadily toward the climax of the Consecration. We peer into that which lies beyond, while in undertones of quiet gravity the priest recites the Communicantes. There is a new scene upon which the keen vision of faith dwells. Suddenly we are brought into the company of the elect; a stately procession passes before our soul's eyes; Mary, the Mother of God, the Apostles, martyrs, and confessors; and we are put into communication with all the saints who stand before the throne of God.

> Earth breaks up; Time drops away
> In flows Heaven with its new day
> Of endless life.

In the Mass, Christ draws all to Himself as a common center. He is in all believers, and it is through Him that they are what they are — members of the body of Christ.

In order to conceive the part we play in the drama of Calvary, painstaking consideration should be given to the vital truth of the Mystical Body and our rôle therein. By union of our intention we make our Lord's great acts of praise, prayer, reparation, obedience, our own. Our Lord made this plain when He said: "I am the vine, you are the branches." He is the head, we are the members of His mystical body. "The whole Christ is head and body: the head the only begotten Son of God, and His body the Church — all its members on earth, in purgatory and in heaven. Our Lord receives His full completion in being united with all of us, His members. Therefore the Church is called the pleroma or complement of Christ, just as the body completes the head, or the crew completes the ship, or the nave the choir of the church."

But let us go back to the vine idea, which is our blessed Lord's own teaching. As the branches make the vine's life their own, and make their own the fruit of the vine, so we, being in close touch with the vine, by our presence at Mass, by our union with Christ, by sanctifying grace, assist in the great drama to God's honor and glory as well as for the good of our own soul.

We are not the only ones in church at Mass time. Besides those who kneel with us there are other guests at the sacred banquet; others united with us. Those are they whom we see not with the eye of the body but with the eye of the soul. In the divine drama which the Church enacts around the altar they have due place. The Church visualizes them for us. She wants us to make of them real friends. So they are summoned before us. With them we communicate, them also we commemorate.

Who are they? All those who in the past have received and believed in our Lord. With them we now join, and participate in their praise, prayer, and thanksgiving; we unite our intentions with theirs. Now, indeed, we are no more strangers but fellow citizens with the saints and domestics of God (Ephesians ii, 19). Being united in communion with the saints, let us try to live and think in the infinite, in order that we may appreciate what it is to be members of the household of the Faith, sharing in common with the saints. The Communicantes places us in wish, in faith, in reality, with our brethren in sainthood. "Their great

THE TWELVE APOSTLES

Early Christian art almost invariably represents the Twelve as seated or standing on either side of our Lord.

names flit past like palaces on a river brink, their bases washed by the pouring liturgy." In a single sentence rippling with light and glory they move before us. One by one, we meet them, are introduced to them: Glorious and ever blessed Virgin Mary, the blessed Apostles and martyrs, and all the saints. Some day we shall see them face to face, but now their fair forms appear in the fields and spreading courts of faith. It is all just like a little glimpse of heaven, alight with God and near at hand His holy saints, our brethren.

Communicantes, et memoriam venerantes, in primis gloriosæ semper Virginis Mariæ, Genetricis Dei et Domini nostri Jesu Christi;	In communion with, and honoring the memory, especially of the glorious, ever Virgin Mary, Mother of our God and Lord Jesus Christ;

sed et beatorum Apostolorum ac Martyrum tuorum, Petri et Pauli, Andreæ, Jacobi, Joannis, Thomæ, Jacobi, Philippi, Bartholomæi, Matthæi, Simonis et Thaddæi; Lini, Cleti, Clementis, Xysti, Cornelii, Cypriani, Laurentii, Chrysogoni, Joannis et Pauli, Cosmæ et Damiani, et omnium sanctorum tuorum; quorum meritis precibusque concedas, ut in omnibus protectionis tuæ muniamur auxilio. (*Jungit manus.*) Per eumdem Christum Dominum nostrum. Amen.

as also of Thy blessed Apostles and Martyrs, Peter and Paul, Andrew, James, John, Thomas, James, Philip, Bartholomew, Matthew, Simon and Thaddeus; Linus, Cletus, Clement, Xystus, Cornelius, Cyprian, Lawrence, Chrysogonus, John and Paul, Cosmas and Damian, and all Thy saints; by whose merits and prayers grant that we may in all things be defended by the aid of Thy protection. Through the same Christ our Lord. Amen.

Of the helpfulness of this intercession prayer, Communicantes, there can be no doubt. It is time, then, that we should stir up our consciousness of the communion of saints, and tune our hearts to their songs of light. Look over the list of those who have holy mention in the Mass. As the names of some were recited in the Canon, the word "canonize" came to designate the act of entering such and such a one's name in the liturgical list; and saints whose names were so entered were said to be canonized. At least those whose names are in the Mass ought to be familiar to all, not by name only, but their lives; who they were, when they lived, how they fought the good fight, kept the faith, loved Christ, and are now enjoying eternal happiness in the presence of God. To communicate with them means conferring with them, putting our life in sweet concord with theirs; using our will and intention to get in touch with them, as we would do with our friends and companions. Not the pen or wire but prayer is the medium between us, the senders, and the saints, the receivers. Impart your cares to them, communicate your hopes, dreams and desires, cal-

COMMUNICANTES

culations, problems, that you may use their influence and bring to bear their intercession in your behalf. How profitable to grasp the character of these important personages. The better we know them, the more apt we are to go to them.

In the past, Catholics in certain places of Europe used to pray to their special patrons, and put certain saints in the list. Thus the local saints, like Denys, Gregory, Benedict, Eleutherius are found in some old-time Communicantes. But the list we use is the one used in Rome, most of the saints on it being Roman; that is, they lived in Rome some time or other. Well may our needs be imparted to these heavenly petitioners. They are the actors in the drama of our religion to whom our Lord has given leading parts; and for this reason they are commemorated in the fixed portion of the liturgy. Notice how the names of twelve martyrs follow the twelve Apostles:

1. Mary, Our Blessed Mother.
2. The twelve apostles, mentioned by name.
3. The three popes of the first century, the first bishops of Rome, after St. Peter (39-64). See II Timothy iv, 21; Philippians iv, 3. All three popes were martyred for the faith. Linus was pope from 64-76; Cletus (76-88); Clement (88-97). In the early part of the second century these names were put into the Mass.
4. Celebrated martyrs of the first four centuries.
   Xystus or Sixtus, pope from 117-126, and martyr. Thirty-three of the first fifty-six popes were also martyrs.
   Cornelius, a bishop of Rome in days of persecution by Decius; martyred 252, Sept. 14.
   Cyprianus (third century) convert, bishop, martyred 258, Sept. 14. (same day as Cornelius).
   Laurentius, a deacon of the Church in Rome, martyred in Valerian persecution, 258.
   Chrysogonus, a noble Roman, martyred under Diocletian, 304.
   Joannis et Paulus, martyrs of the Roman Church, 362.

174 THE MASS

Cosmas et Damianus (third century) brothers, physicians, sometimes called the "silverless" martyrs, because they would not accept pay for their medical services.

It is like a short litany, but it ends up with "and all the saints." These we ask to intercede for us, to beg God to apply their merits to our souls that we may reap the richest fruits of the Mass. The Church commends them to us for

EARLY SYMBOL OF CHRIST AND HIS APOSTLES

consideration, bids us make their acquaintance. No time is more suitable than the present for a study of those canonized saints, their lives and times. Look them up in the "Catholic Encyclopedia." What we should be doing all through life is learning more about these saints of God, the world's greatest heroes and heroines, "divine artists in the moral order."

1. What is a coliseum, a catacomb, a hecatomb? 2. Give the names of three girls of your age, or three boys of your age, who were martyred for the faith and tell their history. 3. What Roman emperors are identified with the persecutions of the early Christians? Just how long did the more dreadful ones continue? 4. Why is our Lady called the Queen of Martyrs?

XXIV

HANC IGITUR — QUAM OBLATIONEM

On beginning the Hanc Igitur the priest spreads his hands over the oblation so that the tips of his fingers reach as far as the middle of the pall. Then the bell is rung once. At the conclusion of the prayer he rejoins his hands, and draws them toward himself, saying the Quam Oblationem. The oblations are blessed, three crosses being made over the host and chalice, followed by one cross over the host, and another above the chalice — all done with the right hand while the left rests on the altar. He next joins his hands, and bows his head at the sacred name with which the blessing ends.

The Hanc Igitur is a general intercession made just before the coming of Christ on the altar. As that moment draws near a bell rings once. "Behold your Lord cometh! Lift up your voice with strength; lift it up; fear not!" At the near advent of Jesus the faithful take pains to have everything ready. And you will note during these last precious minutes of preparation that: (1) the priest invokes the Godhead to accept the oblation, that is, the bread and wine, displayed on the holy table; (2) he prays for peace, safety of soul, and final perseverance; and (3) the objects of the Action are laid before God, who is asked to make the oblation ✠ blessed, approved, ✠ ratified, ✠ reasonable, and acceptable, that for us it may become the ✠ body and ✠ blood of Jesus Christ, our Lord.

All this is for our Lord. The very words of this prayer have the ring of welcome and earnest appeal. A ceremonial movement makes that more clear insomuch as it suits the action to the words. If you look attentively, you can see the hands of the priest stretched out over the oblation. By this gesture along with the prayer for the acceptance of the gifts, bread and wine, he emphasizes the presentation of oblation. Were you about to offer a gift would you not point to it, or hand it over to the beloved one? So it is here. It is as if we were, and we are, giving back to God His gifts before He gives us the greatest of all gifts, His beloved Son. The moment is near for your soul to lean forth to give and receive the greeting, to grasp, as it were, the stretched-out hand of Christ veiled in mystery, and now so near.

There ought to be just that spiritual attitude during the Hanc Igitur. As once God's people had to wait for God between Egypt and Canaan, so now we are waiting for His beloved Son. We have brought these food offerings to God. We have solemnized our covenant with Him whereby the rights and duties of Fatherhood on the one side and of Sonship on the other are created and renewed. Even more. Included in this intercession is the memory of all the faithful. It is incumbent on us to join our forces and unite in Christian brotherhood; pray for the living and the dead; and remember the saints.

Hanc igitur oblationem servitutis nostræ, sed et cunctæ familiæ tuæ, quæsumus Domine, ut placatus accipias; diesque nostros in tua pace disponas, atque ab æterna damnatione nos eripi, et in electorum tuorum jubeas grege numerari. (*Jungit manus.*) Per Christum Dominum nostrum. Amen.	We therefore beseech Thee, O Lord, graciously to accept this oblation of our servitude, as also of Thy whole family; and to dispose our days in Thy peace, preserve us from eternal damnation, and rank us in the number of Thine elect. (*He joins his hands together.*) Through Christ our Lord. Amen.

HANC IGITUR — QUAM OBLATIONEM 177

What a glorious invocation! Most of us must feel that of all times this is the one for such a complete request, such an all-inclusive petition. The humbler of heart we are, and the more urgent in our request, the greater the graces and the more manifold the blessings that will flow to us from the Mass. Let our minds move with the Mass, and join the welcome worship. The Mass, as we know, begets in us, through Christ, praise, expiation, thanksgiving, and intercession; but here intercession is the dominant note. How sad it would be if we were to lose this opportunity by omitting our intercession. "Among the various duties imposed on us by our vocation none is more akin to privilege than the duty of intercessory prayer. To be able to intercede with God is justly considered one of the glories of the saints in heaven; it is a glory in which we on earth share, according to the measure of our worthiness. Nothing more truly marks off the really religious person from the merely respectable than the manner in which this privilege of intercession is appreciated and used; for intercession implies a vivid sense of God's presence in the world and of the world's relationship with God." Should it not be our duty, then, to make this intercession?

Directly in the Consecration Christ will hear our prayer, will accept our offering and change it into His own body and blood. After this long period of waiting and praying and anxious expectancy, the food offering will become the very Bread of Life, the true Bread from Heaven. "I am the living bread which came down from Heaven." And now He is on His way. Lest we forget, then, let us make haste in our own preparation. Beg God to remove all obstacles to His triumphal entry into our midst; ask Him to fill our hearts with due reverence and devotion; plead with Him to accept our poor oblation:

| Quam oblationem tu, Deus, in omnibus, quæsumus, benedic ✠ tam, adscrip ✠ tam, ra ✠ tam, rationabilem acceptabilemque facere digneris: ut nobis cor ✠ pus et san ✠ guis fiat dilectissimi Filii tui Domini nostri Jesu Christi. | Which oblation do Thou, O God, vouchsafe in all respects to bless, ✠ approve, ✠ ratify, ✠ and accept; that it may be made for us the Body ✠ and Blood ✠ of Thy most beloved Son, Jesus Christ our Lord. |

But now let us go back to the fourfold request of the whole family of the faithful: (1) graciously accept our oblation, we beseech Thee, O Lord; (2) dispose our days in peace; (3) command that we be delivered from eternal damnation; and (4) number us in the flock of Thine elect.

All four of these pleas are rich in thought and entreaty. Look into them, and you will see vividly the need for them. Once our Lord told Peter: "Feed my lambs, feed my sheep." But for this very purpose He is now coming Himself. "The Mass is the daily direct and immediate interposition of God on earth, to work a wonder of beneficence which can only be paralleled by His Incarnation."

If this truth were only grasped by us, how impressed, how anxious, how utterly undivided would be our attention at this very moment! Even now the Good Shepherd is on the threshold of our altar, all but among us who have come together to greet Him. He is coming, and it is for us to see to it that nothing troubles His graciousness, nothing delays the swiftness of His approach, nothing stands in the way of His accepting both our oblation and ourselves. He knows us; we are soon to know Him. Into the midst of His flock He shall presently descend from heaven, mystically to shed His blood once more on our altar. If we are ready for Him, His presence will prove our happiness, our love, our joy. What time more propitious, therefore, to put the last touch on our preparation for the progress of the Great Shepherd, to remove the last obstacle from the road made for the passage of the King; to petition Him for each and every member of the flock foregathered to hail Him.

It was the practice of kings in the East to have a road made for their triumphal march. The glorious approach of the

TRIUMPHAL PROCESSION
Arch of Titus.

royal presence was announced by heralds in the distance, who commanded that the way must be left open, that all obstacles should be removed (Isaias xl, 3-8). The long-sustained trumpet blast is heard, a forerunner appears to see that the way the king is advancing shall be put in good condition. All this recalls John the Baptist's announcement of the coming of Christ. You have read how the great precursor stood on the edge of the desert and crowds came from everywhere to hear him.

Thus did the Baptist proclaim the coming of the Messias, "the kingdom of heaven is at hand. Prepare ye the way of the Lord, make straight his paths" (John i, 23; Matthew iii, 1–12). This was a summons to make level the soul's road for the King of kings, to have human hearts ready for the entry of Christ. That is just what we do as, spiritually expectant, we await the approach of our Saviour. Could anything be more solemn, more thrilling, more divinely dramatic than this paving the way for Christ, our Lord? At this instant of the Mass, frail and impotent creatures that we are, we must look to His grace and help to be less unworthy to welcome Him.

Consider further the fourfold request in this part of the Mass. We say "Graciously accept our oblation, we beseech Thee, O Lord." The situation portrayed in our prayer corresponds to the spiritual reality. Follow the Hanc Igitur every way. All of it is both interesting and important. Examine the reasons why the Church thus prays. Our gifts, the bread and wine, are on the altar; what God wants more than our gifts is our hearts, ourselves. The congregation must be in an inward and outward condition worthy to meet and greet Him when He comes. This prayer is, so to say, a signal to the flock in the sheepfold, to the Church anxiously awaiting the coming of the Good Shepherd. The flock knows its need of the Shepherd. "I know mine, and mine know me. As the Father knoweth me, and I know the Father; and I lay down my life for my sheep" (John x, 14–15). The oblation on the altar will soon become the sacred body which was once rent by forces of evil, and the precious blood which was once shed for all sinners.

Next we beg God "Dispose our days in Thy peace." Of course, there is no true peace except it come from our Lord. "And coming, he preached peace to you that were afar off, and peace to them that were nigh" (Ephesians ii, 17). Notice how our Lord sought out men of good will. The angels at His birth had said: "Peace on earth to men of good will," and Christ in His public life addressed Himself to those who were well inclined and gained them. This is how Christ began the Church. By His grace working secretly in their hearts, the first flock was formed. The chief relation of the shepherd to the flock is just this. Rightly, then, do we plead with Him: Guide our feet in the way of peace, give us good will, make us well inclined to Thy holy will, that we may do it as the angels do it in heaven.

One White Shepherd of Christendom, as the Pope, the representative of Christ, is called, told us the sort of peace to pray for: "Now faith teaches that peace consists in the practical recognition of the supreme authority of the Creator over all the works of His hands; second, in the assured prevalence of the spirit over the senses; third, in the sincere and practical love of our neighbors" (Benedict xv). For this, the extension of God's kingdom on earth, we should implore those helps and graces needful. No place is so fitting for this petition as the Church, no time like Mass. And this is the ripe time to make our plea for peace. If Christ is near us, deep down in our soul will be a calm confidence that all is well, though the surface of our life may be disturbed with passing hopes and fears.

"Command that we be delivered from eternal damnation." With wide eyes, looking for the blessed hope and coming of our Saviour, Jesus Christ, we make this poignant appeal. It says over and over again what need we have for our Lord. It proves more; namely, that we realize our need. Woe to the man who thinks he can do without Christ. Not so with us, for we run to Him. The One we sue for help is the same "Who gave himself for us, that he might redeem us from all iniquity, and might cleanse to himself a people acceptable, a pursuer of good works." Listen to the words and commands of our Lord. "I am the good shepherd. The good shepherd giveth his life for his sheep. And when he hath let out his own sheep, he goeth before them: and his sheep know not the voice of strangers" (John x). Shepherding is used as a symbol of God's care for man, both in the Old Testament and in the New Testament. Nowhere is the shepherd more really the saviour than in the land which Jesus loved, over whose blessed hills His sacred feet trod. "In such a landscape as Judea, where a day's pasture is thinly scattered over an unfenced tract of country, covered with delusive paths,

SHEPHERD'S CLUB AND CROOK

still frequented by wild beasts and rolling off into the desert, the shepherd and his character are indispensable. On some high moor, across which at night the hyenas howl, when you meet him, sleepless, far-sighted, weather-beaten, armed, leaning on his staff, and looking out over his scattered sheep, every one of them on his heart, you understand why they make him the symbol of Providence; why Christ took him as the type of self-sacrifice."

To save us from eternal damnation Christ comes in the Mass. He wants to be to us a Good Shepherd and guide us safely through the wilderness of this world, and into His true heavenly fold. The object of His coming, at the Consecration, is to lead His flock to regions of life and peace and pleasant pasturage. To His flock He gives grace and strength, knowledge and life eternal. If only they stay near Him and obey His command, there shall be no want

HANC IGITUR — QUAM OBLATIONEM

to them even amid trial. Every flock, however, must have its trial, must be exposed to the vicissitudes of life. There are beasts and robbers who attack them. "The wolf catcheth and scattereth the sheep" (John x, 12). "The thief cometh not, but for to steal, and to kill, and to destroy" (John x, 10). Satan and his forces bent upon evil are the foes of the sheep and of the shepherd. Yet our Good Shepherd reassures us: "Fear not, little flock, for it hath pleased your Father to give you a kingdom" (Luke xii, 32).

Never was there such a fearless shepherd as our Saviour. Have you thought of Him in that way? In the old days, before Christ came, there were bad shepherds "who did not visit what is forsaken, nor seek the scattered, nor heal what is broken, nor nourish that which standeth" (Zacharias xi, 16). Not so with our Lord. The fact is that He is the Good Shepherd in every sense of the word. He knows us through and through; He comes to us and is all to our soul that the good shepherd is to the least of his flock.

THE GOOD SHEPHERD

Now in the East, Isaias relates, a shepherd often carries the smaller lambs on his bosom, or under his arms, or in the folds of his cloak (Isaias xl, 11). This same prophet foretold just what Christ would do for His followers: "He shall feed his flock like a shepherd: he shall gather together the lambs with his arm, and shall take them up in his bosom, and he himself shall carry them that are with young." Christ is ever on the lookout for the young of the flock; His voice will keep them near to Him. He will prepare a table for us, in Holy Communion, against them that afflict us (Psalms xxii). If the Lord rules us, we shall want nothing; He will convert our souls, lead us on the paths of justice, for His own name's sake, and save us from eternal damnation. For though we should walk in the midst of the shadow of death we need fear no evils since He is with us (Psalms xxii). How apt, then, is the prayer in which we beg Him to deliver us from the countless foes that surround us in this life; evil foes that conspire to lead us away from the Good Shepherd toward the brink of eternal damnation.

A SHEEP BETWEEN TWO WILD BEASTS

"Number us in the flock of thine elect." By the application to our souls of the merits gained by Christ on the Cross, we become bona fide members of Christ's flock. That flock may be little, in contrast with the myriads of people in the world, but it is the flock of the Good Shepherd. Christ has placed Himself at the head of the flock. One flock, one Shepherd. The eternal Father decreed: "I will set up one shepherd over them, and he shall feed them, and he shall be their shepherd." Nothing is clearer than that Christ is the Shepherd of our souls. Alas! that some abandon the Good Shepherd only to run to and fro like frightened sheep in search for they know not what. Yet He calls them back. "I know mine and mine know me." Even now He is come to feed the flock of God. Even now He comes to be the nourishment of our souls and to rule the Church which He hath purchased with His own blood

THE GOOD SHEPHERD

Very rare carving in nicolite.

(Acts xx, 28). But God (who is rich in mercy) hath quickened us together in Christ (by whose grace you are saved). And hath raised us up together, and hath made us sit to-

HANC IGITUR — QUAM OBLATIONEM

gether in the heavenly places, through Christ Jesus (Ephesians ii, 4, 6, 7). For He is the Lord our God: and we are the people of His pasture and the sheep of His hand. Come let us adore and fall down: and weep before the Lord that made us! (Psalms xciv, 6, 7).

1. Explain the grace of final perseverance. 2. Write a theme on "Christ, the Good Shepherd." 3. Do you know any hymns on this subject? 4. "I know mine and mine know me." Explain this text. 5. What do you understand by divine providence, special providence, political providence? 6. Who are the shepherds of God's flock? 7. Can you name seven false shepherds who loom large in Church history and tell why they are to be branded hirelings?

XXV

CONSECRATION

Holding the host with both hands, the priest pronounces the words of consecration secretly, distinctly, and attentively. Then kneeling upon one knee, he adores the sacred Host; next, rising, he elevates it, and replaces it upon the corporal, kneeling once again. The bell is rung thrice.

The priest then pronounces the words of consecration over the chalice, holding it slightly elevated. That done, he replaces the chalice on the corporal. Making a genuflection, he adores; then rising, he elevates the chalice, and replacing it upon the corporal, makes another genuflection. The bell is rung thrice.

The Consecration! This is the great central act of the Mass. You can readily understand why the Church surrounds it with the most impressive ceremonies. Well for all of us to know just what they mean, word for word, act for act. The Last Supper and what followed, the awful scene of the Crucifixion, took place once in far-off Palestine. But our Lord wanted it to be continued for His followers, always and everywhere. So He instituted the holy sacrifice of the Mass. Fain would He have us all gathered about his altar, as the three Marys and John the Beloved were grouped at the foot of His cross; and for this did He allow the scene of His mercy and love to be reënacted every day in the Mass.

As you follow the words of the Consecration in your prayer book you note that the ritual makes it unmistakably clear that our Lord is now about to descend upon our altar and offer Himself in a great act of worship. Directly we shall

CONSECRATION

have Him with us Himself. Hence from now on we must keep in mind both the presence of Jesus and His sacrifice. Lo! He is coming to renew the offering of Calvary for us and for our salvation. Once more will He be the victim and offer up from the depths of His sacred heart the act which signifies atonement.

With the Consecration comes the holiest, the most divine moment of the Mass. It is the time when Christ visits us as the Prince of Priests. "He is the Great High Priest Who is ever offering up His meritorious sacrifice, and the Mass is the earthly presence of it." Endeavor, therefore, to bring yourselves up to some understanding of this tremendous act. And do not forget that the offerers of the sacrifice of the Mass are as follows: First, our Lord Jesus Christ, in whose name and place the priest stands and speaks. After Jesus the priest himself is the chief offerer. Next come the people, who also offer through, and with, the priest. They have their part, since they are of the mystical body of Christ. Christ, the priest, the people — all offer up a sacrifice to God, the Father Almighty. Partakers, therefore, with Christ, we can cast all our life, thoughts, actions, sufferings with Christ's and present them to the Eternal Father as one great act of obedience.

"Do this in commemoration of Me," said our Lord at the Last Supper. This is what is done here and now. Just as it was the custom at the Pasch to rehearse God's mercies to the chosen people in the deliverance from Egypt, so in the new Pasch, the Mass, we commemorate our deliverance through the death of Christ; we tenderly recall what Christ did at the Last Supper and on the cross.

In the Consecration we have the renewal of God's love for us. Once more He has compassion on the multitude, coming down from heaven just as of old He came down from the mountain to meet the crowds waiting for Him. "Of this action of the Infinite God the priest is the true minister. Although God does it all, yet the priest also does it." No wonder, then, the priest's voice drops to a whisper as he calls to mind the event of the Last Supper, takes the bread as Christ took it, raises his eyes to heaven just as our Lord raised His eyes to heaven before the breaking of the bread, and repeats the words of our Lord. The supreme moment at hand, the priest, every motion subdued to reverence, recites what Christ did and said at the Last Supper.

Qui pridie quam pateretur, accepit panem in sanctas ac venerabiles manus suas, et elevatis oculis in cœlum, ad te Deum Patrem suum omnipotentem, tibi gratias agens, bene ✠ dixit, fregit, deditque discipulis suis, dicens: accipite, et manducate ex hoc omnes.	Who, the day before He suffered, took bread into His holy and venerable hands, and with eyes lifted up toward heaven, unto Thee, O God, His Almighty Father, giving thanks to Thee, did bless ✠ break, and give unto His disciples, saying: Take, and eat ye all of this.
Hoc est enim corpus meum.	*For this is My body.*

When the priest says over the bread these words of our Lord: "This is My body," at that moment, the heavens open, the choir of angels is present for the solemn act of Jesus Christ who comes on our altar Himself. The mystery of Bethlehem is renewed. "Heaven and earth intermingle and the highest is joined with the lowly." At that tremendous instant the priest holds in his hands the Victim of Calvary, he perpetuates the offering of Jesus Christ.

The bell rings three times as the priest, (1) genuflecting, adores the sacred Host, (2) rising elevates it, then places it on the corporal; and (3) once more bends his knee and adores. As soon as the sacred Host is raised on high, just as our Lord's body was lifted up high on the cross and offered as a sacrifice to God, we adore Him. And the whole court of heaven unites with us in hushed adoration at this holiest moment. The Mass is Calvary over again. Did you ever notice how, on a stormy night, a flash of lightning will light up a whole street or the trees on a hilltop? You can liken the elevation of the Host to that, in so far as it flashes into the worshiper's mind just what happened on Calvary. There, in very truth:

> Our Lord hung upon the cross
> And the people stood beholding . . .
> And they sat and watched Him . . .
> And they put over His head the cause written:
> "This is Jesus the King of the Jews."

Truly this *is* Jesus! Here, then, we have Him on our cross-altar. So when the elevation takes place, look with love and reverence on the Host, the divine Victim, held aloft in the priest's hands. Look to Him, "the author and finisher of our faith, who having joy set before Him, endured the cross, despising the shame." Bring this home to your mind over and over again. From the highest heavens He comes to us in the Mass. Think of that! God is now on our altar, and God is love. So He ought to be loved. Adore Him. Speak to Him, beg His mercy for your parents, your friends, for all who may need your intercession.

After adoring the sacred body of our Lord, the priest, intent on the words, continues the Consecration. Again his voice drops to a whipser and his head is bowed. He first calls to mind what our blessed Lord did when He took the chalice at the Last Supper; after which come the very words of Consecration which Christ used, whereupon the wine is changed into the precious blood.

| Simili modo, postquam cœnatum est, accipiens et hunc præclarum | In like manner, after He had supped taking also this excellent |

calicem in sanctas ac venerabiles manus suas, item tibi gratias, agens, bene ✢ dixit, deditque discipulis suis, dicens: Accipite et bibite ex eo omnes: *Hic est enim calix sanguinis mei, novi et æterni testamenti; mysterium fidei: qui pro vobis et pro multis effundetur in remissionem peccatorum.* Hæc quotiescumque feceritis, in mei memoriam facietis.	chalice into His holy and venerable hands, also giving thanks to Thee. He blessed ✢ and gave it to His disciples, saying: Take and drink ye all of this: *For this is the chalice of my blood of the new and eternal testament. The mystery of faith: which shall be shed for you and for many, for the remission of sins.* As often as ye do these things, ye shall do them in remembrance of Me.

Again the bell rings thrice, as the priest adores the precious blood of our Saviour.

"In the Blessed Sacrament of the Holy Eucharist," says the Council of Trent, "after the consecration of the bread and wine, there is contained truly, really, and substantially, under the appearance of these things of sense, our Lord Jesus Christ, true God and true Man. For it is not inconsistent that our Saviour should sit forever in heaven at the right hand of the Father, according to the natural mode of His existence, and that His substance should nevertheless be present with us sacramentally in many other places, by a mode of existence which, though we can scarcely express it in words, we can apprehend with minds enlightened by faith, and which we ought to believe."

Prior to this definition the Church had already at various times insisted that the body and blood of Christ are present, not by representation, appearance, or figure, but in their reality, identically the same as they were born of the Virgin Mary and sacrificed for us on the Cross.

We scarcely need to be told now that the Mass is the continuation of the sacrifice of the cross. What our Lord did at the Last Supper, the priest does in the Mass. Then our Lord comes on the altar. Thus in the very form and

CONSECRATION

manner in which Christ gives Himself to us, His death on Calvary is set forth. Not now is it a physical death, to be sure; none the less it is a figurative shedding of blood. The altar, as we have seen, becomes another Calvary. It is not merely an image of the cross; it is the cross itself, with the sacred body which was nailed to it and the divine blood which flowed on it for us. It is the slain Christ we commemorate, and in the Mass we show forth the Lord's death till He comes. This blood of Christ, shed for us, is truly said to ask pardon for us. "This is My blood of the new and eternal testament." As the sprinkling of the sacrificial blood set the seal to the ancient covenant, so now "the Precious Blood of Jesus seals His New Covenant of the New Law of Charity; the law of Fraternal Love." "With desire have I desired to eat this Pasch with you." So our Lord said, and so He does in the Mass. That is why we do Him homage.

This is the heart of the Mass; the very core of the sacrificial act has been reached! "What a marvel has been wrought on this mystical table! Where is now the bread? Where the wine? These no longer exist; an invisible fire has come down from heaven, touched and changed their substance, and it is replaced by the body and blood of Jesus Christ. By virtue of this omnipotent word the incarnate God is born again upon the altar; the word of the priest has given Him a new life, a new existence, and behold there He is before us in the form of a victim." Lest this great truth be passed over in our daily lives, Catholic boys and girls ought to consider how the sacrifice of the Mass is substantially the same as that of the cross: the same act of obedience unto death being an act of praise, of thanksgiving, of expiation, of intercession.

	Victim	Priest	Oblation	Purpose
On The Cross	The Lamb of God laden with the sins of the world. I Timothy ii, 5-6.	"Thou art a priest forever according to the order of Melchisedech."	Jesus Christ offered Himself, accepting in His heart the bloody death which He suffered.	To offer to God the highest act of worship, to give Himself for us as the victim. To win for us pardon, graces, atonement.
In The Mass	The same victim offering Himself to the Father, a mystical renewal of His death to take away the sins of the world.	The same Priest, the Son of God, daily offering Himself by the ministry of Man.	He offers Himself once more, interiorly, mystically, to His Father.	The Mass has the same four ends as the cross, viz., praise, thanksgiving, expiation, intercession.

Christ is now sacramentally present on our altar. "No wonder," writes a great bishop, "you set apart a holy and terrible place, consecrating it with solemn rites — that you erect a stone, an altar, and pour on it the mystic unction — that you burn the symbolic incense, light the lamps of faith . . . surround your ministrations with ancient ceremonies and the prayers of the saints of old." No wonder we spread out the finest linen, and try to provide the most precious vessels, the chalice of gold, and the paten of which a poet-priest, Father O'Donnell, sings:

> A little golden cradle
> It waits for Mary's Son
> Until my words give birth to Him
> Each day's expected One.[1]

For He is all to us, Jesus Christ, who now resides on our altar. God-made man is the Victim who alone can per-

[1] *Cloister and Other Poems*, Rev. C. L. O'Donnell, C. S. C.

fectly honor and glorify the Father, can fittingly thank God for all His gifts to mankind. The drama of the Mass has reached its highest, holiest point. We are all in the presence of the august King, and we worship just the same as if we knelt at the foot of the cross on Calvary nineteen hundred years ago. This is by far the greatest act of our day; nay, of our life.

What time more proper to offer our homage to the Eucharistic Christ. You know what homage denotes. Homagium means *I am your man*. In the Middle Ages, the days of feudalism, the vassal placed his hands between the hands of his lord, and swore loyalty to him, saying: "I am your man." This was called "doing homage." Similarly when knighthood was in flower, in the good old days of chivalry, the young candidate for knighthood spent the night in church before the Blessed Sacrament.

CEREMONY OF HOMAGE

The new vassal is putting his hands between those of his lord.

> The sweet vision of the Holy Grail
> Drove me from all vainglories,
> And earthly heats that spring and sparkle out
> Among us in the jousts, while women watch
> Who wins, who falls; and waste the spiritual strength
> Within us, better offered up to Heaven.[1]

Now is the time for us to pledge ourselves to Christ, to offer Him reverence and obedience. Now is the time for

[1] Tennyson, *The Holy Grail*.

us to be loyal subjects of our Lord. Fealty was the fidelity that the vassal and the knight promised on oath. They were sworn to personal service. So be it with us. Adore, then, and praise God really and truly present on the altar. Say to him:

> Master, go on and I will follow thee
> To the last gasp, with faith and loyalty.[1]

You know that devotion signifies the setting of one's mind and imagination at work upon a mystery; it also means the keeping of one's heart firm toward God and ready to do His will. This is to worship God. Now you strengthen your devotion, your faculty of worship, by exercising your mind in prayer and your heart in religious feeling. Those who are lazy at prayer gradually lose that faculty; it is no longer firm and strong, it becomes skin deep, flaccid, like a muscle little used. We must never let that happen in our case. Not passing prayer merely, but deep, fervent worship. True Catholics are always devout and very much so at the moment of Consecration; for then the Most Holy is come. That visitor is God Himself. Think of it! No wonder the people in the west coast of Ireland salute our Lord aloud at the Consecration and say "A hundred thousand welcomes, O Lord." Their voices, said an onlooker, sounded like the waves of the sea.

Some years ago a non-Catholic was telling how he went into a church and stayed there for Mass. What impressed him was the marked devotion he witnessed on every side. "When the bell rang," he said, "I felt the awe of the moment, the hushed silence, the secret prayer. Everybody seemed intent on some great business all their own." This surprised the stranger, but it does not surprise us. It would

[1] Shakespeare, *As You Like It*.

be odd should any Catholic whisper or cause distraction at such a holy time when every mind is centered on Christ. If we believe, as we do, that the King of kings is come to visit *us*, and the greatest leader in the world wants to meet *us*, why should we not be alert, quick, ready to receive Him? Have eyes and mind, then, for nobody except your Saviour. It is only right that the doors of your heart be thrown open to receive Him.

Well may we ask ourselves: how can anybody be indifferent at such a time? Can any one forget what has just come to pass? Lest we forget, let us be on the alert. No grown-up Catholic with any reverence would do other than keep his soul's eyes clear and his heart intent upon the divine Guest. It does matter how we are conducting ourselves during these precious moments. We cannot too often tell ourselves that. Possibly the reason some prayers are not heard is because they are so carelessly said. The trouble is that some young people at prayer do not ask, they do not really seek. "Ask and you shall receive," declares our Lord. "Seek and you shall find." If we want God's help, we should seek it with zest and pay no attention to anything else. That must be the way we pray when God comes to us in the Consecration. Pray, then, and earnestly. When the Consecration bell rings lift up your heart, and keep your eyes upon the Host.

"When," writes Cardinal Mercier, "the celebrant has accomplished the liturgical act of highest excellence, the Consecration, and when, according to the rubrics, he elevates the sacred Host in a manner so as to render it visible to the assemblage of Christians, it is not fitting that they should remain with heads bowed to earth. The elevation is made for them — tell them. Wherefore, that they should humbly follow with their eyes the sacred Species, at the elevation of the sacred Host and of the chalice containing the precious blood as well."

Look at the Host! Pius X, on May 18, 1907, granted an indulgence of three hundred days once a day to all the faithful who gaze at the sacred Host when it is elevated during Mass, or exposed on the altar, and say at the same time with faith and devotion, "My Lord and my God." There is also an indulgence of seven years and seven quarantines for each recitation; and a plenary indulgence is granted to all who religiously practice it once a day during the week. Join the movement forwarding this pious practice. When the priest shows the Blessed Sacrament to the people, be sure to raise your eyes.

Look at the Host! That is our privilege nowadays, so let us make good use of it. Once on a time, as you know, this most sacred of all acts, the Consecration, took place behind drawn veils. The congregation saw nothing, heard no words, for the whole ceremony was concealed. Gradually this curtain disappeared, the veils were taken away. That is what you would expect. The worshipers wanted to see the whole drama of Calvary. That they so willed is not surprising. Love was the high aim in their hearts, a love which wanted to be vividly reminded of the real Presence. Nor was that all. Some time afterward a new and beautiful rite took place. The Bishop of Paris, Eudes de Sully (1196–1208), introduced the custom of the elevation. Heretofore the Host was elevated, ever so slightly, not at the Consecration, but just after the Pater Noster. But from this time on, as the words of Consecration were said the priest lifted up the Host high enough to be seen and worshiped by the congregation.

Look at the Host! It is surely a great privilege to fix one's eyes on the Host at just this time. Catholics in the Middle Ages considered it very important to see the Blessed Sacrament at the Elevation. Also, they set a needed ex-

CONSECRATION

ample for all who were to come after them. "If the people had not seen the Blessed Sacrament," says Father Fortesque, "they thought they had not properly heard Mass and waited for another; they came in for that moment and went out again; boys were let out of school for a moment to see the Elevation; sometimes they crowded and strained their necks to see the Host elevated." Theirs was surely a high aim, a dear wish, though they sometimes carried it too far. For if the Host were not seen by them "the rude people of the countrey," so ran an old account, "in diverse partes of England will crye out to the priest."

No doubt it was this eager desire to see the elevation that gave rise to the custom of ringing the bell. First at the Sanctus, so that the people could leave off their work and start for the church; next, just before the Consecration, so that they might enter the church in time; then at the elevation, in order that they might see the Blessed Sacrament. In the later Middle Ages bells[1] were used very much. There were two, sometimes three, kinds in use:

1. A little hand bell, called the sacring bell, like the one the altar boy rings. 2. A middle-sized one, that hung in the roof over the sanctuary, the rope reaching down near the server who rung it. It was called the Sance (Sanctus) bell. 3. The great bell of the church, which was tolled when the sacred Host was raised at the Consecration to let the people far and near know that our Lord had come upon the altar.

1. What is the main idea of the elevation of the Blessed Sacrament?
2. The priest is not allowed to lift the Host into public view till it has

[1] Bells were used by bishops from very early years. Handbells are preserved, which are said to be as old as the fifth century. The book of Armagh tells how St. Patrick conferred on St. Fiac episcopal ordination, presenting him with a bell, as a distinguishing mark of his office. One of the oldest bells extant is known as the bell of St. Patrick. It was given to the Church of Armagh by St. Columba. Made of thick sheet iron, six inches high, it has a loop at the top for the hand.

been consecrated. Just when is the bread truly consecrated? 3. In parts of France you may hear many bells rung during the Mass. The French love the tinkling of bells and have them rung at the beginning of the Mass, the Offertory, and at different spaces throughout the Holy Sacrifice. How often is the bell rung in your Church? How often is it called for by the rubrics?

XXVI

UNDE ET MEMORES

Transubstantiation! This is the greatest miracle on our earth — this divine condescension, this coming of our Lord Himself into our very midst. The Real Presence is with us — He whom God has sent! The divine Victim is with us by the will of His Heavenly Father and by His own wish. With His own lips He said that one day when talking to the multitude. It happened after the feeding of the five thousand. When the crowd, hours in search of Christ, at length found Him, they said: "What shall we do, that we may work the works of God?" Our Lord answered them: "This is the work of God, that you believe in him whom he has sent. . . . I am the bread of life; he that cometh to me shall not hunger: and he that believeth in me shall never thirst . . . and him that cometh to me I will not cast out. For the bread of God is that which cometh down from heaven and giveth life to the world. . . . And this is the will of my Father that sent me: that every one who seeth the Son, and believeth in him, may have life everlasting" (John vi).

The lesson is one of God's love for every one of His creatures, and of His goodness in giving us the bread of life.

"The Lord is sweet to all: and his tender mercies are over all his works.
The Lord is faithful in all his works: and holy in all his works.
The Lord is nigh unto all them that call upon him; to all that call upon him in truth" (Psalms cxliv).

To encourage our love and longing for divine truth, Jesus instituted the Mass. He desired to aid our weak, faltering faith, to stir our memory, to keep us in mind of Him, not with shadowy remembrance but with vital faith born of His Real Presence on our altar. What more could He have done for us?

At the Last Supper, our Lord gave a command: "Do this in commemoration of me." The Mass, age after age, is the answer to that divine request. The Church in this part of the Mass shows how mindful she is of her Master's wish. She is full of the divine Presence. Jesus now occupies her whole heart, her whole soul. Does He own ours? The divine Victim, crucified and dying on the cross, should be the object of all our faith, hope, and love. No paltry worship, now, but an offering of our Lord and of ourselves, of all we are and all we have to the Father. This is the mind of the Mass.

The Unde et Memores shows that we are aware, keen, alert, eager, kneeling at attention. No longer are we like children — thoughtless worshipers. Intent upon doing homage to Him, our aim is to be of one mind with Christ. It is just, then, that we should represent to ourselves the sorrows and griefs, the stripes and humiliations that our Lord suffered, for by those very things were our souls healed and ourselves made worthy to receive Him. Here Christ wishes us to recall all that. True to His wish, the words of the Mass utter what our hearts feel:

Unde et memores, Domine, nos servi tui, sed et plebs tua sancta, ejusdem Christi Filii tui Domini nostri, tam beatæ passionis; necnon et ab inferis resurrectionis, sed et in cœlos gloriosæ ascensionis:	Wherefore, O Lord, we Thy servants, and likewise Thy holy people, calling to mind the blessed passion of the same Christ, Thy Son our Lord, His resurrection from the grave, and glorious as-

UNDE ET MEMORES

offerimus præclaræ majestati tuæ de tuis donis ac datis.	cension into heaven, offer unto Thy most excellent Majesty, of Thine gifts bestowed upon us.

But those gifts, once mere bread and wine, have become, by consecration, the body and blood of Jesus Christ, and are now offered to the Heavenly Father by none other than Jesus Christ Himself present on our altar. Remembering Christ we, too, offer this sacrifice coöfferers with Him:

Hostiam ✠ puram, hostiam ✠ sanctam, hostiam ✠ immaculatam, panem ✠ sanctum vitæ æternæ, et Calicem ✠ salutis perpetuæ.	A pure ✠ Victim, a holy ✠ Victim, an immaculate ✠ Victim, the holy ✠ Bread of eternal life, and Chalice ✠ of everlasting salvation.

Surely no more truthful and glorious tribute to the Holy Host than this one, and in language destined for immortality. Now you can see how the Mass is essentially a remembrance of Christ's death. The Real Presence is with us, in the transubstantiation effected by the words of consecration. That is why the crosses made over the Holy Host betoken our memory of Calvary, our realization that the same Victim is now with us to bestow blessings, the graces of the Mass, for which we ask. Note this also. When friends meet, one of the first things done is the recounting of past experiences or adventures. No wonder, then, when we meet with the divine Victim on our altar, we pass in rapid review these great events: His passion, resurrection, and ascension! They constitute a triple triumph to be kept in mind. Meanwhile we do honor to the divine Victim; we have Him actually in our mind, keep Him before our soul's eyes as He passed through His passion to His glory that He might go before us to show us the road to heaven. Having the Most Holy in our midst, we celebrate His divine victory over death, begun on Calvary, confirmed when He rose again, completed when He took possession of His throne and prepared a place for us. Happy for us that we can do just this, for great is the value of such remembrance.

As we revive these thoughts of Christ and of His triumphs, we speak consciously of our inheritance: we Thy servants; that is, members of Thy household. Ours is a big household, and the Church is the home. "Christianity," a convert once said, "is not merely an idea, it is also a community. It is a Church as well as a religion. Its office is to bring men into a polity in belief of the truth. Hence the ancient expression, 'Corpus Christianorum' — the Christian people. St. Chrysostom speaks of the creation of this Christian people as the one miracle of Christ which no heathen could gainsay."

Think of the present number of Catholics in the world. Find out for yourself where the Church is strongest. You will find that in the American possessions the total is 29,015,-774. In the British Empire there are 14,439,941. Of especial interest is it to note that in many big cities, provincial centers, confessions are regularly heard in Chinese, Dutch, Flemish, French, German, Hungarian, Italian, Lithuanian, Maltese, Polish, Russian, Portuguese, Spanish, and other languages. The number of Catholics in the world reaches the figure of 316,858,975. Big? Yes, yet small in comparison with the millions who have not heard of Jesus Christ and His Church. It is sad to think how dark their souls must be in this life. For them we ought to pray every day in the Mass. Thank God for the devoted missionaries who go to the ends of the earth to win the heathen to the faith of Christ. Catholic boys and girls should make it a point to know all about these foreign missions. Altogether there are thousands of men and women who give up their lives to be missionaries far away from their native land.

UNDE ET MEMORES

Now, perhaps, we can better understand the world-wide Church — Civitas Dei — comprising so many tongues and peoples, the world over, in which we have the inestimable privilege of being citizens. "Now therefore you are no more strangers and foreigners; but you are fellow citizens with the saints and the domestics of God" (Ephesians ii, 19). Moreover, just in the measure that we are alive to our part in the Communion of Saints, and recognize with growing knowledge our kinship with others — the faithful on earth, in purgatory, in heaven, all centered in Christ on our altar; in so far can we share in the passion of Christ, love Him better and offer with Him the holy sacrifice.

Happy are we if by grace we truly belong to the Church; unhappy, if we are utter strangers to holiness. To be holy is to be near God. The Mass will help make us holy, a more vital union with Christ being possible where we have His continual presence. He has for us both help and sympathy. Before the gaze of the divine Victim on the altar the whole congregation lies open, with its past, present, and future. As from the cross, so now His outstretched arms reach to include us, His heart yearns to feed us with His lifeblood. Our relation to Him is, at this time of the Mass, altogether unique, and it is well to be mindful of His passion, resurrection, ascension — all for us. "I am the way." The divine Leader is there to show us the way and lead us. No army in the field can exist long unless it is in touch with its commander. We are in the field, united under Him so that we think, feel, act with Him. In Him we live and move and have our being. There is an organic oneness with Christ and we are united closely with Him, who is the Head and Form of the Living Church, whereof we are members. Holy Communion, the coming of Our Lord Himself into our very being, will render that oneness, that mystical union, even more wonderful; it will extend the life of Christ in our souls, reinvigorate us in the graces of the resurrection and ascension, so that we can say with St. Paul: "I live, yet not I, but Christ liveth in me."

No wonder, then, we call ourselves "God's holy people," in this prayer. Christ Himself has spoken of "His kingdom," "His flock," over and over again. St. Peter describes Christ's disciples as a *gens sancta* — a holy people. Mindful of this, we are gathered together; we kneel as a bodyguard in the presence of that victim of love, burning with all the energy of the divine Spirit Who fills Him; nay, transforms Him into the "Pure Host, the Holy Host, the Immaculate Host" that is on our altar. He is with us now, for He has made Himself "the holy bread of eternal life and the chalice of everlasting salvation." Such is the meaning of the Unde et Memores.

Having grasped the meaning of this great truth, the next thing is to realize our duty. Here we must ask ourselves how our conduct measures up in this part of the Mass. Upsoaring feelings will not bring anybody to heaven, unless they are followed by duty well done, by actual fidelity to our Lord. Do we mean what we say? The real significance of Unde et Memores is "we are mindful, considerate of Christ." We are not "memores" (mindful) if our eyes are wandering, looking here and there, at Jack's old suit, or Jane's new hat. Yet it is a sad fact that some do that, just as if nothing happened in the Mass to engage their steadiest attention. That is not the way to keep faith with our divine Visitor. It is our duty here to be seriously attentive, and give all our attention to our Lord just come upon the altar. Now is our opportunity to beg our Lord to make us true to our holy religion always and everywhere, remembering that our religion is not a matter of feeling, but a concern of the will; not mere promises, but rather the doing of our duty. Certainly we should be careful of our deportment; more careful to think of our Lord's life, death, resurrection; most careful to plead with Him for our own welfare, that of others, of the public, of the whole Church.

Another consideration is weighty in this stage of the sacrifice. The Mass makes vital the truth of the fatherhood of God and the brotherhood of man. Let us have a clear idea of that truth of the fatherhood of God and the brotherhood of man. The kingdom of God is indeed founded on that truth, and we, the children of the kingdom, are banded together for the common purpose of making possible on earth the reign of Christ in human hearts. "Thy kingdom come" is our standard, nothing being dearer to our hearts than the wish that all men might belong to the kingdom. The Blessed Eucharist is the sacrament of unity, one faith, one Lord. In order to belong to the kingdom, subjects must show faith in, and loyalty to, and acceptance of Jesus Christ. "No man cometh to the Father, but by me" (John xiv, 6). We know that love of our religion is bound up with love of Jesus Christ, and love of our Lord is bound up with love of our neighbor. "If you do not love your neighbor whom you see, how can you love God whom you do not see?" So we must love all people, because Christ commands us to do so; because He Himself set the example and gave us the two great commandments. If you would have the whole truth of this matter, read John xiv. There is the very heart of the gospel of the fatherhood of God and the brotherhood of man, centering in Christ, our Lord. The unique fact of Christ's teaching is that it rests upon Himself, His own personality. "I am the vine, you are the branches; . . . unless you abide in me you cannot have life . . . without me you can do nothing." Allegiance to the personality of

Jesus Christ, then, is absolutely necessary. That came straight from Jesus Christ Himself and His Apostles preached it everywhere. More than that, He gave us the means thereto by instituting the Eucharist. By the Mass only can the craving for nearness, the satisfaction of ardent, devoted affection, be realized. In short, the Mass makes more easy the reign of God in our hearts, the only thing eternally worth while. The Mass was to be the rendezvous, the appointed place of meeting for His loyal followers, and Communion a banquet of brotherhood.

Being loyal to our Lord means being loyal to all that is just, good, and true. It will help you to love God and your neighbor all the more, when you keep in mind the great truth that Christ on our altar draws all to Him. We are His holy people. The Communion of Saints stands out everywhere in the holy sacrifice, but nowhere so shiningly as here, where the congregation prays as a corporate whole, speaking through their priest. Never can we forget our incorporation in that community nor the way the Mass extends and intensifies that membership. The Mass ties us together with cords of love, firm knits us in bonds of Christian brotherhood. There is no gainsaying it, the brotherhood of man is nowhere so deeply realized, so truly proclaimed, as in the Mass. That is why the Mass is the soul of our religion. "If they took the sacrifice of the Mass out of our religion, then religion would fade, would droop, would die and become soulless." There never was a time, there never will be a time, on this planet, there never can be a period in the story of man's life, without sacrifice offered in recognition of God's supreme dominion over His creatures. And this great gift, the Mass, which Jesus gave to the world, remains for all generations.

As in every Mass "we offer unto Thee Thine Own of Thine

Own in all and for all"; so upon this sacrifice we now in our day beg God to look. This, you can see, is the prayer of all, of the Mystical Body.

Supra quæ propitio ac sereno vultu respicere digneris: et accepta habere, sicuti accepta habere dignatus es munera pueri tui justi Abel, et sacrificium patriarchæ nostri Abrahæ: et quod tibi obtulit summus sacerdos tuus Melchisedech, sanctum sacrificium, immaculatam hostiam.	Upon which vouchsafe to look with a gracious and favorable countenance, and to accept them, as Thou wert pleased to accept the gifts of Thy just servant Abel, and the sacrifice of our patriarch Abraham, and that which Thy high priest Melchisedech offered to Thee, a holy sacrifice, a spotless victim.

Supra quæ, said when we are one with Christ, is a prayer that God may receive this sacrifice, as He received the sacrifices of Abel, Abraham, and Melchisedech. In a retrospect of faith we glance backward to those sacrifices so pleasing to God, in so far as they foreshadowed the great sacrifice at which we are granted the privilege of being present and partakers. All those great men of old are one with us in worshiping God.

THE SACRIFICES OF ABEL AND MELCHISEDECH

What we are to note from now on in the Mass is the marvelous way in which the living Christ binds us more closely to Himself, stirs our consciousness of the Communion of Saints, urges us to join ourselves through prayer with all the members of the household of faith, living and dead. Undoubtedly the very words of the Mass make that plain. By our presence at the Holy Sacrifice, by our union with Christ we become with the priest coöfferers of the Victim. We are one with Him, in a wondrous oneness. The appreciation of this fact in its bearing upon the oblation is a special study. The divine Victim, the same One who was immolated on the cross, we offer in reality to the eternal Father. We offer, think of that! And we offer that Victim, not only in the state which is most acceptable to God's justice, but also in the state which is most grateful to His love. Furthermore, offering the divine Victim for the second time, we ask God to accept this pure, holy, and immaculate Host, even as He accepted the gifts of the field from Abel, the self-giving of Abraham, the bread and wine from the hands of Melchisedech. And we pray further:

Supplices te rogamus, omnipotens Deus, jube hæc perferri per manus sancti Angeli tui in sublime altare tuum, in conspectu divinæ majestatis tuæ: ut quotquot ex hac altaris participatione, sacrosanctum Filii tui Cor ✛ pus et San ✛ guinem sumpserimus, omni benedictione cœlesti et gratia repleamur. Per eundum Christum Dominum nostrum. Amen.

We most humbly beseech Thee, Almighty God, to command these things to be carried by the hands of Thy holy angel to Thy altar on high, in the sight of Thy divine Majesty, that as many as shall partake of the most sacred Body ✛ and Blood of ✛ Thy Son at this altar may be filled with every heavenly grace and blessing. Through the same Christ our Lord. Amen.

During this prayer, the priest bows down profoundly, then kisses the altar, and finally makes the sign of the cross over the body and blood of God's Son. You know what the crosses signify — they are fraught with blessings. An appeal that God may receive our sacrifice, the self-offering of the Communion of Saints, it is both beautiful and mystical. There could hardly be any greater proof of this than the way in which saints and scholars, through the Middle Ages down to our own day, have tried to explain the *Supplices te rogamus*. The phrase Thy heavenly altar (*sublime altare tuum*) points to heaven. But a moment ago the priest was recalling the ascension of our Lord into heaven; thither the Saviour went to prepare a place for us; there He abides forever on the right hand of the Father. We keep that truth in mind when saying this prayer. "If you be risen with Christ," says St. Paul, "seek the things that are above; where Christ is sitting at the right hand of God: Mind the things that are above, not the things that are upon the earth" (Colossians iii, 1–2). Naturally Catholics go in spirit from the altar where Christ is here with us really and truly, though sacramentally, to that high heavenly altar where He is present in His glorified body, reigning forever, as He "sends forth judgment unto victory." "Jesus Christ, the first man in heaven, wants His fellow men there." And we wish to reach there; so we ask that our merits in this Mass will go before us; that God will take note of our part as the sacrifice is conveyed to His heavenly altar.

We are here face to face with a really wonderful mystery: one that fills us with awe for the very holiness of the sacrifice where angels crowd round the altar and earth is brought closer to heaven. We pray that the fruits of the sacrifice be secured to us, as we plead that this Mass — even our own poor part in it — may be acceptable to God. "We most humbly beseech Thee, Almighty God, to command these things to be carried *by the hands of Thy holy Angel* to Thy altar on high." What a glorious prayer, yet how mystical! Angels' notes are again heard. Their presence is, so to say, barely revealed; but the soul's eyes catch a glimpse of them as their wings brush upon the text of the Mass. Nothing is more beautiful than this joining of the holy angels with our sacrifice. All during our Lord's life on earth, angels were never distant from Him. Gabriel at the Annunciation, choirs of them at Bethlehem, the angel of comfort at Gethsemane. Of these we know from Holy Writ. Must there not have been myriad angels round about Mount Calvary, just as they are at our altar here and now? What wonder that we think of them in the presence of Christ, ready at His nod, to serve, even as they

CHERUBIM

were close at hand on the Mount when Satan tried to tempt our Lord (Matthew iv). Angels, then, come to our mind and into our prayer in this part of the Mass.

In past days, people used to pray thus:

"Receive upon Thy reasonable altar in heaven for a sweet smelling savor, into Thy vastness in heaven, through the ministry of Thy holy angels and archangels, like as Thou didst accept the gifts of the righteous Abel and the sacrifice of our Father Abraham and the two mites of the widow."

Such are the very old words of the Coptic liturgy of St. Cyril. But in our Mass we pray, "per manus sancti angeli tui." Here it is pertinent to ask: who is "Thy holy angel," the angel of the altar? It is a question that the wisest man could not answer offhand. "Many medieval writers," says Father Fortesque, "discussed who the angel might be. Some think it is St. Michael; others say it might be the priest's guardian angel. St. Thomas explains it to be the angel in Apocalypse viii, 4: 'And the smoke of the incense of the prayers of the saints ascended up before God from the hand of the angel.'"

What can we add to that? We know by this time how profound is this mystery. Which of us can hope wholly to understand those words, so deep, so wonderful, so stupendous? But this we know: that the Mass is one with that eternal sacrifice offered on God's heavenly altar. Nor can there be any doubt that we have a part in that sacrifice. So here let us ask that the good God may receive our poor part — our hopes, our praise, our prayer, our self-giving — "by the ministry of Christ on His heavenly altar for an odor of sweetness." Also let us ask, in the words of the Supplices, that all who open their hearts to receive the divine Victim may be filled with every heavenly grace and benediction, and may thus be drawn, by angels, as it were, nearer and nearer to their heavenly home.

While the above prayer is addressed to the Father, it is through the intercession of the Son. The sign of the cross is made over the gifts on the altar to show that they are the real body and blood of Jesus Christ. For the Mass, never forget, is another Calvary, and brings the blessings of the cross, the merits of our Lord's passion and death. Throughout this part of the Mass, it is Christ who pleads with us and for us, He being the great Intercessor. Therefore, when you hear or say the words, "Through Christ our Lord," think of the solemn, majestic pleading of our Saviour. He shed His

212 THE MASS

precious blood for us and for our salvation, and constantly intercedes for the forgiveness won for us on Calvary's heights. He promised to grant us whatever we should ask in His name. That is why we ask for all favors through Jesus Christ. Here we are gathered round Jesus, the Victim, in His most meritorious act. Even now His redeeming blood is pleading for us, as once upon Calvary. And now as our own remembrance of Christ is intensified, we beg Him to keep us and ours in mind and give us His divine help.

1. "An angel of God" is mentioned in the text of the Mass. Can you tell what are the duties and privileges of the angels? 2. What was the relation of angels to the ancient sacrifices? Read Genesis iv, 4; viii, 20–21; Apocalypse viii, 3–4. 3. Read the article on angels in the "Catholic Encyclopedia." 4. How would you explain to a non-Catholic what is meant by the word "Catholic"? 5. Are you able to give any information as to what is being done by Catholic missionaries, priests, and sisters in China, India, Africa, South America, the South Sea Islands, Alaska?

ANGEL

XXVII

MEMENTO ETIAM

The priest, saying "Memento etiam," slowly separates his hands, and soon joins them at the words, "in somno pacis" — a gesture of peace and rest. Then he raises them to his face, inclines his head, and fixing his eyes on the Sacred Host prays for the dead. He next raises his head, holds his hands extended, and continues the prayer. Toward the end he once more rejoins his hands.

E pluribus unum — in union there is strength — is the motto of our country. It is also the motto of the Church, though in a much wider sense; above all this is true of the Mass. The sacrifice of the Mass is the sacrifice of the whole Church along with Jesus Christ, offered to God in mystical oneness. The offering made in the Mass is both the body of Jesus Christ, real and natural, and His mystic body, which is the Church. While Jesus is offered for us He does not absolve us of the obligation of offering ourselves with Him.

The Head — Christ now on the altar

The Mystical Body { The Church in heaven / The Church on earth / The Church in purgatory

Keep that divine fact well in mind. The sacrifice of the whole Church — the Church in heaven, the Church on earth, the Church in purgatory. Therefore, the souls in purgatory communicate and participate in the Mass when the Church offers herself in sacrifice with Jesus Christ.

The Church on earth is a thoughtful mother. Her aim is to stir sympathy for the poor souls, and lead us on to an ever fuller understanding of our Christian brotherhood and its responsibilities. She knows how forgetful are her living children of the ones who have gone before them into eternity.

Tombs hewn in the rock

So she sets aside this part of the Mass in order to urge us to do our duty by them. An immediate obligation flowing from membership in the Communion of Saints is ours. Of a truth, we of the Church on earth ought to pray for the departed souls. If our membership in the Communion of Saints is vital, there must be united effort; there must be earnest service in behalf of the needy ones. The Church never forgets them in the Mass, so anxious is she that they receive the merits of the Son of God who now renews His death on the altar. While her mind is occupied with the

MEMENTO ETIAM

divine Victim, with love, with heaven, she gives utterance to her dear wish for the dead. They all pass before her eyes.

Memento etiam, Domine, famulorum famularumque tuarum N. et N., qui nos præcesserunt cum signo fidei, et dormiunt in somno pacis.	Be mindful, O Lord, of Thy servants and handmaids N. and N., who are gone before us with the sign of faith, and rest in the sleep of peace.
Ipsis, Domine, et omnibus in Christo quiescentibus, locum refrigerii, lucis et pacis, ut indulgeas deprecamur; per eundem Christum Dominum nostrum. Amen.	To these, O Lord, and to all that sleep in Christ, grant, we beseech Thee, a place of refreshment, light, and peace; through the same Christ our Lord. Amen.

"Remember, O Lord, Thy servants and handmaids." . . . Those souls really exist in the mind of the Church, since they are of the family of the faithful. They have their part in the sacrifice. They unite with the Church on earth and the Church in heaven to make the offering in the Mass. Nevertheless they cannot help themselves into heaven; but we can help them. And so in this prayer we ask relief and deliverance for them, the faithful in purgatory, that they may enter into the Communion of Saints in heaven. "Give them," we pray, "a place of refreshment, light, and peace." In other words, "Take them into heaven!"

What a plea! What a holy remembrance! Nearly nineteen hundred years have found the Church doing just this. A wise, ancient mother, she never overlooks the least of her children; she never forgets the needy. *In memoria æterna erit justus* is her motto. An uncommonly thoughtful mother, she holds the just in eternal remembrance. Over and over again, all the faithful dead come before her, the little and great, rich and poor, ignorant and enlightened, all who have gone before us, countless generations of them back to the very beginning. Faith and love bridge the silence of centuries. Languages come and go, but this prayer, so strongly appealing to the heart of God, is still heard over all the Catholic world in the interests of the dear dead. Clustered about Christ we plead for them that they may share in the fruit of the sacrifice and receive its application. Jesus Christ is on our altar, and as we offer Him to His Father we beg for those graces and benedictions in behalf of the poor souls.

DIPTYCH OF THE FIFTH CENTURY
(Cathedral of Milan.)

The early Christians were wonderful in their remembrance of the dead. Very ancient traces appear of the observance of a day for the commemoration of "the souls of all those who have died in the communion of the body and blood of our Lord." St. Chrysostom speaks of those who made commemoration of a mother, a wife, or a child. They knew, by faith, that whether living or dead, all faithful were alike living members of Christ's Church. They had on their altars a *diptycha mortuorum,* or tablet containing the names of the faithful dead; and they often read aloud their names in prayer to keep alive the spirit of Christian brotherhood. Back in the dim days of the Catacombs you find inscriptions commemorating the dead, such as, *Heraclius quievit in sæculum; Lucem tuam divinam da Deus et requieiem; Beatissimo martyri Januario. Damsus episcopus fecit.*

In the Catacombs the inscriptions were engraved with a

chisel and then colored red; or they were scratched with a nail; or again they were smeared in charcoal, in hope that when persecution had passed away they might be recorded in a more permanent form. Thus you find letters are engraved, sometimes painted on the marble. Their execution varies from extreme neatness and even beauty, as in the lettering employed by Pope Damasus in the fourth century, to extreme ugliness, as in the case where good souls, slaves and rustics, knew little of the art of engraving and yet were full of faith.

This external side of their religion was but a sign of their interior, spiritual fellowship in the faith. It is a fact that the early Christians, whether learned or illiterate, had a deep love, an abiding memory of their faithful departed. Always in the Mass, those who were gone were congregationally prayed for and in the most touching way remembered.

A good Catholic will be sure to take part in the solemn appeal for the poor souls, since in a true sense we are their keepers. Be sure to keep them in mind. Here in the Mass, the Church wants to make us see her Memento, study it, learn it, make it our own. All must feel the duty of remembrance. Never let it be said that we are selfish or slothful in this matter. A Catholic who neglects praying for the poor souls in purgatory is sadly wanting in that vital faith which shows itself in works of charity. Many are ungrateful toward their dead; they pray for them seldom or never. Wider awake, with a clear idea of what is wanted, let us think about the dead and pray for them, thus accomplishing one of the ends for which Christ instituted the holy sacrifice — intercession.

That they cannot help themselves is certain, yet we can help them; so it is for us to show a spirit of unity and cooperation. Instead of stopping idly to wonder where they may be, let us seek to hasten their rest by rendering them the help of our prayers. This is to show practical interest in them. Ask Christ to apply to their souls His own precious blood. That is what the Church asks; thus should all her children do.

By giving us the sacrifice of the Mass our Lord has put into our hands the key to the treasury of His merits. Let us use the key for our own and for the benefit of the holy souls. Too bad if we were ever to pass this part of the Mass without remembering the dead, especially our own. Where but here should we be of one heart and voice with the Living Christ and His Church? "It is a holy and wholesome thought to pray for the dead." But nowhere is it more holy, more wholesome, more profitable so to pray. Where but here, with Jesus in our midst, should we ask our Heavenly Father for mercy? Where but here should we ask Him to wipe away all tears from their eyes and admit the poor souls into His kingdom? Like condemned exiles in prison cells who hear the appeals of friends for their freedom, the holy souls will be eternally grateful to us for our worthy prayer in the Memento etiam of the Mass.

ENTRANCE TO THE CATACOMB OF ST. DOMATILLA

The same faith makes them our brothers, so we ought to be attached to them by the substantial tie of prayer. The

MEMENTO ETIAM

Church places the welfare of the dead in the care of the living. In simple, graphic language she visualizes for us: "Those who have gone before us with the sign of faith." She wants us to love and help them. The value of the prayer is just that. The souls in purgatory become real and permanent acquaintances of ours. We recognize them in the company of the Communion of Saints. Remember to assist the souls in purgatory in every Mass that you hear. Assist them for God's sake, for their sake, and for your own sake. The measure of mercy you show will be the measure of mercy you shall receive. May this be said of each of us.

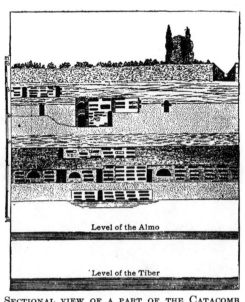

SECTIONAL VIEW OF A PART OF THE CATACOMB OF ST. CALLIXTUS

Many such catacombs have yet to be thoroughly explored.

> Thou art praised for thy science, thy art and thy grace,
> For the courage so high that belongs to thy race,
> But when all is admired, and all has been said,
> There is nothing surpasses thy love for the dead.

1. Sympathy with the poor souls enables one to do much for them. How? 2. "Say it with flowers" is a familiar billposter. How can you do that spiritually to show your love for the dead? 3. Next to the Mass

THE MASS

what devotion is most helpful to the holy souls? 4. What customs exist in the Church aiding the memory of the dead? 5. Have you ever read of saints who saw purgatory in vision? Who are they? 6. What immortal poet attempts to describe purgatory? Have you read him? 7. Mention several other means, besides Mass and prayer, of aiding the poor souls.

XXVIII

NOBIS QUOQUE PECCATORIBUS

The first three words of this plea are spoken in a moderate voice while the priest strikes his breast with his right hand. The other words are recited secretly with the hands extended as usual in the long Eucharistic prayer. At the end of this part the priest's hands are joined at his breast.

Nowhere else in the world should people be more calm and collected, knowing what they are about, than when at Mass. Neighbors, kneeling together, we are fully aware of our misdeeds, yet pleading with our Heavenly Father, and asking our dead for help as we bow our heads in sorrow before the divine Victim — such is the spirit of the prayer now to be said. Those words, Nobis quoque peccatoribus, signify sorrowful remembrance. At their mention you notice how the priest strikes his breast, bends his head, raises his voice. The raised voice is to recall the faithful to united prayer, the striking of the breast is a gesture of sorrow and unworthiness, while the bowing of the head, as Pope Benedict XIV says, is because "our Lord bowed His head when He died, and here we remember the dead."

It behooves us to look well into this prayer. Its words and acts most fittingly tell how we feel in this part of the Mass. Like soldiers in serried ranks, the faithful kneel in their pews. They have come here for forgiveness, for encouragement. They ask God to pardon them through the merits of the divine Victim on the everlasting altar.

With deep humility they admit their unworthiness; they call themselves sinners. In the same breath they count upon the aid of the saints. Well they may do so, for the saints will surely assist. As for those blessed helpers who are remembered, the very names of a few are uttered — exactly as if a few more of our friends were being singled out in the presence of Christ as we converse with Him in prayer. And all the while Christ is there interceding for us.

Tomb of a Crusader

Nobis quoque peccatoribus, famulis tuis, de multitudine miserationum tuarum sperantibus, partem aliquam et societatem donare digneris, cum tuis sanctis apostolis et martyribus; cum Joanne, Stephano, Mathia, Barnaba, Ignatio, Alexandro, Marcellino, Petro, Felicitate, Perpetua, Agatha, Lucia, Agnete, Cæcilia, Anastasia, et omnibus sanctis tuis; intra quorum nos consortium, non æstimator meriti, sed veniæ, quæsumus, largitor admitte. Per Christum Dominum nostrum.

Also, to us sinners, Thy servants, confiding in the multitude of Thy mercies, vouchsafe to grant some part and fellowship with Thy holy apostles and martyrs; with John, Stephen, Matthias, Barnabas, Ignatius, Alexander, Marcellinus, Peter, Felicitas, Perpetua, Agatha, Lucy, Agnes, Cecilia, Anastasia, and with all Thy saints, into whose company we beseech Thee to admit us, not in consideration of our merit, but of Thy own gratuitous pardon. Through Christ our Lord.

Now, let us consider this stirring prayer. The spirit which breathes in it is one of sincere petition. By making this poignant appeal we express the hope that we may be made worthy to join the ranks of the blessed company of

NOBIS QUOQUE PECCATORIBUS

the saints. What we beg for is part and fellowship with them. But, to dwell with them one day we need their help, their intercession, their inspiration. Otherwise how can we hope to succeed in our exacting duties; how win our way to enrollment in the heavenly legions? Only one way, and that is to show ourselves good soldiers, to prove the stuff that is in us. Soldiers are mustered in, trained, then sent out into the service. So it is with us. Our duty is to stand together for the cause of God, as good soldiers of Jesus Christ, as people who please Him when they have engaged themselves. Not to do this is to prove disloyal to our Lord, to be deserters to the cause of Christ, to forfeit the kingdom of heaven. Heaven forbid that we should ever end that way. Of old the Ephraimites deserted the cause of God when they were most needed.

> The sons of Ephraim who bend and shoot with the bow: they have turned back in the day of battle.
> They kept not the covenant of God: and in his law they would not walk.
> And they forgot his benefits, and his wonders that he had shewn them.
> They were turned aside as a crooked bow.
> And God chose not the tribe of Ephraim. But he chose the tribe of Juda, Mount Sion which he loved. (Psalms lxxvii, 9–11, 57, 67–68.)

Ephraim, turned aside from God, was like a deceptive bow that shoots its arrow in the wrong direction. It could not be depended on; it made no sure shot; its aim was crooked. Then the prophet, Osee, said: "Ephraim is joined to idols; let him alone" (Osee iv, 17). By some this has been considered the most terrible text in the Bible. But even more terrible was the judgment pronounced by Christ upon the Pharisees: "Let them alone, they are blind, and leaders of the blind. And if the blind lead the blind, both fall into the pit" (Matthew xv, 14).

That these two warnings were meant for us is beyond doubt. They do, after all, mean a lot for us. We may well dwell upon them. There are many cowardly Christians about, many blind leaders nowadays. Not to know this, or to forget it, is religious ignorance. Catholic students fool themselves badly by thinking they can follow false leaders and still be loyal to our Lord; or that they can serve Mammon and serve God at the same time. It is impossible to do so. No one being a soldier of God entangles himself with false idols or false leaders. If we deny God, He will also deny us. For very fear of this we run to God, beg of Him light, help, encouragement, and the strength to be good soldiers.

What we are really asking for in the Nobis quoque peccatoribus is to be good Christian soldiers. We all despise a coward, a traitor, a slacker, or a deserter. And we want to be good soldiers. During the last war the present writer received a letter from one of his doughboy friends, a Catholic school product. Part of it read: "I had the honor of serving at Mass a week ago in a very pretty little church near where we are located, and to-day I received Holy Communion. Pray for me that I may be a good soldier and not show yellow."

We want to be the same sort of soldier for Christ that that lad was for his country. And a soldier he certainly proved himself. Of his heroism, the captain of the 312th Infantry, 78th Division, wrote to his pastor:

This is the first opportunity that I have had to write you a story of the heroic self-sacrifice of an Albany boy, whose early life and character were molded in the Cathedral; a boy who laid down his life on the battlefield under circumstances that for true heroism has few parallels in the history of the war. I refer to the death of Parker G. Dunn.

When Parker entered the army at Camp Dix last April he was assigned

NOBIS QUOQUE PECCATORIBUS

to our regiment. His interest in his work and his natural abilities and keenness soon won him a place in the intelligence section. He sailed with the regiment in May and went through all the hardships of the campaign and had the reputation of being a good soldier. His immediate commanding officer had commended him to me several times for his general efficiency.

During the St. Mihiel drive he was in the thickest of the fighting and no matter where he was placed he did his duty fearlessly and he did it well. When our division went to Argonne, I met him on the road one evening and he expressed himself as being anxious to again get into the fray. It was in the Argonne, too, that he proved his valor and made the supreme sacrifice.

On the morning of October 23, our regiment was occupying the hills just north of Grandpré. The first battalion was ordered to attack. During the advance, the battalion commander from his P.G. saw that it was necessary to give one company in the attacking line information of the progress of another company. On account of the severe machine-gun and artillery fire sweeping the area over which the messenger would have to travel, the major hesitated to order any runner to make the trip. It did not seem possible that any one would cross that field alive. Private, first-class, Parker G. Dunn, overhearing the major's remarks, volunteered to act as a runner although he was a member of the intelligence section and there were runners available. The duty that he volunteered to undertake gave every appearance of having a fatal termination.

"Sir, I would deem it a great honor to be permitted to carry the message."

Thus spake Parker Dunn to the major. He was given the message and started out while the major and other officers watched his progress. After advancing a short distance he was wounded. With his high sense of duty still paramount, he pressed on and fell wounded the second time. Still undaunted, he rose and staggered on. After proceeding a few yards further he was killed. Had he stopped when he fell the first time, he might have lived; had he stopped when he fell the second time, he might have lived; but no, his sense of duty was so high that it was "do or die," and he died gloriously. After the advance his body was recovered and Parker Dunn was buried on the hill near Grandpré where he fell.

Such was the glorious career of a Catholic boy who had learned well the lesson that is taught in every Catholic classroom — "For God and country!" This is the spirit. Have you noticed how often the soldier idea, taught in every Catholic school, is mentioned in the sacred Scriptures? In the Book of Wisdom, Almighty God is represented as a great warrior: "The Almighty Word lept down from heaven; from thy royal throne, as a fierce conqueror, into the midst of the land of destruction, with a sharp sword, carrying thy unfeigned commandment." Fiery words, aren't they? But God has enemies who have to be overcome, age after age, evil foes that war upon the good.

Regular Catholics, therefore, are just like an army. They are enrolled in the Church militant. All their lifetime they struggle against evil. Not necessarily in the open, but always in the secret trenches of the soul. For every soul is a battlefield, temptation being the tactics, the maneuvers of the enemy: "For our wrestling is not against flesh and blood; but against the rulers of the world of this darkness" (Ephesians vi, 12). It is the business of every Catholic to know just what weapons the enemy employs. Victory can be won only at the cost of courage and vigilance. What sort of soldier are you? Have you heard and obeyed the call to arms? The command rings clear. In Con*firm*ation, note that word "firm"; much strength was given to you so that you would prove courageous in your duty. Holy Communion increases your desire to serve and makes you grow strong in spite of trials. By going often you are enabled to be a more faithful soldier, readier to carry out orders accurately and obey commands. But have you done all that? To say the whole truth, none of us has done as well as he ought. Think of how you have acted in times of temptation. Sometimes you have stumbled, sometimes fallen. An evil thought enters your soul's house, and you let it stay there until it makes itself at home. Then, how difficult

NOBIS QUOQUE PECCATORIBUS 227

to throw it out. Had you given it no quarter, the peril would have died then and there. But you were weak, and you lost. That was because you forgot that your soul was the battleground of temptation, and you took your foe for a friend.

In view of this, we must open our eyes, look over the field of life, and arrange our forces as we prepare for the struggle against sin. Any soldier in a battle must keep his head, must steady his hand as he points his weapon. Can you not see the need for more help in all this? It takes a strong soldier to put up a good stiff fight in life's battle. Is not temptation the proof of our spiritual mettle? Yet how often we fall before it. Why? Because we do not feel and act, pray and fight as if we were bound to win. Have you not seen some go from bad to worse? Have you not heard of such and such a one who has failed in his Catholic duty? Catholics throwing themselves into the struggle with life sometimes lose their faith. They fall down, fail in their duty, quit going to church; and unless God comes to their aid they are lost and their souls, once good and beautiful, become more and more battered and tarnished by evil.

Plainly, without God we can do nothing. Hence the need of the Mass where the Master will put courage into our soul; where the Captain gives light, grace, strength. Our Lord, of course, instituted the Mass for just that — the defense of our souls lest they succumb to the foe.

These truths will be all the more evident from our further studies of the aim and purpose of the holy sacrifice. At all stages of life's struggle our Lord on His altar gives strength and courage and saving grace. This is a life lesson we all need to learn. How important, then, to hear Mass often and well. Unless you do, you will grow weak, lukewarm, become a cowardly deserter, a Catholic failure. No use to hope that you will be able to wrestle with sin, and win out when the temptation seizes you. For if God is not on your side, down you are sure to go, down to disgraceful defeat. The danger is that Satan in the fury of his rage will have you in his power before you are half aware of it. Against this danger the Nobis quoque peccatoribus warns us, as it sends us in quest of help from our Lord and His trusty soldiers, the saints. As long as we keep near them we are safe. There are no better friends to be found.

Finally, get in touch, the close touch of prayer, with those special saints mentioned in the Nobis quoque. They are spiritual soldiers of the highest type. Their names will live through the wear and tear of time; for they are canonized in the Mass. To them we pray, that they may help us to be good soldiers, to endure, to carry on in the name of our Lord. They dared to serve, and on them the Captain relied. Many were the battles in which they had to fight and overcome the dark foe. But they were faithful to the Captain's clear command; so great was their love and interest in the task before them, that they defended their battery to the last ditch. All of them have the distinction of having fallen in action and won their eternal reward. That is why we pray to them and ask their intercession. They can strengthen our sense of service, they will help make us sterling soldiers. Looking down upon this earth, the old battlefield where their crown was earned, they will hear our prayer and we shall all be better for knowing them.

Historically, St. John the Baptist leads in this list. Born a short time before our Lord, his whole life from babyhood was consecrated to the service of the Messias. So he stands at the head of the little company that first fought and died for Christ. They were the spearhead of that great army which was to deploy down the ages, fight the good fight, and keep faith with the Commander. Endlessly that army was to move forward in the world in a great campaign for Christ. But John was, so to say, head of the intelligence department of the first corps. You can find the news notes of his battle-record in Matthew iii, iv, xiv. In A.D. 29 he was beheaded by Herod, dying shortly before his divine Master.

St. John the Baptist

St. Stephen was the first martyr after the death of Christ. Another gallant soldier; such courage as he exhibited could only come from on high. As John defied Herod, so Stephen was fearless in the face of the Jewish mob. He fought evil to a finish and fell in action, A.D. 36. The mob stoned him to death, yet he prayed for them with his last breath. The details may be found in Acts vi, vii.

St. Matthias, an Apostle, served long at the side of Our Lord. What an honor! His, too, was the honor of being a member of that band of seventy sent out to skirmish for souls. "Go," said Our Lord to them, "Behold, I send you as lambs among wolves." Matt. x, 16. After the Ascension, according to Acts i, 15–26, Matthias was promoted to the high rank of an Apostle. As to his subsequent missionary activities the reports are vague and often conflicting; but a very old tradition tells of this very courageous soldier of

Christ entering into the interior of Ethiopia to preach the gospel of the True Light to the barbarians and cannibals buried there in the heart of darkness.

St. Barnabas was another apostolic-hearted leader. A levite of Cyprus, he sold all his lands, brought the money, and laid it at the Apostles' feet. Then he attached himself to St. Paul and not only mustered into the service of his Master many a good soldier, but himself shed his life-blood for the great cause. On his active life, Acts iv, 36; xi, 22; xii, xiii, xiv shed light.

St. Ignatius of Antioch was a great bishop and energetic soldier of the Faith, who carried out every order of Christ, obeyed every command, and grew strong in his sufferings. He was ready, nay, anxious to be ground to death for his Master's glory. On his way to the end, having been haled to Rome for trial, he wrote: "From Syria even to Rome I fight with wild beasts, by land and sea, by night and by day, being bound amidst ten leopards, even a company of soldiers, who only wax worse when they are kindly treated." Not long after he reached Rome he won his crown of martyrdom in the Flavian amphitheater.

St. Alexander (Pope 106–115), a Roman by birth, ruled the Church during dark hours. Born into an age where Christians, and their leaders especially, had to suffer for their faith, this vicar of Christ, the fifth in succession from the Apostles, proceeded in the performance of his duty, commanded the growing Christian army in the face of pagan foes. All the early Popes had to struggle against fearful odds, but duty was duty; so Alexander exposed his life and feared no danger. He stuck to his guns, refused to retreat, and died for his Lord. He was decapitated in Rome on May 3, 115.

St. Marcellinus was a priest who fought the good fight.

Imprisoned for his zeal in the Faith, every effort was made to have him renounce his divine Master and go over to paganism. But it was no use. The prison where he was cast had no light, no food, and the floors were strewn with bits of broken glass to add to his sufferings. That sort of trial did not shake his spirit. He fought Satan to a standstill, and was put to death at Silva Candida, in the time of that agent of the devil, Diocletian.

St. Peter, an exorcist who would not stand for error or evildoing. A judge, Serenus, put him into prison for preaching the Christian faith. While there Peter cured the jailer's daughter who was possessed by the devil. On hearing that the jailer's whole family had gone to Marcellinus to be instructed in the true religion, the judge seized both Peter and Marcellinus, imprisoned them together, and left them in chains and tortures, till finally their heads were cut off.

St. Felicitas, a valiant woman of Carthage in north Africa. She was a slave in the household of St. Perpetua, and, together with her mistress and three other Christians, met her death in the amphitheater of Carthage on March 7, 203. Notice now how well all of them bore the shock of awful death with undaunted courage. "At the demand of the pagan mob the fearless five were first scourged; then a boar, a bear, and a leopard were set at the men, and a wild cow at the women. Wounded by the wild animals, they gave each other the kiss of peace and were then put to the sword."

St. Perpetua was the other valiant woman of that fearless five. She was a young married lady of noble birth. Her father was a pagan, her mother a Christian; two of her brothers were Christians, the third dying a pagan. When thrown into prison because of her faith, her pagan father sought to sap her Christian courage, and promised to save her life if only she would give up her faith. While still in prison her baby was born. Then she had a vision, "in which she saw herself ascending a ladder leading to green meadows, where a flock of sheep were browsing." This was a premonition of her martyrdom, which shortly followed.

St. Agatha, the beautiful, high-souled Sicilian girl, smiled in the bitter face of death. The love of God is the soul's greatest beauty. And she had just that. During the Decian persecution (250–253) she was seized and thrown into prison. A Roman senator, Quintianus, sought her hand, when he sat in judgment against her. But she had no use for his promises or threats, nor did she give up the love of God for all the earth had to offer her. Indeed, she preferred death to dishonor. She met torture without flinching. Mindful of her Master, and moved by the memory of Christ crucified, she stood strong under the many cruelties practiced on her, and died a glorious martyr in Catania, Sicily. To-day the people of Sicily venerate her and seek her aid against the eruption of Mt. Ætna.

St. Lucy of Syracuse in Sicily was born about the year 283 and grew up to venerate St. Agatha, who had been executed fifty-two years before. A valiant young woman, never afraid to sacrifice the things of time for eternity, generously she gave of her riches to God's poor. Like Agatha, she was in love with Jesus, the All-True, the All-Good, the All-Beautiful. God gave her great beauty of face and form; but more beautiful still was her soul, which looked upon Jesus with the same loving eyes as the Apostle St. John. When only twenty years of age she suffered all sorts of trials, but showed a fine contempt for death, with a love for our Lord that was honey-sweet, all-consuming. Neither fagot, nor flame, nor the batteries of questioning judges moved her.

She was beheaded in the year 303 and thus won her crown of virginity and martyrdom.

St. Agnes was a singularly beautiful character. This twelve-year-old Roman maiden, virgin and martyr, lived in the third century. Few have been more honored; for she was another leader of the white-clad company of early Christian martyrs who bore the tests of repeated trials for their religion. For her the truths of faith and purity stood high and clear and she boldly declared herself a follower of Christ. This mere girl was subjected to the most horrible cruelties, yet she stood her ground, undaunted. When, at length, her fierce heathen foes were burning her to death, she veiled her chaste body by means of her long flowing hair. Thus she won her martyr's crown. On account of her virginal innocence you see in her pictures a lamb.

St. Cecilia was the rich, beautiful, brilliant daughter of a Roman senatorial family. Imbued from childhood with the living spiritual power of God's grace, she was early stirred to the highest thoughts and noblest aims, and she wished to yield all for the sake of Christ. Her life, as written in the "Acts of the Martyrs," is a stirring record of high endeavor and the courageous following out of God's purposes. A Christian from her infancy, she insisted on preserving her innocence and would yield to no cause save Christ's. The black storm cloud of persecution did not dismay her. All the pressure brought to bear upon her was in vain. She did not view with alarm the death that faced her. To-day there are thousands of musical societies named after her, and she is honored everywhere as the patroness of church music.

St. Anastasia was another valiant woman who enjoyed great prominence in the early Church. The daughter of a Roman *vir illustris*, she showed her readiness to meet danger in carrying out her Christian duty. With a firm foundation of eternal life she could fight for the freedom of the children of God, and die for her Master. On Christmas Day she was visiting the faithful on the island of Palmaria when she was captured and beheaded. A special Mass used to be said in her honor on our Lord's birthday.

So much, then, for this gallant company of martyrs — fifteen in all. It is to be noticed that all of them are somehow linked up with the Church in Rome; also, that here in

ANGEL WITH CROWN

the Mass we have a fixed scheme just as in the Communicantes. We should understand once for all that it is most profitable to know all these saints and pray to them. Purer pulses never beat than theirs. And we, who pray to them, how much do we know about their divine adventure, their soul-stirring heroism, their transcendent disdain for the baits and rewards the pagans held out to them? Do we give them room in our mind? Certainly we might read and reread their lives till we nearly know them by heart. You will find much about these saints in the "Catholic Encyclopedia." It gives one accurate accounts of those soldiers and the scenes of their campaigns; scenes which stand out softly and delicately, flamingly and terribly, and are the inspiration of the ages. Well for us if we revive among ourselves a practical love and devotion to them. Dip into their lives, their world life; there is so much of value in them for all of us. One must be very sorry for those Catholics who are ignorant of the lives of such saints. No group of people could possibly be more interesting — or more inspiring.

1. Explain with reference to this part of the Mass: the more fervent the prayer, the richer the fruit. 2. In studying their lives, what did you notice about the saints in the above list as regards their ages, sex, order, state of life, customs, traditions? What special sacrifice did each make? 3. What do you know about the career of the Church in north Africa before the Saracens came? Against what odds did that Church have to struggle? Name five great saints famous in that Church. 4. One is struck by the parallel between the saint and the soldier. Why is the Christian life compared with a warfare? What are the like ideas? 5. Give the difference between a heretic and an apostate, an infidel and an agnostic, a pagan and a Catechumen. 6. Mention six ways in which the modern boy and girl can exhibit courage.

DIADEM

The martyrs were "clad with justice and judgment, as with a robe and a diadem" (Job xxix, 14).

XXIX

PER QUEM PER IPSUM

In the Per quem hæc omnia the priest makes three crosses with his right hand over the Host and chalice, saying at the first cross, "Sanctificas"; at the second, "Vivificas"; at the third, "Benedicis."

For the second elevation, he uncovers the chalice, genuflects, and rises. With the Host he makes the sign of the cross three times over the chalice, from rim to rim, saying at the first cross, "Per ipsum"; at the second, "et cum ipso"; at the third, "et in ipso." Then he forms two other signs of the cross, over the corporal. Now comes the second elevation, and the concluding words of the canon, "Omnis honor et gloria."

Near the end of the Canon we come, almost abruptly, upon a most interesting invocation. The worshiper's is a noble privilege; it is also a responsible one. Our duty, then, is to look into this. The prayer Per quem hæc omnia, offers something of a puzzle. On close inspection its words bewilder us. "These gifts," it says, when the word "gifts" does not signify the divine Victim. What gifts, then? At one time there occurred at this point in the Mass a blessing of the fruits of the earth. There is no doubt that some of the old Sacramentaries prescribed a benediction of fruits of the earth in the Mass. We know, of course, that there were many special benedictions of things given outside the Mass. Such were the blessings of wine, bread, salt, ashes, palms, incense, candles, Easter eggs, etc. Thus we read of St. John's wine, St. Mark's bread, so called because of the saint on whose festival these things were blessed. Or, of oil that was blessed for baptism, for confirmation, for the sick. Then, too, ashes were blessed for use on Ash Wednesday, palms for Palm Sunday, candles for Easter Sunday. These blessings took place apart from the Holy Sacrifice.

In the Mass itself the gifts blessed were many and various; in fact Pope Eutychian (275–283) ordered "that only fruits of beans and grapes be blessed on the altar." Grapes were blessed on the feast of St. Sixtus (August 6), beans on Ascension Day. Of the latter blessing we still have this prayer. We take this in the form used far back in the sixth century.

EUCHARISTIC BANQUET

Benedic Domine et has fruges novas fabæ . . . in nomine Domini Nostri Jesu Christi, per quem hæc omnia Domine semper bona creas, etc.	Bless us, O Lord, and these new fruits of the beanstalk . . . in the Name of our Lord Jesus Christ through Whom Thou dost always create, etc.

This prayer makes it clear that the gifts were upon the altar and that God was asked to confer His own blessing on them. Nor was this custom new. History has on its dim pages many a line that tells of such gifts offered to God. As to the setting apart of the first fruits to be blessed, that goes very far back. It must not be forgotten that "Cain offered, of the fruits of the earth, gifts to the Lord" (Genesis iv, 3). But Cain's heart was bad, and his offering was not acceptable, as was Abel's. "But to Cain and his offerings he had no respect: and Cain was exceedingly angry, and his countenance fell" (Genesis v, 5). How could the Almighty bless him when he was evil-minded and jealous of his brother? Any offering worth while must be accompanied by good will, by gratitude implying love of neighbor; for the blessing of an offering is an acknowledgment of God's goodness together with the desire for His glory and praise.

Again as we come down the long dark valley of ancient history we see, even among savage nations, the custom of offering the first fruits. Not until this was done did they believe the rest of the crop to be lawful food. The ancient Hebrews had a cereal offering. This consisted of wheat or barley or flour. A mixture was prepared, oil and frankincense were added, and a portion of the whole was burned upon the altar, while the priest used what was left. It is interesting, furthermore, to read in 4 Kings iv, 42: "And a certain man came from Baalsalisa bringing to the man of God (the prophet Eliseus) bread of the first fruits, twenty loaves of barley, and new corn in his scrip." That was in the ninth century before Christ.

When our Lord came, full of grace and truth and light, and when He instituted the holy sacrifice of the Mass, commanding that it be continued in commemoration of Him, it is not surprising that the early Christians should have taken it upon themselves to make offerings of their own in the Mass and asked God's blessing upon them, even as the ancients did. So, since the end of the fifth century, they had such a blessing here in the heart of the holy sacrifice.

But now comes a question. Was this custom of blessing the fruits placed on the altar universal in the Church or only local? We are not so sure of that. At any rate, it was done in many churches and there were more ways than one of blessing. Cardinal Bona, a great liturgist, was of the opinion that whatever was to be blessed, oil or honey, beans or grapes, was brought up to the altar by the deacon, whereupon the prayer was said which referred to God's creating and vivifying power. That our prayer, Per quem hæc omnia, is a relic of a past custom there can be little doubt. It is quite clear, if you compare it with the old prayer given above. Their similarity of word and spirit is proof, and one may ask whether our prayer is but a fragment of the old prayer.

Per quem hæc omnia, Domine semper bona creas, sancti ✠ ficas, vivifi ✠ cas, bene ✠ dicis et præstas nobis.	By Whom, O Lord, Thou dost always create, sanctify, ✠ quicken, ✠ bless, ✠ and give us all these good things.

" 'Per quem hæc omnia bona creas (Thou createst).' God the Father created all things through the Son, Jesus Christ. "All things were made by Him" (John i, 3) — and thus also bread and wine, which are converted into the body and blood of Christ. We need not confine the sense of the words to the first creation of all things, but this same power of God is continually renovating the fruits of the earth and of the vine. *Sanctificas* (Thou dost sanctify). In Jesus Christ the gifts brought to the altar become sacred and set apart from common use. *Vivificas* (quicken, or vivify). God through Jesus Christ vivifies the bread and wine, converting them into His body and blood, which are the real food or nourishment of our spiritual life. *Benedicis et præstas nobis* (bless and give us). God through Jesus Christ vivifies and sanctifies, and diffuses His heavenly blessings upon the bread and wine, and thus blessed by transubstantiation they are given to us that they may impart true life to our souls and preserve it in them — *per ipsum* (through Him). Christ is the true mediator between God and man — *et cum ipso* (and with Him). He is equal to God the Father — *et in ipso* (and in Him). He is consubstantial with the Father

— *est tibi, Deo Patri*, etc. (there is to Thee, God the Father Almighty, in the unity of the Holy Ghost, all honor and glory). All honor and glory is given to God the Father *through* the Son, *with* the Son, and *in* the Son, and in the unity of the Holy Ghost, who, proceeding from the other two Persons, is equally adored, praised, and honored with them for ever and ever."[1]

All serious students ought to look well into this for, as we said, each part of the Mass is meant to be of help — and it will do us all good to study and talk it over. It is difficult for most of us to understand people bringing their gifts in church to be put on the altar. But it must not be forgotten that in the long ago the churches were not so big, or the crowds so great, or life so complex as ours. The early Christians were so thoroughly grateful to God; it was believed that everything they had was not half enough to give back to the Giver of all. In Acts ii, 44–45, you can read about their utter unselfishness. Here is a lesson in gratitude to which we may well give much attention, a lesson we must learn if we would be of one mind with the Church. Even though the gifts once present on the altar are no longer there, the words and signs still remain. Why does the Church still retain them? Because He who blesses all is there. The Great Giver, God Himself, is present. With the Giver we include all His gifts, and so we raise our hearts in gratitude for all we have received through Christ.

Speaking largely, then, the Per quem hæc omnia is a thanks to the Giver for His gifts. Everything we have we owe to God through Christ our Lord. That is only truth. And it would be very sad if we were to forget to return thanks when the Giver is on our altar. Can you not see how wise the Church is in retaining this prayer, how well

[1] Arthur Devine, Passionist, "The Ordinary of the Mass."

PER QUEM   PER IPSUM

these words voice our acknowledgment to the Blessed Sacrament? "Through Christ, our Lord" — thus it can be stated in four words. Through Him "every best gift and every perfect gift comes down to us from heaven." He is the source of divine goodness, of every blessing. Included in these blessings are the fruits of the earth, all human excellencies and all supernatural graces. We must thank Him more and more. No one can do that fully, but each should do his part. Do not fail to give thanks to God for such gifts, but most of all and greatest of all, for the gift of Himself in the Holy Sacrament. To give such thanks is to revive our faith, and to do much for our Lord's honor and the profit of our own soul. One wishes that it were possible for every boy and girl on their way to young manhood and young womanhood to embody their thanks in this prayer. This is the very thing our Master wants most. We therefore do well to raise our hearts in gratitude for all we have received through Christ who is now on our altar, in our very midst. "For of him, and by him, and in him, are all things: to him be glory forever. Amen" (Romans xi, 36).

Just as the Canon draws to a close, a singularly beautiful rite takes place. The soul of the Mass, one can say, is summed up in its two sentences. A doxology is said and the Host is once more elevated. That you may the better understand what is said and done note well the solemn words and acts. They go hand in hand — act and word. First of all, the priest genuflects; then taking the Host in his right hand for the Elevation and holding the chalice in his left, he makes thrice the sign of the cross over the chalice, saying:

Per ip ✠ sum, et cum ip ✠ so, et in ip ✠ so est tibi Deo Patri ✠ omnipotenti, in unitate Spiritus

Through ✠ Him, and with ✠ Him, and in ✠ Him is unto Thee, God the Father ✠ Almighty, in

✠ Sancti, omnis honor et gloria. Per omnia sæcula sæculorum. Amen. | the unity of the Holy ✠ Ghost, all honor and glory. Forever and ever. Amen.

This is a scene of daily occurrence on our altars. Its twenty-six words afford a remarkably complete résumé of the Mass. We are rightly curious to know the meaning of these words, acts, crosses, so swift, so full of meaning, declaring the whole truth of the sacrifice. All of us want to be informed about matters so sacredly important. Being a devout Catholic means keeping faith with the Holy Sacrifice, implies knowing the acts of the Mass and attending to them with reverence. The whole Mass is a key to endless treasures. Master each part: it is new every day, and for you every day. Could anything be more solemnly beautiful than this part? No imagination could invent a more solemn ending to the long prayer of the Canon; such a close may well engage our closest study.

1. With the Host the priest makes three crosses over the chalice, signifying that all blessings flow from the divine Victim on the altar. "Through Him, and with Him, and in Him" are words that stir our faith and enliven worship, seeing that the Host and chalice contain the same Jesus Christ who was slain on the cross, and who offered three prayers when dying.

2. With the Host the priest makes the next crosses outside the chalice, saying: "To Thee, O God, the Father Almighty, in the unity of the Holy Ghost." By these words and acts you can see how the sacrifice of the cross of Jesus Christ is the highest gift that can be offered to the honor and glory of the Divinity. The sacrifice of our Lord's body and blood is offered (crosses outside the chalice) to the Father and the Holy Ghost. Thus the Holy Trinity, Father, Son, and Holy Ghost are honored in this glorious doxology.

3. The priest lifts the holy offering, Host and chalice. By this second elevation, this lifting up of the great Victim as once He was lifted on the cross, is expressed the honor and glory we should pay to God. "All honor and glory," says the priest at this uplifting — the gift of the cross

PER QUEM   PER IPSUM

to the Father and the Holy Ghost. Once this elevation was so high that all could behold chalice and Host.

4. Having knelt in adoration, the priest rises, places the pall on the chalice, and says: "For ever and ever." This is said in a loud voice, and is called ekphonesis; that is, the part that is said audibly as in contrast to what is said secretly.

5. "Amen" the altar boy answers in the name of all; and here the Canon ends.

Thus ends the Canon of the Mass with the glorious doxology and the elevation — all to prepare the faithful for Communion. Never forget that the Consecration and the Communion are the very essence of the holy sacrifice. After the words of Consecration there was an elevation, but this second one was far older than that. Indeed this one we have just been studying is ancient, since the ninth century or even earlier. In commenting on the second elevation, Father Griffith says in his book, "The Mass":

Up to the twelfth century, there was no other elevation in the Mass of the body and blood of Jesus Christ except this. The priest raised the Host and the chalice sufficiently high that the people might see and adore Jesus Christ by Whom all honor and glory is paid to the Trinity. This ceremony took place a short time before the Communion and was very solemn. The gates of the sanctuary were opened, the heavy curtains which concealed the sanctuary during all the Canon were drawn aside, and the priest presented the sacred mysteries to the adoration of the faithful; but since the custom of elevating the Host and the chalice after the consecration has been introduced, this second elevation is no longer so solemn; the priest raises the chalice and Host slightly above the altar to preserve a vestige of the ancient custom.

We should remember, then, that at one time this second elevation was the very central part of the Mass. Since the center of gravity has been shifted, so to say, to the Consecration, the greater elevation immediately after the words of the institution occupies our closest attention. As we come to the end of the great consecratory prayer of the Canon, it is evident that the Church wants the faithful to look upon our Lord in the Blessed Sacrament with the same tender regard as the Apostles displayed during the great discourse at the Last Supper, or as did the sinners who waited long for His coming. This is the reason why the Church still retains the second elevation. It summons before us once more the self-giving of our Saviour. It is an invitation to adore anew Jesus in the Blessed Sacrament. Time now to express deep desire that our Lord be very near and dear to you, and you to Him. To say the doxology with earnest intent at this elevation is to open your heart wider for the worship of God. Happy is he who, like the eager Peter, having waited for the coming of the Messias, welcomes him with: "Thou art the Christ, the Son of the Living God!"

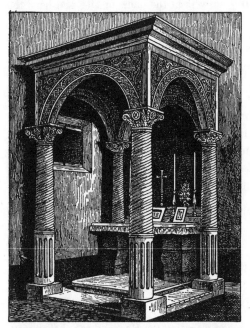

CIBORIUM OF ST. APOLLINARE, AT RAVENNA

What soul-stirring acknowledgment! What warmth of welcome! The arms, as it were, of belief and loyalty are extended in cordial salutation to the divine Master. The need for us is to do the same with unbounded spiritual hospitality. And our holy Mother wants the divine presence to be felt in the heart of every worshiper. We have here the chance of reviving all the warmth of spiritual welcome displayed at Consecration time when our Lord came to win all hearts. Imbued with that selfsame living faith, let us keep faith with Christ, and offer Him our act of reverence and worship. So doing, the better will be our preparedness for the reception of our Lord at Communion time.

As in the Mass there is praise and thanksgiving, so in our hearts there should be the same; so, also, when we leave the church our joy should be translated into everyday life, in our dealings with our fellow creatures.

1. Put into a few lines your idea of what you should do at the second elevation. 2. What present-day Catholic custom resembles somewhat the ancient blessing of fruits? 3. In this part of the Mass the priest makes five crosses. Can you explain? 4. Ancient customs of sacrifice cast penetrating beams of light on the prayers and acts of the Mass. Can you explain? 5. Lest you forget, it may be well to review what you studied some time ago about the Sacrifice of the Mass and the Sacrifice of the Cross. Are they the same? Wherein do they differ?

XXX

PATER NOSTER

After the second elevation, the priest having genuflected, says "Per omnia sæcula," etc. As he says "Oremus" he joins his hands and inclines his head toward the Blessed Sacrament. And when he comes to the Pater Noster, he disjoins his hands, holds them extended before his breast, and with his eyes fixed on the Host recites aloud the greatest of all prayers.

A Catholic teacher, Brother Leo, has well said: "The dramatic instinct — the instinct that urges us to play, to impersonate, to act out, to make believe — is a legitimate human instinct. . . . Mother Church encourages and utilizes and perpetuates that instinct in her soulful and impressive liturgy."[1] Nowhere is this more evident than in the use, place, and setting of the "Lord's Prayer." The Church recognizes, and wants us to recognize, the vital and salutary value of this the greatest prayer in the world. Being the most sacred of all prayers, it has a place in every Mass the world over. This was so from the very early days. Thus will it go on till the end of time.

Let us make sure that we in our day appreciate this beautiful prayer, first in its setting, next in its profound significance. Sometimes boys and girls recite it in a monotonous, singsong fashion because they fail to realize how wonderful it is. They forget that to pray is to think, to attend, to hold the mind lovingly to its object, and not let words simply go on and on without thought. If they could be brought to realize that when saying the Lord's own prayer in the Mass they are "actors in the most wonderful and im-

---

[1] Brother Leo, "Religion and the Study of Literature."

pressive drama in the world," their devotion would be increased; nay, they would want to put their whole mind, heart, and soul into it. Certainly there is need for us to do just that. If all of us who are intelligent Catholics will only remember that we have a contract to pray for the living and the dead, we shall make the Mass a test of how that faith is kept. Then, too, the "Lord's Prayer" will assert itself in this part of the Mass with growing intensity.

It is well to recall here the divine origin and the circumstance of the first "Lord's Prayer." The scene was a low, square-shaped hill near the Lake of Galilee. Thither had come a band of disciples, intrepid and fervent, thirsting for truth and God. They had left behind them the city with its attractions in order to climb the mountain and seek Christ. For Him they had left their friends. Nothing but the longing to do God's will was now theirs. Their sincerity and sacrifice were soon rewarded. Lo! our Lord was in their midst. He had come down from the Horns of Hattin, where He spent the night in prayer, to hear them and teach them. On their asking Him how to pray, He gave them the "Our Father."

Centuries afterward, we, too, come seeking Christ, thirsting for His truth; and we, too, are in His immediate presence. The King on our altar is also our Teacher. With deep faith in the mystical union of Christians in Christ we are called upon to say the very prayer our Lord taught His disciples. But as a sort of introduction to the prayer we beg God to allow us to say it. That shows that we are aware alike of its wondrous dignity and of our privilege.

Oremus. Præceptis salutaribus moniti, et divina institutione formati, audemus dicere:

Let us pray. Instructed by Thy saving precepts, and following Thy divine directions, we presume to say:

Pater noster, qui es in cœlis, sanctificetur nomen tuum: adveniat regnum tuum: fiat voluntas tua sicut in cœlo, et in terra: panem nostrum quotidianum da nobis hodie; et dimitte nobis debita nostra, sicut et nos dimittimus debitoribus nostris: Et ne nos inducas in tentationem. Sed libera nos a malo. Amen.	Our Father, who art in heaven, — hallowed be Thy name: Thy kingdom come; Thy will be done on earth as it is in heaven. Give us this day our daily bread: And forgive us our trespasses, as we forgive those who trespass against us. And lead us not into temptation. But deliver us from evil. Amen.

During this prayer the priest joins his hands and inclines his head toward the Blessed Sacrament. He has his eyes fixed on the Host when saying this, the greatest of all prayers; as if he must not lose sight of our Lord. He is preoccupied with the Host; his mind is centered in Christ, their wills are one, and discord is absent from his heart. This is as it should be, for the prayer itself, said in the presence of the Great High Priest, is intended to express "a unity in love of God and loyalty to God and the purpose to do the will and seek the kingdom of God." That must be our aim, since this prayer implies our fellowship with Christ and with one another. Our Lord and His Church, remember, are at one in this — the greatest petition in the world. Faith, hope, love unite in the "Our Father" which "combines every divine promise, every human sorrow and want, and every Christian aspiration for the good of others."

There was a time when this prayer was said at the end of the Mass. But Pope Gregory I (590–604) moved the "Our Father" to its present place, before the Communion. "It seems very unsuitable," he said, "that we should not say the prayer handed down by our Redeemer Himself over His body and blood." It is necessary for us to recognize the tremendous importance of saying the "Lord's Prayer." We ought, also, to take time and thought to study that prayer. Do so, and you will see its unity, symmetry, completeness. You can see, too, the doctrine of the Holy Trinity shining out in all the glory of Christ's revelation of His Father, Himself, and His holy spirit.

Observe in this perfect prayer the divine proportion and exquisite development.

1. The first half has reference to God, the second half to us. (Just as in the Decalogue and the two great Commandments.) 2. The triplets correspond in both — the first petition is addressed to God the Father, the second to God the Son, the third to God the Holy Ghost. 3. If you follow the six petitions you will notice how they begin with the glories of heaven, go on to life on earth, and end with the powers of hell. What a panoramic sweep is this! No prayer in all the world is like it. 4. Observe how petitions I and II are worship, III is praise, IV is impetration; V-VI are propitiation. How beautifully are the ends of the sacrifice here expressed!

It is much easier to grasp the beauty of the "Lord's Prayer" if you have gained a good idea of its background as shown in St. Matthew vi, 9 sq. In the Mass we are gathered about Christ just as the disciples were grouped about their Master when He told them how they should pray. At that time our Lord came and taught them to pray. Now our Lord is here to help us as we pray. In the Judgment, our Lord shall render us according to the way we have lived up to this prayer. Hence the value — nay, the necessity — of justly weighing its precious words. It is everything to have acquired and to possess a deep understanding of this model prayer, the badge of true discipleship. Let us analyze it part by part.

"Our Father." Not "My Father"; for now we are brethren of Christ, our divine Brother is present on the altar.

> Thou hast on earth a Trinity —
> Thyself, my fellow man, and me;
> When one with him, then one with Thee;
> Nor, save together, Thine are we. [1]

Ours is a society whose members are mutually responsible for one another's welfare. Every time we say this prayer it should remind us that we are brothers, belonging to a holy Church, joined together in Christian fellowship. Nowhere is the idea of the fatherhood of God and the brotherhood of man so perfectly realized as here in the Mass. Understood in its present significance, this "Our Father" is to be said by us in company with Christ. He is on the altar, pleading to His Heavenly Father for us. The spirit of the Son, God will give us, indeed has given us; but He will bestow it on us in greater fullness at Mass time so that we may be able to cry from the depths of our hearts: "Abba," that is, "Father." This is just what God wants of us. With Christ, the priest and people ascend in prayer to heaven where God dwells in glory with His saints.

"Who art in heaven." Touches of home! Heaven is the place we must have in view when we pray to Our Father. The abode of God is a place of light and joy and everlasting happiness. What is it like? Eye hath not seen, nor ear heard, nor hath it entered into the heart of man to conceive the definite reality. Yet God in His goodness, sometimes allows us just a little taste of heaven even in this life. As a man once put it: "Some one, St. Peter or another, leaves the gate ajar for a second . . . " Our acquaintance with heaven surely begins in our own soul, but that is a far-off acquaintance. The reality is yet to come. None the less, every one of us must hope, work, love, and strive for that nearer and nearer future.

[1] Father Tabb.

Nothing could be more natural than this quest of the soul for its eternal home with its Heavenly Father. Just as a bird has its homing instinct, so each soul away from its home in this vale of tears, needs must seek somehow its true home. Try, as any one may to make a heaven of this world, there always will be in the human heart that home-hunger for heaven. Our Heavenly Father put that in every heart. "Thou hast made us for Thyself, O God, and our hearts will never be at rest till they rest in Thee." That should come to our mind when we say : Our Father Who art in heaven.

No boy or girl can afford to neglect this prayer, nor fail to think of the hereafter. In youth, life looks far ahead. But, as St. Ignatius used to say, as short as the past is, the future will be. The day is soon to come when life is over. What then? Heaven, let us hope. Then, be it your daily prayer, to your Heavenly Father that His divine Son, Our Lord present you spotless before the presence of His glory with exceeding joy (Jude i, 24). It is very important that we both take deep interest in heaven and make good investments there. By Baptism we have been called to "an inheritance incorruptible and undefiled, and that cannot fade, reserved in heaven" (I Peter i, 4).

A devout Catholic writes :

When I was a boy, among the books in my nursery was one which told the simple story of a little fellow who stood in the fields and watched the clouds sweeping by overhead, until there entered into him a longing to follow the clouds and to discover to what far bourne they drifted.

The story of the boy who watched the clouds and wanted his dreams to come true is the story of all of us. But we of the faith are fortunate in this, that we know the part we must play and the road we must take, if we would come in the end to that place where our home is prepared, and the best is true.

Look upon life, then, as a road upon which we journey in the direction of heaven: "for a city that hath foundations; whose builder and maker is God" (Hebrews xi, 10). Each one is bent upon this divine adventure. He strikes hard patches in the road, rain and fog come every now and then, storms and sunshine. Yet one must never lose hope, for faith shows the way, and grace gives the courage and strength to go on. One has but to shoulder his duty day by day.

Next, mark well, the way by which you will be able to reach that place. "I am the door," says Our Lord. "By me, if any man enter in, he shall be saved and he shall go in, and go out, and shall find pastures" (John x, 9). Christ, then, is the One "Who is able to preserve you without sin and to present you spotless before the presence of His glory with exceeding joy" (Jude i, 24). Every one of us has the glorious opportunity of drawing nearer to Our Lord in the Mass, of going in and out the true door. "If any man minister to me, let him follow me; and where I am there also shall my minister be. If any man minister to me, him will my Father honor" (John xii, 26).

Surely, there is no better way of reaching the Father through the Son than in the Mass. Thus the Mass provides a foretaste of heaven. Have you not felt that, and tasted the fruits of supernatural grace? Truly on our altar a host of angels surround the Eucharist Christ and the spirits of the just are assembled for praise. In the Mass we echo the praise heard in heaven, just as the shepherds echoed in their hearts the angel chant as they sped on their way to Bethlehem. Our altar is Bethlehem restored. The heavens have bent down and the Just One is with us in the Mass. "For a Child is born to us and a Son is given to us" — the Son of God. An immense horizon opens before faith's eyes and our souls are joined in praise and worship with the

Queen of Heaven, the angels, martyrs, virgins, penitents, hermits, crusaders, missionaries, saints, kings and queens, canonized children. Indeed we kneel at the threshold of heaven, as we now pray to Our Father, the Lord of Heaven and Earth.

"Hallowed be Thy name." Consider carefully those words. This is a prayer that God's name, that is, God Himself, may be regarded holy by all creatures both in heaven and on earth. The angels and saints are forever praising God in heaven, and our dearest wish is that He may be rightfully worshiped here on earth. Christ is doing that here and now in this prayer on our altar. Our duty is to join with Him in one mind and one heart, worshiping God's infinity, His majesty, His holiness, His love; prostrating our body and soul before Him.

EGYPTIAN PRIEST PLAYING A HARP
(Tomb of Rameses II.)

We "hallow" God's name when we reverence His holy Word and obey His Commandments, worthily receive His Sacraments, obey the commands of His Church, are reverent toward His ministers, pray to His saints, and when we attend to His whisperings in our conscience.

Earlier in the Mass, you will remember, we had a sacred recollection of the souls in purgatory, or "hallowed memories of the dead"; next we had sacred memories of the saints, whom we "hallowed." But now we hallow the name of God, or make that name sacred in our mind, as we set our will to do His will on earth.

Of all our duties the first is to hallow God's name. We do this by pleasing Him in our conduct, and thus we will earn His love and graces in return. The attitude every true girl and boy adopt toward their own earthly father is much what they should maintain toward their Heavenly Father. A Catholic teacher has well said:

> Probably the strongest desire in any child and its strongest motive is the desire for esteem, especially of its parents and more particularly of its father. Hegel tells us the approbation of the parents represents to him his own better will, and has in consequence a rightful claim on his obedience. This judgment mirrors him to himself, and reflects his own worthiness or unworthiness. Gradually, by contact with his teachers and others, whom he looks upon with respect and reverence, his conscience is being formed, "till the rule and measure of self-respect is transferred from without to within." His standard now is the idea of the right, the true, the just. This culture of the will in education is far more important than culture of the intellect. Will is of the essence of man's personality, in virtue of which man is man. He has learned to know his duty, and all his powers have been disciplined and developed for its accomplishment.

"Thy kingdom come." After the petition for God's glory comes the petition for His kingdom. The hallowing of God's name leads directly to the coming of His kingdom. It is curious how well known are the stories of human kingdoms and how comparatively little known are the truths of God's kingdom. When we were small, did we not think more often of God, His angels, His presence, than we do now? No wonder Christ so loved little children. They are so good, so trusting in Him, the world over. A Catholic traveler [1] writes:

> After the World War, I saw refugee children feeding on roots and grass. The Polish forests were filled with lost and wandering people, who had no subsistence except what the ready earth gave them. But why is the root of the fern so sweet and palatable? Because when the

---
[1] Charles Phillips in the *Catholic World*.

Holy Family was fleeing into Egypt, and the Divine Infant cried with hunger, the fern offered its roots to Him to eat, "even though it knew it must die if its roots were taken." And why is the thistle leaf spotted? Because the Mother of Jesus spilled some of her mother milk over it one day when she was nursing her Baby.

Why does the lightning never strike the hazel? Because when Mary —"like a frightened quail," as the legend quaintly puts it — was fleeing with her Child from Herod, the hazel offered her its shelter, "though it knew the sword of the wicked king would cut away its branches to hunt for the fugitives." So likewise the aspen always trembles, because it was cowardly when Mary sought its shelter. And the cuckoo must ever be a bird without a nest, because it wished to win the favor of King Herod by calling out to him to betray the hiding place of the little Christ.

What do we know about the kingdom of heaven? Are our ideas of it musty and vague, or clear and well defined? It seems indeed that the Jews had some ideas of it that were quite wrong. Their idea was that the coming of the Messiah meant a golden reign, a millennium. They had the notion, born of their national aspiration, that it meant the pulverizing of Roman imperialism; a victorious war of vengeance, prompted by God, upon the Gentiles; a triumph followed by the setting up of a Jewish kingdom in Jerusalem where the purified people by their sheer goodness would attract all the natives of the earth into their community — a kingdom whose king was God. Now Christ, God's Son, changed and corrected that idea.

During the three years of His public ministry He chose and trained His Apostles. The kingdom, He told them, is already begun. Men may enter it if they will cast aside self and sin. Only then will God reign in human hearts. There are many qualities in the kingdom, mysterious and elusive (Matthew xiii). In time this will come clear. He instituted the Sacraments, especially the Holy Eucharist, so that He would be always present on earth amidst his growing kingdom. After the Resurrection, He founded a visible Church. The Mass was its center, the source of His perpetual presence. There were ample means to keep His teaching and His spirit alive among men. Had He not bestowed His Holy Spirit, which would never let His Church err in its teachings? He made St. Peter, His successor, the visible head of the Church. He saw to it, from heaven, that the infant Church would be "the visible expression, the flesh-and-blood embodiment, of the kingdom of God." And it always has been to this day, and will be to the end of time. For so Christ promised: "Thou art Peter; and upon this rock I will build my church and the gates of hell shall not prevail against it. And I will give to thee the keys of the kingdom of heaven" (Matthew xvi, 18-19).

The early Christians accepted these truths. They lived for them; they died for them. And how they loved Jesus and His Apostles! The Mass, the martyrs, testify to all this. Even the poorest rustic who was a Christian gave utterance somehow to his affection for Christ and His Church, "built upon the foundation of the Prophets and Apostles. True to the teachings of Christ, the lives of His first followers changed the course of nations. They made for the freeing of slaves, the elevation of women, the amelioration of life, the spread of righteousness and peace and joy in the Holy Ghost. What is all that save the coming of the kingdom?"

No one who reads the history of the Catholic Church diligently can say that he is unable to see what Christ meant by His kingdom. The grand old Church is really an extension of the life of Christ. She lays down His laws, interprets His will for us, makes clear to us His mind and words. In short, she is the visible organization established by Christ to promote slowly and through much suffering and persecution, the kingdom of God, and to impart

PATER NOSTER

to all men, though it takes ages, the religion which He came on earth to establish. During the last twenty centuries the Church has carried on in the interests of Christ's kingdom, steadily unfolding the truth committed to her keeping. Her history is a continuous record of difficulties overcome by the indwelling Providence in her. Of that record one reads with wonder and amaze. The gates of hell have never been able to prevail against her, try as they did. She is to-day a world-wide community of Catholics, active and vigorous, ready to fight for every word, every idea, every teaching given her by Christ: "going forth teach all nations." And her work in the ages to come will be "to make the earth as full of knowledge of the Lord, as the waters cover the sea."

"Thy kingdom come!" To help in this is our duty. Duty well done is much like diving when you go swimming. It looks hard at first, but it is not. What you have got to do, in duty as in diving, is not to stand shivering on the brink of effort. Plunge in at once. Do not wait! The thing is half done when you go about it that way. It will not help to stand and shiver and sigh. Anything worth while in this world costs effort. Until we have jumped into this work and done something for Christ's kingdom we remain conspicuous slackers. The whole earth is our Lord's, but we have to extend His kingdom in it. For this we pray every time we recite the "Lord's Prayer." Not only must we pray, we must also work for Him, and the coming of His kingdom. The reign of Christ in our hearts and in the hearts of others will be the one way of recovering this earth's allegiance for its Owner. Bent upon this, you are helping to make God's kingdom come.

In order to promote His kingdom, our Lord instituted the Mass. He wanted to keep His spirit alive among us, to give us grace, to strengthen His followers in all ages, until the end of the world. The Mass is the power house whither we repair to get strength, the armory where we get our courage and fresh ammunition for the fight against evil. If you go often to Mass, you will have more enthusiasm, you will welcome self-sacrifice, you will not be afraid to fight for the kingdom. But if you stay away from our Lord, you may easily become one of those who help make this world a worse place to live in instead of a better.

"Thy will be done." To us this means doing our plain duty! The doing of God's will is simply obedience. Just that, and nothing else. Here in the Mass we are at school, so we must learn our lesson from the divine Master. Twelve-year-old Jesus taught that lesson long ago to Mary and Joseph as well as to the doctors in the temple. Living service is what God wants, actions that square with His will. Your conscience reflects God's will, so the first thing to be sure of is that you have a clear conscience; and the next thing is to do what it says. Then you will be conforming your will to the will of God, and carrying out His will in action. This is true loyalty; standing on moral worth and social service, taking no part with selfishness. That is not always so easy. It requires much grace and courage and strength. There is another kind of loyalty, which is mere lack of moral courage to take sides with God. It takes another side, not God's side, and thus finds it easy to do contemptible things with self-satisfaction. That sort of loyalty — which is disloyalty to God — thinks ill of people and readily commits grievous offenses. It takes the low

STAMP OF THE TENTH LEGION

side of the mind, where the ideas of deceit, selfishness, and cowardice crawl in; where whims, likes, and dislikes crop out. Such false loyalty sticks to the lower soul; it will wink at abuses; it aids in dishonesties; it cheats, copies, tells lies; it will do things which are contrary to conscience. In the end there is sure to be harm done, never good. One cannot be on the side of Christ and the cheat at the same time. Nor can you be indifferent to sin if you want to be a friend of our Lord. "No man can serve two masters; either he will love the one and hate the other or he will sustain the one and despise the other." Our loyalty to God's will must be open, honest, fearless.

Sometimes amid the experiences of life God *wills* that we should suffer pain and sorrow. "If any one will come after me, let him take up his cross and follow me." Christ wants us to march and fight with Him for the same causes — true ideas, good men, honest conduct; charity, humility, obedience. To do that is to do God's will. Our will being "of the earth, earthy," has to be lifted up Godward. It is harder than "chinning" a horizontal bar in a gymnasium. One has to lift himself up to it by sheer strength until it becomes easy. Life is God's gymnasium. Your daily duties ought to be taken as a sort of gymnastic "stunt" in which you would be ashamed of yourself if you fell down. There are weight-tests of character, and you must expect that your soul adventures there will be strenuous; indeed, without strenuosity one can accomplish little in this world. Let us learn to understand our duty, and fit our acts to it, no matter how hard it may seem. Doing hard things gives you moral muscle. Some day you may need all that strength — when big crosses come, big trials take place. Strength of character, somebody said, consists of two things — power of will and power of self-restraint. It requires, therefore, for its existence, strong feelings and strict command over them. So we have to train ourselves in trials to rise to God's will.

There is reason to worry if we find that our will is out of line with God's will. We should know better than that. Our life work is to make our own will straighten out until it becomes parallel to God's will. In that direction lies true success. You will never begin to know what true peace of heart is until you begin to do God's will in everything. Measure up to the divine purpose in your life! We must be able, and then prove our strength in daily conduct. We have the strength by the grace of God, but it has to be used intelligently. This is no easy task, for we like to have our own way and to follow our own will. So in the "Our Father" we beg the grace to do God's will here on earth as the angels do it in heaven. Christ and His angels are on our altar, so no time is more propitious than now for asking assistance. If each of us is earnest and sincere in this matter, and anxious to do the divine will, God will help us more and more.

"Thy will be done!" Judged from what Jesus said and did all through the days when "He came in and went out among men," our Lord's whole aim in coming down from heaven was to do the will of His Heavenly Father. "In the head of the book it is written of me that I should do Thy will," ran the old, old prophecy. This He ever did. In fact the very first recorded utterance of our Lord (Luke ii, 49) shows that the thought ever in His mind was: "Thy will be done on earth as it is in heaven." The Finding in the Temple tells us that. For when Mary told Him that she and Joseph were looking for Him, our Lord with quiet repose replied: "Did you not know that I must be about my Father's business?" Later on He declared "My meat is to do the will of Him who sent me." That, then, was the whole work of Jesus — to do the will of His Heavenly Father. That, too, is your work and mine. The big business of our life is to do God's will.

Allegiance to the will of God can be explained in the following diagram. It will keep your path safe, and your view clear. It reads:

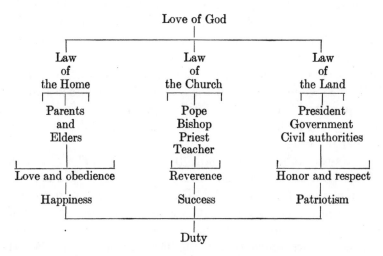

Our duty to the will of God is thus made plain. These are the cofactors, all requiring calculation in your arithmetic of obedience. Examine them in part and see how they contribute to the total product of duty. Take away any one of them from your sum, and you will not get the answer, the total resultant that God wants — the solution of the problem of obedience. Love of the will of God is what helps. No love of God, no love of His will, and no desire to do one's duty. Take away the heat from the center and the circumference will not long retain its warmth. Boys and girls who do not love God run away from God's will. Failing in that, they fall short of their threefold obedience. They may be promising, pretentious, but they are not obedient. They are not honest with themselves, nor with God; and they have a muddle-headed idea of what the will of God really is. In fact they take no pains to find out, so self-centered are they. Hence, life is sure to be for them a long, hard, mean path later on. No wonder they grow up to be lukewarm Catholics, ingrate men and women, undesirable citizens. Let us be blunt doers of the word as well as sayers, loyal to the will of God, ever acting on the principle of devoted service. "It may sometimes look hard, very hard, to do God's will, but we will find it much harder not to do it." Are we not better off for having done the good things, the just and the true? Whip your will into good acts. Then you will become a strong and perfect Christian — a soldier of Jesus Christ.

"Give us this day our daily bread." Bread! The food of our soul as well as the food for our body. We are dependent upon God for both. But for the bread of our souls we are now most anxious, as we kneel in the presence of Him who is the living bread that cometh down from heaven. Indeed we are much in the plight of Lazarus, who lay at the rich man's gate desperately ill (Luke xvi, 20). He wanted bread for the body. Bread for the soul is much more important. That bread is the living Christ, who is love incarnate. With the bread of life and understanding He shall feed us to make us strong in Him. And He shall help us to "see life straight and see it whole." More than that. If we eat of Him our soul shall live for ever and ever. For he that eateth hath eternal life; and it is this soul life that we must have, else we die from bitterness, cynicism, disappointment, selfishness. Without the living bread man's soul slowly starves, no matter how well his body may be cared for; for love is the life of the soul. As the food is, such is the life. And if God is the food of our soul, then its life will be Godlike — full of love and sweetness, active with courage and helpfulness.

When one of your classmates is sick, you visit him. The physician has come in to see the patient, has ordered certain medicine; and once the sick person has begun to recover from his illness, a diet is prescribed. Without food and nourishment the sick boy could never gain health and vigor. He would remain weak and ailing in body; weary and heartsick because he cannot regain his strength. Now all that has to do with the body. But it is much the same with the soul when sin makes it ill and infirm. Unless the divine Physician is called in, the soul will stay sick and suffering. But when He comes, and brings the bread of life, then the soul quickly comes back into a state of health, vigor, and strength, seeing that it is nourished with the food that gives life. Our Lord says to the soul: "I am thy health." And He is, so that when He heals us, we are healed indeed.

"Give us this day our daily bread!" The early Christians were so anxious for the food of their soul that they went to Mass every day. The Acts of the Apostles (ii, 46) describes how they broke bread from house to house. They had Mass in the upper room of various houses, just as Christ had said the first Mass in the upper room. But soon there were overflow meetings everywhere. There were so many converts to Christianity in those early days that there was not room for them or for the services of the Mass in one house; so they met in smaller companies at different places. There the holy sacrifice of the Mass was celebrated, following directly upon what they called the Agape, or Love Feast, in which they prayed, sang hymns, and ate together.

Remember these Christians were sorely persecuted, yet by the Mass and its graces they were made calm, serene, cheerful, courageous, full of faith. They were ready to court death and agony to be with Christ, so strong was their soul from the daily bread they had received in Holy Communion. Indeed, for us as well as for them, the sacramental effect of Holy Communion will be to put encouragement and sweetness into life. The bread of sweetness is the Blessed Sacrament, whereas selfishness is always sour, bitter, disappointing.

AGAPE OR LOVE FEAST
From an ancient sculpture at Milan.

"Give us this day our daily bread." One of the mysteries of life has been the slowness of mankind to make use of the great means of light and strength afforded in the Mass. Surely any one can see how sad is this state of affairs in our world at the present time. All are God's creatures, but many have yet to come to the knowledge of the truth. Especially that truth of the near and personal presence of the Son of God, the bread of life, on our altar. Turn to John i, 9–12, and see the facts.

"Give us this day our daily bread." May not you be in sore need of help from our Lord — help for your body, or for your soul, or for both? Is it sensible to forget what

Christ said: "Ask and you shall receive. Seek and you shall find"? The big thing is this: when you are in distress, go to the One who can help; when your soul needs grace, light, strength, courage, betake yourself without delay to the Blessed Sacrament, the source of all these things. Should you stay away then the loss is yours. Those who think they can get along without Christ will one day come upon a sad awakening. During the restless days of youth there is special reason for repairing to the sources of strength. We should not be slow of mind in regard to such an important matter. We need Mass, need it very much. Our souls hunger for the daily bread. Some, alas! are prone to forget this; they do not value Mass highly or make sacrifices to attend it; their tendency is to go only when they have to — no oftener. That is saddening; sadder still to hear the miserable pretext on which they try to excuse themselves. No one can say that he can do without the daily bread of the soul. It follows, then, that our chief duty, during school days, is to make His words our own. No lessons have one millionth the value of His. You can find them any time in your New Testament. Make sure that you do not miss them.

"And forgive us our trespasses, as we forgive those who trespass against us." This is an agreement made with God. You do this, and we shall do that! "Turn away Thy face from my sins," we say to God. And He will do that on condition that we turn away our face from the offenses of others, forget their misdeeds, and not nurse the hurt they may have done us. To forgive one's enemies is the act of a real Christian and the very opposite of the world's way. No wonder wars are rife and nations far from peace. They will not forgive, they will not forget. Have you ever realized that Christ makes that the one condition of our being forgiven ourselves? "With what measure (of mercy) you mete out to others, in the same measure will it be meted out to you." Read what our Lord did to the unforgiving Pharisees who wanted to stone a poor sinner (John viii, 1–12).

To seek revenge is forbidden us. "Vengeance is mine," sayeth the Lord, "I will repay." By Baptism, some one has said, we are enrolled in a "League of Mercy." We are to do good to all, but especially to those of the household of faith. Of all human evils the worst is that a man should hate his fellow man. Hatred destroys all the beauty, the magic, the peace that lie within our human life. Therefore, did Christ teach us to pray: "Forgive us our trespasses as we forgive those who trespass against us." We simply must forgive others. Our Lord's command is "pure, enlightening the eyes," making the task easier. The people who think that they can go on heaping up dislikes, resentment, hatred, prejudice, and still get to heaven are sadly mistaken. They must have forgotten what Christ taught: "Love your enemies; do good to them that hate you; pray for those who persecute and calumniate you." We realize, of course, that this is hard, but it is the sure sign of a Christian. In that way you will show the true spirit of Christ. You cannot be a real Christian, a follower of Christ, unless you really forgive people the injuries they may have done you. And forgive them in such a way as to show that the past is forgotten, absolutely forgotten. In no other way can you so truly prove that you are broad-minded, tolerant! In no other way can you say the "Lord's Prayer" right.

In this part of the prayer we declare to God that we forgive our neighbor's trespasses. But do we? Many who use these words may not mean them in the least. Many others simply lie when they tell the All-Knowing that they hate no one. Let us not be like that, dear Lord. Help us to bear one another's burdens, and so we shall fulfill the law. Kneeling here in the Mass we want our Lord to know that we desire to do just what He asks of us; then He will do for us what we ask of Him. The will to try — this is what He loves in us. If people have been unkind or unjust to us, we shall forget it, wipe it out of our mind with one act of generosity, of superb forgiveness. That is what He has done for us times beyond number. That, too, is the grace He gives us in the Mass — a grace of peace and good will.

Lastly, we beg of God: "Lead us not into temptation." God does not Himself tempt His children. Far from it. "Let no man, when he is tempted, say he is tempted by God. For God is not a tempter of evils, and He tempteth no man" (St. James i, 13). But God does permit us to be tempted, else how could we show that we are loyal to Him? It is a manly thing to fight for what is right and not

ST. MICHAEL

The archangel is first designated by name in mosaics of the fifth century.

let evil conquer your soul and make you a moral coward. Next time you are tempted, keep that in mind. The overcoming of a temptation, however painful and difficult, is finer and more strengthening to our souls than any other victory in the world. Indeed, it is the victory of free will, faith, and God's grace over the world, the flesh, and the devil. There, in fact, are the three sources of temptation. Evil has its own methods, and let us be on our guard against them. It gets in its deadly blows by means of the *world,* the *flesh,* and the *devil.* Mark well the three foes. Do not for one moment imagine that they will leave you to your peace.

The world, that is, the trials and sorrows of life from without. If you go by the world's methods, you will think crookedly and act crookedly. What are these methods? Ambition to get on by foul means : soul-smashing discouragement because one meets with hard trials, failures, or disappointments: anger and jealousy at the success of others: weariness in the practice of virtue when you see how bad people appear to prosper and you are tempted to follow their example. They will tell you they have "made good," but really they have done evil. In their hearts they know they are lying. There is many a boy and girl living a dull, idle, spoiled life to-day whose best chance was lost when they began to act dishonestly and deceitfully and continued in that way till they developed the habit. They now look back at their early days with wistful longing and wish that they had been true to their better selves. There is time still for them to get back on the right track, if only they will go to our Lord. He will teach them to see life straight.

EVE AND THE SERPENT
(Rheims)

The flesh, that is, from within. Many of our temptations arise from self-love and carelessness. Evil desires, for example, of dishonesty, stealing, impurity, deception, visions of ill-doing wickedly reveled in. A bad desire may become the mother of sin, and that babe of sin will have been born and waxed ever so strong scarcely before you realize it is grown up.

Satan. The direct assaults of the devil, the evil one, who seeks to lure us away from a good life to a bad. That is the way of temptation. Satan exists and he is busy. Be on your guard against his tactics; they are ever so clever. "For first a bare thought comes to the mind, then a strong imagination; afterward delight and evil motion and consent. And thus, little by little, the wicked enemy gets full entrance, when he is not resisted in the beginning. And how much the longer the man is negligent in resisting, so much the weaker does he become in himself, and the enemy becomes stronger against him" (*Imitation of Christ*, Book I, Chapter XIII, Paragraph 7).

"But deliver us from evil. Amen." A hint of need; nay, a cry for help in the face of danger. So it is. Evil foes, as we have seen, rise up against us and seek our soul. That happens often in life. True, the conditions, the tactics, of the warfare, change for each soul from decade to decade. As we grow older, fresh evils threaten. What, then, are we to do? To gain more strength, of course; and to arrange our forces so that our foes may gain the least possible advantage. These three enemies we have to face in this life. Indeed, God allows them to try out the spiritual fiber of which we are made. So we here ask for what is most needed in this fight — God's help. To fight down those forces by the help of God's grace and strength is what we now pray for. "Life," said a great sage, "is far more a wrestling match than a dance." Clearly, we have to wrestle with evil, with temptation all our life long. But listen to what the Apostle says: "Let no temptation take hold on you but such as is human. And God is faithful, who will not suffer you to be tempted above that which you are able: but will make also with temptation issue, that you may be able to bear it" (I Corinthians x, 13). Temptation is like a wrestling match with one who tries to waylay us, rob us of our spiritual strength, and down us in the mire of sin.

SYMBOL OF OUR REDEMPTION

"Watch and pray," says our Lord, "that you enter not into temptation." Understand, we should never seek temptation, never court the near occasions of sin. But if we cannot avoid encountering a temptation, we must then pray hard, meet it, exercise our virtue to the fullest, and fight it to a standstill. How shall you be crowned unless you fight, and be valiant in the fight? Watch, pray, fight! At all events God and you make a strong team. The world, the flesh, and the devil all together cannot beat that combination. You must fight temptation and by God's grace you will gain the upper hand. When temptation shows its face, remember the things of God you have been taught. When the hour comes for the fight between desire and duty, be strong.

DEVIL

A Gnostic symbol of the spiritual enemy of God. The image, human and serpentine, has the head and face of a lion. The human form and expression are noteworthy. This bronze is in the Vatican collection.

1. The highest aim of education is to make for the soul's immortal destiny. Can you explain this? 2. Write a theme on the following suggestive editorial:

WHAT IS THAT BOY BEING RAISED FOR?

Johnny writes his name on the neighbor's car; he throws sticks at cows; he does almost anything except shoot the teacher. Johnny is in thousands of our homes, and his parents are sure to say: "Oh, let him have his fun. You can't expect a boy to behave all the time!" Two thirteen-year-old boys set fire to several Grand Rapids factories, "just for the fun of it." It cost nearly a half million dollars. There is nothing in all the world finer than a real boy. And he's much too good to raise for a reformatory or a jail (*Collier's Weekly*).

3. What to your mind are the reasons for your parents sending you to a Catholic school? Write a theme on this, and tell us the whys and wherefores. 4. The following elements go to the making of your character: inherited physical qualities, temperament, surroundings, education, religious influences, the use you make of your will in choice, the grace of God. Of all these, which seems to you the biggest factor?

XXXI

LIBERA NOS QUÆSUMUS

During the Libera nos quæsumus, the priest draws out the paten from under the corporal, rubs it a little with the purificator, and signs himself with it. He then kisses the paten at the upper edge next his hand, and places it under the Host. For a short time the Host rests on the paten as in a golden dish.

Next follows the Libera nos quæsumus, a short address to the Blessed Sacrament, asking that Christ keep us from all sin and wickedness. Written by the Church in faith, illuminated in colors of life and hope, and shot with the pure gold of remembrance, this prayer is exceedingly beautiful.

Libera nos, quæsumus, Domine, ab omnibus malis, præteritis, præsentibus, et futuris: et intercedente beata et gloriosa semper Virgine Dei Genitrice Maria, cum beatis Apostolis tuis Petro et Paulo, atque Andrea, et omnibus sanctis, da propitius pacem in diebus nostris: ut ope misericordiæ tuæ adjuti, et a peccato simus semper liberi, et ab omni perturbatione securi. Per eumdem Dominum nostrum Jesum Christum, Filium tuum, qui tecum vivit et regnat, in unitate Spiritus Sancti Deus.

Deliver us, we beseech Thee, O Lord, from all evils, past, present, and to come: and by the intercession of the blessed and glorious Mary ever Virgin, Mother of God, together with Thy blessed Apostles Peter and Paul, and Andrew, and all the saints, mercifully grant peace in our days: that, aided by the help of Thy mercy, we may be always free from sin, and secure from all disturbance. Through the same Jesus Christ, Thy Son our Lord, Who liveth and reigneth with Thee in the unity of the Holy Ghost, one God.

The priest in a low voice makes this plea which, you can see, repeats the substance of the last petition of the Lord's Prayer. It is what rightly ought to be called an epilogue. The Libera nos quæsumus is the liturgical epilogue to the Our Father, an iteration of what we want, what we so much need. To pray is to think, to attend, to hold the mind lovingly to its object; and here like little children who say again what they have already said, we, the children of God, beg and beg in a fixed, determined way. What has already been stressed is even more clearly expressed — the evils past, present, and future from which we seek to be delivered through the intercession of our Lady, Saints Peter, Paul, Andrew, and all other saints.

St. Andrew

Those names are but a few of the multitude of witnesses of the Holy Sacrifice. Our mind would be overwhelmed by the thought of naming even a part of them, so we select certain noted ones. Mary, the Queen of all Saints, Peter and Paul are already well known to every Catholic. Next comes Andrew, whose name means "the manly one," and who has proved a good protector. Andrew is noted among these because he was the brother fisherman with Peter, first to be called to follow Christ (John i, 40–42); and so he is invoked by name with Mary, Peter, and Paul — great intercessors, all of them.

There is a wealth of beauty in this prayer said so softly, as if the plea were dying down, in the deepest emotion of appeal, to the very bottom of our hearts. Evils crowd about us in this life like a mob bent upon doing damage to our soul; so we want Mary, Peter, Paul, Andrew, and the saints to crowd them out, and keep them away. They will be our protectors, if, in this part of the Mass, we plead for their help.

Libera nos, quæsumus Domine! Here is a most important consideration: Christ is our great Intercessor, our powerful Protector. We call Him brother — our Elder Brother. And He is all that — "nearer to us than a brother, closer than hands and feet." From time to time this is forgotten. Not all of us have appreciated this privilege of nearness. Every work of ours that runs counter to Christ is both an injury to our soul and a disloyalty to our Savior. From such we need to be made free. And Christ our Lord is our great Protector, or Liberator. We want to be delivered from evil — past, present, and to come. Only by going to Christ can that be done. Unless we come to that conclusion signally and keep it in our mind, we shall be the sufferers.

"Come to me, all you that labor, and are burdened, and I will refresh you" (Matthew xi, 28). It will pay to keep that invitation in mind and go to Him when evil threatens to get the better of us; in other words, when we are near sin. Go straight to Christ. "Go to him early in the morning, and let thy feet wear the steps of his doors" (Ecclesiasticus vi, 36). Ask Him to deliver you from all evils — past, present, and to come. Remember the case of the daughter of Jairus: how her father went straight to our Lord for help — and received it. Nothing could serve us better than to keep that incident in mind. Read the accounts of it in Matthew ix, 18–26, Mark v, 22–43, Luke viii, 41–56.

The same soul drama so powerfully presented in the Gospel scene goes on in our own inner life. What we here seek for our soul is to be compared with what Jairus sought for his daughter — freedom from evil, from the death of the soul. That Christ will surely grant us, if we have faith. Moreover, since all sin is spiritual sickness, mortal sin is death of soul. The daughter of Jairus represented a soul fallen into grievous sin, through frailty rather than through malice. Yet our Lord restored that girl to life when recourse was had to Him with lively faith and humility. If we have recourse to His real presence just as Jairus went to Him when He was on earth, then He will come to the help of our soul, raise it up, even though it be dead, cure us of sins past and present, and keep us from evil in the future. Let us not hesitate to make this request of our Lord.

1. Among the most imminent dangers and temptations for high school students are these: Bad companions, bad books, bad movies and dramas. What should be the attitude of a Catholic boy and girl toward each of these?   2. Nothing is more beautiful in youth than sincerity. To be simple and straightforward, seeking the truth and telling it always everywhere, these are the highest attributes of a Catholic student. Name a character in our Lord's day who was sincerity itself; one who was insincerity incarnate.   3. There are three things beginning with an S which have the hiss of Satan in them. They are sin, sloth, and selfishness. Point out how all three spoil Christian character.   4. Explain these words of Emerson: "Shallow men believe in luck, believe in circumstances — strong men believe in cause and effect."   5. Write a theme based on the following: Knowledge comes from the professor and the book, but the character is shaped, rounded, and polished by a variety of agencies lying outside both these.

XXXII

FRACTIO PANIS   COMMIXTIO

For the Fractio panis the priest uncovers the chalice, makes a genuflection, and, rising again, takes the Host and breaks it in the middle, over the chalice. He then places part of the Host on the paten; from the other part a particle is broken off, the rest being placed on the paten. With the particle in his right hand he makes the sign of the cross thrice over the chalice; finally he puts the particle in the chalice, saying in a low voice, "Hæc commixtio."

It is evening in an upper room in Jerusalem. A living silence obtains. Outside, under the starlight, the olive trees are still. They, too, seem awed at what is about to come to pass. The Master, Jesus of Nazareth, has just charged His twelve with the Gospel and their work in the world. And now "taking bread, he gave thanks, and brake; and gave to them, saying: This is my body, which is given for you. Do this for a commemoration of me" (Luke xxii, 19). In the eyes of the Saviour shone an eternal vision. His plans ran ages ahead. And His work on the morrow would consummate the will of His Heavenly Father Who had sent Him. Yet this night, they who were there, how they must have felt the very glory of Christ's self-giving.

Suppose you were of the number of those disciples? After all, the privilege Catholics have is akin to that. The disciples' privilege, it is true, was to hear the first Mass. But we, too, can hear Mass. Doubtless, then, we are greatly honored, for there is nothing in all the world finer than that inestimable privilege. Indeed it was our Lord's will that all of us should be actually present at His mystical death. When at Mass we should never fail to be impressed with the truth of our Lord's infinite concern for human souls. Truly, then — and we cannot too often repeat it — there is nothing in all the world more wonderful than this daily sacrifice, exhibiting as it does God's love and mercy, reminding us of what our Lord did at the Last Supper and in His Passion. Nothing symbolizes this truth so clearly as the breaking of the bread; for it helps one to keep in mind that the Mass is the self-giving of our Saviour; the lifting up of the cross of our redemption; the act of the Sacred Heart offering Himself to the Heavenly Father; the giving over again of that body once bruised, of that heart utterly broken.

Now let us see what is happening. If you are near the altar, you will note that the priest genuflects, takes the Sacred Host in his hands, calls upon the holy name of Jesus, and breaks the Host into three pieces. This action is known as the Breaking of the Bread; it is an important detail which dates from the original Eucharistic service, when Christ said the first Mass the night before He died. Surely, no more significant action could take place.

UPPER ROOM, OR GUEST CHAMBER

But what, you may ask, is the meaning of the Fractio panis? What did our Lord mean by it, for it was His own act at the Last Supper? Let us see if we can grasp the sense underlying it.

At that Last Supper, which was the first Mass, our Lord took bread and changed it into His own body. This He broke and gave to His disciples. Then He told them that they and all who came after them were to keep it in the same form for all time. The next day our Lord's blessed humanity was, as it were, broken on the cross. Now notice how the Breaking of the Bread reminds us of what our Lord did for all of us at the Last Supper and on the cross. The Host laid down on the paten is our Lord's life laid down for the world. "He was wounded for our iniquities, He was bruised for our sins, and by His wounds we are healed." While no bone of our Lord's body was broken on the cross, yet His Sacred Heart was pierced for us. Of the Saviour of the world an ancient prophet had said: "He keepeth all His bones, not one of them is broken" (Psalms xxxiii, 21). But when the soldier stuck his spear in the side of Christ the wound thus inflicted was a large one, for the iron point of the spear such as Cæsar's legionaries carried was both heavy and rough. Hence the Sacred Heart was pierced, broken, so that blood and water came forth from it. In this connection read John xix, 32–37.

CUSPIS

With such a weapon, the soldier opened Our Lord's side, piercing His Sacred Heart.

Virtually, therefore, our Lord's body was broken for us. And this is what now happens in a mystical manner. In the Mass the priest does all that Jesus did, and so he breaks the Host. "The bread which we break, is it not the communion of the body of our Lord?" says St. Paul. It will thus be seen that the Fractio panis is a repetition of our Lord's own act. Let there be no mistake about it. He

FRACTIO PANIS COMMIXTIO

did just this, once at the Last Supper (Luke xxii, 19) and again at Emmaus (Luke xxiv, 13–22). And as our Lord did, so does the priest through His power. That is why the priest, when breaking the Host, says these words: "Through the same Jesus Christ, Thy Son, our Lord, who liveth and reigneth with Thee in the unity of the Holy Ghost, God, world without end. Amen."

The fraction, or the rite of breaking the bread in the celebration of the Mass, is, as we have seen, both a copy of our Lord's action and illustrative of the words of the institution: "taking bread, He blessed and broke . . ." This rite was always carried out in the Mass from the very infancy of the Church in accordance with the wish of Jesus. Indeed, the very name by which the Mass was known in early days was "the Breaking of Bread." In the ancient Mozarabic rite the priest broke the bread in halves, and divided one-half into five parts, the other into four. He then formed a cross with seven of them, putting five in a line to make the stem, and one on each side of the second from the top to make the arms.

The two remaining pieces, Gloria and Regnum, were placed in the paten below Resurrectio, in a line with it. Thus the whole course of our Lord's being, acting, and suffering in the flesh, with the fruits of it, was represented in this symbolic manner. When Communion time came the priest put the particle called Regnum into the chalice, received himself that called Gloria, and used the other particles for Communion, breaking them up as the number of communicants might require. You can see how each part of the broken bread stands for a mystery of our Lord's life. Nothing, then, could be more natural than that, in the earliest form of the liturgy, the breaking of the bread should have been regarded as the climax of the ritual followed, and should have been for the early Christians what the Elevation in the Mass is nowadays for us.

To return now to our Mass, the Breaking of the Bread is accompanied with a desire for peace. St. Paul's great wish for the Romans was: "Now the God of peace be with you all. Amen" (Romans xv, 33). The priest, with this same wish in mind, holds the sacred particle in his fingers, makes three crosses over the chalice from rim to rim, and says:

P. Pax ✠ Domini ✠ sit semper vobis ✠ cum.	P. May the peace ✠ of the Lord be ✠ always with ✠ you.
A. Et cum spiritu tuo.	A. And with thy spirit.

Thereupon the priest drops the particle, the broken part of the Host, into the chalice, exactly what our Lord did at the Last Supper (John xiii, 26). This is to mark the union of the all-holy body and the precious blood of our Lord and God and Saviour Jesus Christ, in His glorious resurrection. Remember that the resurrection as well as the death of Christ is represented in the sacrifice. Indeed, the Mass is the renewal of the sacrifice which Christ, the Eternal Priest, offered on the cross and which He offers now living in heaven.

FRACTIO PANIS   COMMIXTIO

Immediately after mixing the body and blood of our Lord, the priest says:

Hæc commixtio et consecratio Corporis et Sanguinis Domini nostri Jesu Christi, fiat accipientibus nobis in vitam æternam. Amen.	May this mixture and consecration of the Body and Blood of our Lord Jesus Christ avail us who receive it unto life everlasting. Amen.

The whole idea of this prayer of the mixture is to ask for the life eternal earned for us by the body and blood of our Redeemer. "To avail us unto life everlasting"; that is, to strengthen our friendship with Jesus Christ, the victim of love for us, on our altar. We have to come to Him, we believe in Him, we submit to Him. Suppose, however, we are tempted to betray Christ, as Judas did? Can you not see the need for this prayer since we want to stay friends with Christ? We now kneel in the circle of our Lord's friends. We are at His table, His guests, and would fain stay and receive Him into our hearts as the Apostles did at the first Mass. But we have our misgivings; sin can break every bond of love and friendship for Christ. The first step, then, toward love of Christ is fear of sin, fear of offending our Lord and friend. All sin is treachery; it darkens the mind, undermines loyalty to Christ, deprives the soul of peace and calm. So it is against sin we pray, for sin is a traitor's kiss, the kiss of Judas who sat with Christ at the Last Supper. Judas even as he sat there was meditating treachery and sin. Remember he was soon to receive Holy Communion. Yet our Lord gave this vile sinner a last mercy when He offered Judas the chance for repentence in the silent appeal of divine love. Even then the all-gentle Saviour was ready and willing to forgive Judas, but the traitor rejected His offer, and straightway Satan took possession of him.

Observe in the Gospel the mercy of Christ who marked

the traitor privately, not publicly; while warning Judas of his fate, He did it so as not to embitter him. Our Lord whispered to St. John only, and even to him the name was not mentioned. Had the divine Master denounced Judas as a traitor, clearly and openly, the Apostles undoubtedly would have dealt severely with him. As it was, a fierce surge of wrath at the very idea of treachery had risen in the hearts of the Apostles. Their souls were in the grip of a terrible anxiety.

"Is it I, Lord?" they ask, one after another. They are dismayed even when they are indignant at the unknown traitor, and they display a wholesome fear, mistrusting their own weakness. Be sure to study this episode in the first Mass, because therein is a deep personal lesson for all of us. Read John xiii, 18–30, as told by the Apostle himself, who sat next our Lord at the Last Supper.

1. "Courage," somebody has well said, "is not the absence of fear but the control of it." Are you able to make this clear to a child? 2. When did our Lord suffer from the temptation of fear? 3. There is one evil in this world which we should fear. What is it? 4. Explain the text: "The fear of the Lord is the beginning of wisdom."

XXXIII

AGNUS DEI

The Commixtio completed, the priest rubs his forefingers and thumbs over the chalice, and having joined them again, he covers the chalice, and genuflects. Then rising, bowing down, and striking his breast three times, he says in a clear tone the Agnus Dei.

That fear the Apostles felt in the first Mass (mentioned in Matthew xxvi, 20–22; John xiii, 22) was a wholesome fear. Notice how the same note is now struck in the Mass. That should not surprise us, for there is a good kind of fear, very necessary for all. If any one tries to tell you he has no fear, be sure that such a one does not tell the truth about himself. All feel fear some time or other. In fact the very highest form of courage is to be afraid to do a thing — and do it. "Were you ever frightened?" somebody asked a soldier. "Why, I'm frightened half the time; but I'm never afraid," he answered. But it is of wholesome, helpful fear we now speak. "The fear of the Lord is the beginning of wisdom." We need just that; indeed, never are we safe without it.

Had Peter feared, he would not have denied his Master; but he boasted and fell. It would have been better if Judas had feared instead of brazening it out even to the extent of making a bad Communion. What a warning! It should make us pause.

It behooves those who still have any doubt about the need of the fear of God and the importance of the message of the Agnus Dei to make a close study of the career of

Judas Iscariot. Remember that he was present at the first Mass. Even though he listened to the warning of the Master, in spite of all that was said, he sat there blind, unbelieving, and unconscionably fearless. There was no trouble of soul then; that would come later. But not now, for the gates of his soul were closed to fear. Before the Mass was over he went out to betray our Lord.

He had lived in base complaisance to everything that served his own selfish purpose, and now he sold our Lord to the Jews. Into the Garden of Gethsemane he came with a detachment of soldiers followed by the rabble. Then he gave Jesus the traitor kiss — the very kiss that should have been a token of loyalty, a sign of intimacy and cordial greeting. What a betrayal! "Hail, Rabbi!" said Judas. In his excitement the traitor may have even caressed the divine Victim he was betraying. Then Jesus was seized by the mob and made prisoner.

It is not recorded just what Judas did for a time after that, but one can fairly guess. Likely he sneaked about to see what would happen, and when he got news of our Lord's trial, then a terrible revulsion of feeling took place in his mean soul. Still he skulked about on that Good Friday morning watching the procession to Pilate's judgment hall. He heard the shouts of the rabble: "His blood be upon us and upon our children." He was sure that Pilate had condemned Jesus to death.

By this time the sin was entirely committed. It began to be upsetting. He saw it at last in all its horror and it drove him to despair. Those Jews who had bribed him now deserted him, having no further use for the traitor. They had gained their point. The crime was done, and he was left alone, face to face with his awful sin. When rich he was poor, poorer than a pauper. No wonder re-

AGNUS DEI

morse seized Judas. The light of life had gone from his low soul. Nothing mattered, for nothing remained to hearten him. Confronted with the black deed he had done, it was more than he could bear. The terrible prophecy may have run through his mind: "The Son of man indeed goeth as it is written: but woe to that man by whom the Son of man shall be betrayed: it were better for him if that man had not been born" (Matthew xxvi, 24). New terror rose in his heart at that very thought. He must make some sort of open confession. He must get rid of the maggots of avarice that were consuming his very inward being. He had sinned against the all-lovely, all-loving, all-lovable Nazarene even then on the road to His death.

Judas's terror was followed by despair. So powerful became this feeling that it drove him up to the Holy Place of the temple where none save the priests had a right to enter. Though the place was forbidden to him, that did not deter the madman. He flung the money on the floor, crying, "I have sinned in betraying innocent blood." But the other conspirators replied: "What is that to us? Look thou to it." The Jews cared naught for him now. Only when he could serve them as a tool did they make use of him. The treason committed, they threw aside the tool that was Judas. And now, rushing away, the traitor went into solitude, shunning everybody.

JEWISH SILVER SHEKEL
(Obverse and reverse.) These must have resembled the pieces of silver for which Judas sold his Divine Master.

Did anybody notice that skulking traitor as he dodged amid the narrow streets of darkest Jerusalem, a wild look in his eyes? Erased from his mind was all his shrewd sanity. What he could not forget was the black treason smirching his soul. Terror drove him this way and that, as if from danger. The danger existed, but only in his heart full of remorse and regret and sorrow and sinfulness. Madly he seeks to get away from the blame, the result of his treason. He continues his flight without finding rest. No rest for the wicked! With mind unhinged by fright and terror at his deed he continues on his restless way. He pauses, perhaps, a moment to look back on the city and his own sin. There was still time to repent, but repent he did not. The words of Christ were ringing in his ears: "It were better for that man — himself — that he had never been born." This was more than he could bear. Beaten and overcome in mind, incapable of reasoning, he betakes himself to the high road.

By now the sordid traitor is bent on committing suicide. They were going to hang Jesus. Judas, too, must hang. Dark of soul, he would come to an end by his own hand, the hand that held the price of our Lord's precious blood. On, on he hurries, intent upon his own destruction. Up the road that leads to the side of a yawning chasm he rushes, driven by the demon remorse. At last he arrives at a suitable place. Trees hang over the edge of this precipice that looks down into the deep valley of Hinnom. To the branch of one of those trees Judas fixed the rope, took the jump, and hung over the valley; but the rope gave way. Down, down he fell, down along the steep face of the Southern Hill opposite Mount Sion, till he hit one of the sharp, projecting rocks so common there. Upon the rock he was dashed to pieces. Terrible end for one whose silent heart, having emptied itself of all mercy for the All-Merciful, received the reward of its iniquity.

Beyond a doubt that narrative will help keep your mind

AGNUS DEI

clear as to the need of fear. There is many a boy and girl whose best chance is that they have the fear of God in their heart. To those who dwell on the awful details of Judas's fall, a salutary lesson comes — the fear of the Lord is the beginning of wisdom. Had Judas feared and heeded the warnings of his divine Master he never would have come to such a frightful end.

It is highly important for all of us to make sure that we are on Christ's side and not against Him as Judas was even when in the divine Presence. Yes, we must fear lest we, too, fail Christ, fail to "endure unto the end." This fear is a thing to foster; the absence of it points to a dangerous self-complacency. "Fear," says St. Augustine, "is the needle which enters the texture, not to remain itself, but to draw the thread after it"; it leads the way to love. Lest we should be in any danger of betraying our Lord we rightly mistrust our weakness, and in this part of the Mass we beg the Lamb of God to have mercy on us. The Agnus Dei is eloquent of our disturbed mind, of our fear lest any of us should go on to the sacrilege of a bad Communion as did Judas, whose heart was hardened by his habit of sin. That is the only thing in the world we need to be afraid of — sin. That was the way the Apostles felt at the Last Supper. They were troubled of soul. They were beaten and overcome in mind, when they heard our Lord allude to the danger, nay the bare fact of the treachery in their very midst. The thought of it was more than they could bear. Hence, the upset which spoiled their peace of soul; hence, too, the agonizing appeal to the Master: "Is it I, Lord?" That sort of fear was good for them. It put them on their guard, it made them humble, mistrustful of themselves, and entirely dependent upon God. Only by God's merciful help could they stand strong, loyal, faithful. They must stand close to Christ before they can say they are with Him.

As of old the disciples were gathered about Christ, now we are gathered round the altar, and we plead together for grace, mercy, and peace. The tone of our prayer is one of fear — that "fear which trembles at unwonted and sudden adversities which endanger things beloved, and takes precautions for their safety" (St. Augustine). So we fly for refuge to the Lord on the altar and exclaim:

Agnus Dei, qui tollis peccata mundi, miserere nobis.	Lamb of God, who takest away the sins of the world, have mercy on us.
Agnus Dei, qui tollis peccata mundi, miserere nobis.	Lamb of God, who takest away the sins of the world, have mercy on us.
Agnus Dei, qui tollis peccata mundi, dona nobis pacem.	Lamb of God, who takest away the sins of the world, grant us peace.

God loves nothing better than true humility, and to all who are truly humble and sorry for their sins, He is sure to give peace. You must not fail to notice the priest, his attitude and movement, as he recites aloud the Agnus Dei. Observe, too, the striking way in which he resembles the publican in the temple (Luke xviii, 13–14). Just study the two.

The Priest	The Publican
1. Having genuflected (after the prayer of the Commixtio) the priest rises and inclines his head profoundly before the altar.	1. The publican was a humble penitent. He "would not so much as lift up his eyes toward heaven." His heart as well as his head was bowed down.
2. The priest strikes his breast, a gesture of sorrow, because he has grieved that same Lamb of God veiled before him on the altar.	2. "But struck his breast," humbly petitioning for the one thing he most needs.

AGNUS DEI

3. The priest pleads Lamb of God ... For there, before him, is the Immaculate Lamb, Whose blood conquers death and opens to men the true land of promise.

3. Saying: "O God, be merciful to me a sinner."

We have our Lord's word for it that "he that humbleth himself shall be exalted." "Heaven's gates," an English poet beautifully wrote, "are lowly arched, and the humble of heart alone can ever hope to enter there." Wherefore we should be humble and fearful, as were the Apostles at the Last Supper. Then Christ will make us really holy, will purify us by taking away our sins, will grant us peace.

Christ is the lamb of God Who was led to the sacrifice for our sake. A lamb used to be slain to make atonement for sin. Learn all about it (Exodus xxix, 38; Numbers xxviii, 3).

The greatest of Israel's feasts was the Passover, in memory of Israel's deliverance in Egypt (Exodus xii). A lamb, "a male of the first year,

CHRIST, THE LAMB OF GOD
The source of life.

without spot," was offered in the paschal feast. When the lamb was killed, its blood was caught in a gold basin. Then the lamb was taken and roasted whole on a wooden spit. No bone was allowed to be broken. You will note that no bone of our Lord's body was allowed to be broken either (John xix, 33–36). Nothing was eaten until the Passover meal, when the paschal lamb was eaten. Now, our Lord was the Lamb whose death was our deliverance. The paschal lamb was only a figure which represented the true victim until the time when our Lord would come as the Lamb of God. He came and was offered as a pure lamb, innocent and holy; He shed His precious blood in order to wipe away our sins. Ages before our Lord was born the prophet portrayed Him "as a lamb that is led to slaughter" (Isaias liii, 7). This prophecy was in the mind of John the Baptist when he pointed to our Lord with the words: "Behold the Lamb of God who taketh away the sins of the world" (John i, 29, 36). The Baptist was alluding to what Christ would do by being slain as the true Paschal Lamb. Indeed this is just what came to pass. "He was led a sheep to the slaughter; and like a lamb without voice before his shearer, so openeth he not his mouth."

Our Lord on the cross was the true Paschal Lamb, for He bore our sins and was sacrificed: "A lamb without blemish and without spot." "For Christ, our Pasch is sacrificed," says St. Paul. Similarly St. Peter: "You were redeemed with the precious blood of Christ, as of a lamb unspotted and undefiled" (I Peter i, 18–19).

In the Mass, that same Lamb of God, the ruler of the earth, is actually upon our altar. He has come back once more to be mystically slain in order to expiate our sins and draw us to His sacred heart. Hence we pray in the last plea: "Lamb of God, who takest away the sins of the world, grant us peace."

Next follows the triple prayer for peace. This is divided into: (1) the prayer for outer peace; (2) the prayer for inner peace; and (3) the prayer for worthy preparation for Communion.

In the first prayer the priest says:

Domine Jesu Christe, qui dixisti Apostolis tuis, Pacem relinquo	O Lord Jesus Christ, who saidst to Thy Apostles, Peace I leave you,

vobis, pacem meam do vobis: ne respicias peccata mea, sed fidem Ecclesiæ tuæ; eamque secundum voluntatem tuam pacificare et coadunare digneris: qui vivis et regnas Deus, per omnia sæcula sæculorum. Amen.	My peace I give you: regard not my sins, but the faith of Thy Church; and vouchsafe to grant her that peace and unity which is agreeable to Thy will: Who livest and reignest God, world without end. Amen.

The peace of the whole Church. This plea takes us back in spirit to the First Mass. What our Lord promised intimately to His disciples as a fellow man Who was yet true God — that we ask for. We should learn by heart what Christ said, then, to His disciples gathered around the holy table. The precious words are given by St. John, who sat next our Lord. Make sure that they are clear in your mind (John xiv, 27-31). On that night Christ left peace with His followers. As a matter of fact the "Catholic Church to come" was there at that table. Not until Pentecost, however, after Christ's death, resurrection, and ascension, would it be born. But now in this twentieth century the Church, born long ago, and waxed strong, is assembled in part, at Mass. So we pray our Lord to vouchsafe to the Church and to us, of course, that peace and unity which is agreeable to His will.

Remember that peace, outward peace, at least, comes and goes from the Church according to God's own providence. Indeed, the one thing that the Church asks is that we remain true to the spirit of her divine Founder. The Church is in a real sense the Incarnation prolonged; "Christ really lives, speaks, and acts in her, His mystical body. Her whole history is a repetition of the thirty-three years of the Incarnate Word on earth; she loves the hidden life which is so alien to the pomp and display of the world. Witness her religious orders, her hermits, her inner life. She is assailed by the same temptations as our Lord felt when tried after His forty days' fast in the wilderness. The figures of Judas, Pilate, Caiphas, and Herod are continually appearing in her historic life (for example, Martin Luther, Henry VIII, John Knox, *et al*). The Church has even her Gethsemane, her way of the cross, her crucifixion, her burial, and her resurrection. Her life is simply a reduplication of the life of Christ." That truth ought to be better known. Trials of one sort or another the Church has ever suffered. The world will always have a grievance against the Church. "I have given them (the Church) thy word, and the world hath hated them, because they are not of the world: as I also am not of the world." The reason for this opposition on the part of the world, Christ makes very plain (John xvi, 1–4). Yet the Church enjoys peace even in the midst of trials, just because she performs the tasks of Christ and is not dismayed with droopy terror in the face of the foe.

"Regard the faith of thy Church." Consider the Church's strong adherence to everything that Christ has said and done. When it is a question of what our Lord teaches, she is always outspoken, always fearless. Never has she veiled her teaching under the mask of prudence, never proved coward in her fealty to Jesus Christ. This is the victory by which she overcomes the world.

Pause to think of all the Catholic Church has gone through for the sake of Christ. "In the past the Church has triumphed over the Græco-Roman world. She has ridden the steeds of barbarism, and emperors have held her stirrup. The traitors of the Renaissance, the rebels of the Reformation, the French Revolution with its fire and sword left her dead and decently buried. This was the first report. But the special correspondents were deceived, as their successors will be to the end of time." What a glorious passage!

AGNUS DEI

how strikingly true! Try to grasp this great truth of history — the divinity of the Church. Nobody but God knows what will be the future development of our grand old Church. But as a Catholic priest once said, "Is it not evident that the conception of the Catholic Church, of Catholic truth and Catholic holiness, is capable of yet greater expansion; that it has not yet exhaled its sweetest fragrance ; or donned its finest and brightest colors; that the Apostolate of Peter and Paul is far from ended, that their words have not yet gone into all lands, nor their voices reached to the ends of the earth?" Yes, and now the Church is active and vigorous in the cause of Christ. The bark of Peter sails on and on, over all the seas.

ROMAN SOLDIER
With full battle equipment.

The second prayer for peace, this for inner peace, is now recited.

Domine Jesu Christe, Fili Dei vivi, qui ex voluntate Patris, cooperante Spiritu Sancto, per mortem tuam mundum vivificasti, libera me per hoc sacrosanctum Corpus et Sanguinem tuum ab omnibus iniquitatibus meis, et universis malis : et fac me tuis semper inhærere mandatis, et a te nunquam separari permittas. Qui cum eodem Deo Patre et Spiritu Sancto vivis et regnas Deus in sæcula sæculorum. Amen.

O Lord Jesus Christ, Son of the living God, who, according to the will of Thy Father with the cooperation of the Holy Ghost, hast by Thy death given life to the world, deliver me by this Thy most sacred Body and Blood from all my iniquities and from all evils; and make me always adhere to Thy commandments, and suffer me never to be separated from Thee. Who livest and reignest with God the Father world without end. Amen.

The second prayer is for personal peace — the peace of Christ in the hearts of all Catholics. Within the Church, inside the fold, this peace is greatly to be desired. Christ has pledged it to all the faithful. "My peace I leave you, My peace I give unto you," He promises. Now the trouble with many people to-day is that they are looking for peace everywhere but in the right place, the only place where it can be found — in religion and in obedience and union with Christ. All true peace spread from Christ to the peoples and nations that did His will. If men reject Him, "the Prince of Peace," then they will fall under the domination of war and sin, pride and falsehood; they will put around their necks, not the sweet yoke of Christ, but the iron yoke of selfishness, and consequent sorrow. Certainly until men and nations stoutly support Christ and His law, they will never enjoy any permanent peace; let them, therefore, learn this lesson, the most important one that history teaches.

This prayer shows us what that peace of Christ is; not mere earthly joy and prosperity, but the removal of all the elements of discord in the soul. We can best secure peace by adhering to the commandments of Christ, and by never separating ourselves from Him by mortal sin.

The world over, many are without peace because they fail in these two things. Our duty is to make sure that we stand close to our divine Captain and obey His words. *Non enim dormientibus divina beneficia sed observantibus deferuntur!* "You are my friends, if you do the things that I command you" (John xv, 14). No one can resist Christ and have peace. No one can turn his back on the law of Christ and be truly happy. The knowledge and love of Jesus Christ is the very stuff of which peace is woven. All true peace came into the world with Jesus Christ. "Peace

AGNUS DEI

on earth" the angels sang at His birth — peace to men who will do His will.

Finally the third prayer is said:

Perceptio corporis tui, Domine Jesu Christe, quod ego indignus sumere præsumo, non mihi proveniatin judicium et condemnationem; sed pro tua pietate prosit mihi ad tutamentum mentis et corporis, et ad medelam percipiendam. Qui vivis et regnas cum Deo Patre, in unitate Spiritus Sancti, Deus per omnia sæcula sæculorum. Amen.	Let not the participation of Thy body, O Lord Jesus Christ, which I, though unworthy, presume to receive, turn to my judgment and condemnation; but let it, through Thy mercy, become a safeguard and remedy, both of soul and body; who with God the Father, in the unity of the Holy Ghost, livest and reignest God forever and ever. Amen.

The third prayer is preparatory to receiving Holy Communion. Suppose that you were one of the twelve at the Last Supper. Suppose you heard Christ say that there was a traitor in the crowd. Would you not be upset, worried? Quite rightly, then, the priest calls upon the goodness of God, leans upon His divine mercy. Unworthy as the priest is, or indeed anybody is, to receive our Lord, he begs that this Host he is about to receive may be for his eternal benefit and not for his condemnation. Judas's Communion was for his condemnation, because it was a bad Communion. Read carefully Matthew xxvi, 14–28, and you will see that the betrayer of Christ was in mortal sin when he received Holy Communion at the first Mass. No other words can tell better the cowardice of Judas. Then to think of his awful ending as related in Matthew xxvii, 51, and Acts i, 18.

That is what makes us fear. How akin to the spirit of the traitor is that of the bad communicant! There have been more traitors than Judas! Observe how St. Paul scored the bad communicants in Corinth, in the days of the early Church (I Corinthians xi, 21–22). Naturally we ought to detest traitors. But let us not forget that all sin is treason, and mortal sin a betrayal of the divine Master. Those vivid New Testament pictures of people who betrayed our Lord should help instill a salutary fear in every truly Christian heart.

Lest, then, we fall into the Judas sin of betraying Christ by a bad Communion, of receiving with unworthy, sin-soiled lips His kiss of peace, we beg God's help. "Let not," we pray, "the participation of Thy body, O Lord Jesus Christ, turn to my judgment and condemnation (as it did to Judas's) but let it be to me for the safety of my soul, the safety of my body, the receiving of a saving remedy."

1. Explain how Holy Communion is a saving remedy. 2. The early Christians had the utmost reverence for our blessed Lord and for everything associated in any way with Him. Their thoughts were of Him and of His sufferings. They feared to offend Him. Often they used trinkets to keep them in mind of His loved ones; and they wore the Gospel for which martyrs shed their blood. How do Christians nowadays continue such customs? 3. Do you know the origin of the Agnus Dei worn by many Catholics to-day? 4. Are such Agnus Deis sacramentals? 5. Name ten sacramentals not mentioned in your catechism.

XXXIV

DOMINE NON SUM DIGNUS

The prayers for peace have been said. Making a genuflection and taking the Host in his hands, the priest next says the Panem cœlestem; then, slightly inclining, he takes both parts of the sacred Host, and striking his breast and raising his voice a little, he says three times the Domine non sum dignus.

The Mass, we have seen, is a sacrifice, an act of divine worship. Every sacrifice demands the destruction of the victim. On the cross, our Lord's heart was broken and His blood shed, unto the remission of sins. In the Mass there is no real shedding of blood, but there is the mystical separation of the precious blood from the sacred body. Then the Breaking of the Bread is followed shortly by the Communion. It is easy to see, in this, the completion of the mystical destruction of the divine Victim. First the destruction, then the consumption of the Victim. This was done with more dispatch in the early Church. Then they did not have the triple prayer for peace. After the Breaking of the Bread there came at once the kiss of peace followed immediately by the Communion. So doing, the sacrificial acts of Fractio and Cummunio must have stood out in great relief. Indeed, quite quickly the whole movement went on in the Mass till Communion time came; then all the faith-

RELIQUARY

From the fourth century.

ful went up to partake of the Victim from the altar of sacrifice. To their souls, Christ Himself applied the merits of Calvary.

Communion time is at hand. "The chalice of benediction which we bless, is it not the communion of the blood of Christ? And the bread which we break, is it not the partaking of the body of the Lord?" (I Corinthians x, 16.) The priest genuflects, and then takes the two parts of the broken Host in his left hand, using his thumb and forefinger to hold them over the paten. While so doing, he says:

| Panem cœlestem accipiam, et Nomen Domini invocabo. | I will take the Bread of Heaven, and will call upon the name of the Lord. |

Then, striking his breast, in a moderate tone he says three times:

| Domine, non sum dignus, ut intres sub tectum meum: sed tantum dic verbo, et sanabitur anima mea. | Lord, I am not worthy that Thou shouldst enter under my roof: say but the word and my soul shall be healed. |

A perfect prayer at such a time. The centurion in the Gospel used these words. The priest, like the centurion, standing in the presence of Christ, filled with a sense of his own unworthiness to receive the Son of God under the eaves of his soul, nay in his very heart, employs the selfsame words. He says the Domine non sum dignus in all faith, in all honesty, in all humility. And we, too, must do likewise as we acknowledge our own unworthiness and at the same time beg our Lord to say the word that will heal our soul.

Naturally the centurion in whom we see a faith edifying in the extreme, deserves our closest attention. The fine portrait of the centurion whom Jesus loved and openly

DOMINE NON SUM DIGNUS

praised for his faith and honest humility is given by St. Matthew viii, 5-13. We should study his character and imitate him, for the Church uses his very words in the Mass.

"I am not worthy that thou shouldst enter under my roof!" The humility of the centurion sprang from his sturdy honesty and his esteem of our Lord. It will help if we catch his spirit; his humility and his faith. We should do everything to make our soul's house ready for our Lord's coming in Communion. If some important person were to ring the bell of your door, you would not dream of appearing before him with hair disheveled, clothes torn, face dirty, and generally bedraggled in appearance. Nor would you want such a one to find your house full of dust and dirt, full of noise and tumult, the chairs broken, the walls bespattered, everything in disorder. You would feel ashamed of yourself for many a day. But think what it means to have Jesus come to enter under our roof! Our soul is God's house. Have we that house well ordered, beautified, and adorned for His coming? And even if it were the best, we still feel that it is not good enough for our Lord. No mistake could be greater than that of supposing that we are really worthy of receiving Holy Communion. Even the best of us owes it to honesty to proclaim our unworthiness.

"Say only the word." That is what the centurion said to Christ. He was a legionary who had both faith and humility. He knew that just as his own soldiers would be obedient to him, in the same way the armies of angels, the spirits, all diseases — yes, all the powers of nature — would be obedient to Jesus. Jesus could command them all at a word.

There is a manly outspokenness in the faith and loyalty of this man. How truly he esteemed our Lord! "Yet why," he asked himself, "why should I, a mere centurion, the commander of a hundred men, think that I am worthy to receive the divine Wonder Worker under my home roof?" He was not, and he knew it. It was no secret. And he had the humility, the sterling soldier honesty to say so. He had no hesitancy about it. Besides his humility, he had wonderful faith that God could cure body or soul; that Christ was all-powerful. And he was right. This faith rang true; it pleased our Lord who not only praised him for it, but actually said the mere word and healed his servant at a distance. Now you know why the Church canonizes the centurion's expression of faith and humility by placing his words in the Canon of the Mass.

"And my soul shall be healed!" The divine Physician who comes to see us is able to recognize our malady, diagnose it correctly, and cure it with a word. Sin is the sickness of our soul. The divine Physician can read every symptom: the low aims, shabby desires, spitefulness; the whims, mean moods, the whining disposition; the dislikes, small talk, sulkiness. All these spoil the beauty of the soul. They are the blotches that come out on the soul, following the fever of sin — a moral fever. It is a terrible thing to be seriously sick when on one's feet, and not know it. Disease neglected becomes inveterate and often fatal. You have often heard of "walking typhoid." In order to prevent the germs of sin from poisoning the soul all bad

A Roman soldier of the Legion

DOMINE NON SUM DIGNUS

habits should be eliminated at the very beginning. The sick soul needs the divine Physician who alone can supply the remedy for its ills. Be assured that our soul needs to be healed. If we know anything about ourselves, that must be as clear as print. True self-knowledge makes us humble. Humility always implies self-knowledge. People who tell you that they have not an atom of humility are ignoramuses; they know nothing about themselves. They must spend much time minding other people's business, instead of having a care for their own soul. Self-blinded, they develop a colossal conceit. The Scribes and Pharisees were of that type, and our Lord despised and denounced them for it. A Scribe or Pharisee would have told you that he was faultless. You remember the one in the temple of whom our Lord spoke (Luke xviii, 9–14).

SCRIBE

Word for word, he knew the Law and the Prophets, but his piety was legal, not spiritual.

That Pharisee went away, unjustified. That, too, can happen to us in God's temple unless we honestly acknowledge our failings and beg our Lord to heal our soul.

If we ask our Lord to heal us, He will hear our prayer: for Christ loves to find in anybody an uncompromising love of truth and strict personal sincerity. He will do the same for us as He did for the centurion, if we frankly confess our unworthiness and ask Him to change us, to heal our soul. A great deal needs to be changed; many ills, as we have seen, have to be healed in us. These we must eliminate if we would be less unworthy to welcome the divine Guest. "Do thou heal us, Lord, and we shall indeed be healed." Then will soul and body have that health, that *salus*, which comes through close union with Him who is the source of their being.

Communion clearly shows how the Mass is a sacrifice. In very early times there used to be a kind of sacrifice among the Hebrews known as the sin offering. This was intended to restore the worshiper to favor with God after such favor had been forfeited by some sin. A ram, goat, or bullock was slain near the altar, the fat portions were consumed upon the altar, and the offering was presented in behalf of the sinner. Among the special features of this sacrifice was the peculiar disposal of the blood, part of which was placed on the altar of burnt-offering, while the rest was poured out at the base of the altar (Leviticus iv, 1–35). The high priest, of course, was the offerer, and the sacrifice or sin offering was but a type of the great sacrifice yet to come. What was offered in the ancient sacrifice, the victim, was destroyed before God to show that He is the sovereign Lord of all things. But now the divine Victim, the body and blood of Christ, is received in Holy Communion. Christ gives Himself to us that we may be united to Him, identified with Him. In Holy Communion, therefore, the dearest desire of the human heart is realized. "When we feed on our Lord's flesh and blood we are transformed into Him; our body is now His, our soul is His; we cease to be our own. We bear the marks of His body on our own." The desire of fullest union with our crucified Saviour is at last realized.

DOMINE NON SUM DIGNUS

The last great action in the Mass is the Communion. It is the consummation of the sacrifice. Hence the great importance of making a detailed study of the Communion of the priest. Try to get all the ceremony into clear focus. Our aim is to see this part in clear outline without missing its rich detail. Without any confusion you should be able to recognize each part in its place, everything that is said and done. With this aim study the following schema. Here you have an accurate and complete account from which you should quickly comprehend the Communion and duly appreciate the action and words of the priest.

Up to this time three groups of prayers have been said, as it were, in prelude to Communion:

(1) Pater Noster, with its epilogue.
(2) Agnus Dei, with its triple prayer for peace.
(3) Domine non sum dignus, thrice repeated.

The priest prays as he makes the sign of the cross with the Host:

| Corpus Domini nostri Jesu Christi custodiat animam meam in vitam æternam. Amen. | May the Body of our Lord Jesus Christ preserve my soul unto life everlasting. |

Meditating a few moments after receiving the Host, the priest next says with a glow of thanksgiving:

| Quid retribuam Domino pro omnibus quæ retribuit mihi? Calicem salutaris accipiam, et nomen Domini invocabo. Laudans invocabo Dominum, et ab inimicis meis salvus ero. | What return shall I make the Lord for all He has given to me? I will take the chalice of salvation, and call upon the name of the Lord. Praising I will call upon the Lord, and shall be saved from my enemies. |

While saying the above prayer, the priest uncovers the cup, the chalice of salvation, genuflects, takes the paten, sweeps the corporal with it in order to collect any fragments on it, and puts them into the chalice. Thereupon, making a sign of the cross with uplifted chalice before drinking the precious blood, he says:

Sanguis Domini nostri Jesu Christi custodiat animam meam in vitam æternam. Amen.	The Blood of our Lord Jesus Christ preserve my soul unto life everlasting. Amen.

The priest drinks of the chalice, the precious blood moistening his lips, entering into his very heart, which is filled with the presence of God.

After this, and when the people have received Communion, he says in secret the prayers:

Quod ore sumpsimus, Domine, pura mente capiamus; et de munere temporali fiat nobis remedium sempiternum.	Grant, O Lord, that what we have taken with our mouth, we may receive with a pure mind; that of a temporal gift it may become to us an eternal remedy.

When washing his fingers over the chalice, he says:

Corpus tuum, Domine, quod sumpsi, et sanguis quem potavi, adhæreat visceribus meis: et præsta, ut in me non remaneat scelerum macula, quem pura et sancta refecerunt sacramenta. Qui vivis et regnas in sæcula sæculorum. Amen.	May Thy Body, O Lord, which I have received, and Thy Blood, which I have drunk, cleave unto my inmost parts; and grant that no stain of sin may remain in me, who have been refreshed with pure and holy mysteries. Who livest and reignest forever and forever. Amen.

After the priest's comes the people's communion. Just as soon as the priest drinks the precious blood the people who are to receive Communion rise and proceed to the altar. Holy is this hour. It is now the time for them to partake of Christ crucified, to embrace Him with all the power and

DOMINE NON SUM DIGNUS

devotion of their soul. Soon, they know, they will be, in the depths of their soul, face to face with our Lord! Think of it! Indeed we are not worthy. Millions of Catholics from the time of St. Peter to our day have knelt just like that to receive their Lord and God. Sometimes under the earth in the Catacombs; sometimes in the sands at the edge of the desert; sometimes in the jungles, hearing Mass under a palm tree. Pity those who stay away these days of ours. All He asks is repentance and good will. Even so, souls are troubled in approaching the altar since they are so unworthy. Therefore the thing to do is to make sure that we confess once more our sins. All our actions, interior and exterior, should show that we realize this.

If any of the faithful are to receive Communion, the altar boy says the Confiteor. People should do the same, renew their sorrow and contrition, confess and have their sins expiated. The priest takes the ciborium from the tabernacle, turns round to face the people, and pronounces the Absolution. Standing out well in front of the altar, he says:

Misereatur vestri omnipotens Deus, et dimissis peccatis vestris, perducat vos ad vitam æternam. Amen.	May the Almighty God, who alone can forgive sins, have mercy on you, and having pardoned your sins, may He lead you to life eternal. Amen.
Indulgentiam, ✠ absolutionem, et remissionem peccatorum vestrorum tribuat vobis omnipotens et misericors Dominus. Amen.	May the Almighty and merciful Lord grant you pardon, ✠ absolution, and remission of your sins. Amen.

This said, the priest takes the ciborium, turns to the people, and holding the ciborium in his left hand, raises the Host high in his right, saying:

Ecce Agnus Dei, ecce qui tollit peccata mundi.	Behold the Lamb of God, behold Him who taketh away the sins of the world.

And then he repeats thrice:

Domine non sum dignus ut intres sub tectum meum: sed tantum dic verbo, et sanabitur anima mea.	Lord, I am not worthy that Thou shouldst enter under my roof; say but the word, and my soul shall be healed.

What could be more expressive than these words: "Behold the Lamb of God!" and the deep response of the humble soul: "Lord, I am not worthy!" Our present great need is for a clear vision of the real extent of our unworthiness; then we can receive Christ with the humblest of hearts, and the profoundest sense of gratitude that He should deign to enter under our soul's roof and abide with us. Surely we can stand being very very humble at this holy moment, when God's goodness to us is simply beyond imagination.

The priest comes down to the altar rail, and standing before each one about to receive Communion he makes the sign of the cross with the Host; then, when placing the Host upon the tongue of the communicant, he says:

Corpus Domini nostri Jesu Christi custodiat animam tuam in vitam æternam. Amen.	May the Body of our Lord Jesus Christ preserve thy soul unto life everlasting. Amen.

The Christian soul then receives the same body that was sacrificed on the cross. Behold with eyes of faith how Christ kisses and embraces the soul in the sacred Communion; how He pours Himself into human hearts, mingles His pure flesh with sinful flesh; how He humbles Himself to become the food of the souls He has created, that they may be two in one. "Thou in me and I in thee, as the Father and I are one." With our Lord in our heart we may now offer ourselves to the Heavenly Father.

Because our blessed Lord well knew what need every soul

has for the light of life, He instituted the Blessed Eucharist. In His infinite love He actually desired to be with us. "With desire," He declared, "have I desired to eat this Pasch with you." The Church interprets for us the will of Christ; so she urges us to receive Holy Communion. The plain fact is that we cannot go too often. "Unless you eat the flesh of the Son of Man," says our Lord, "and drink his blood you cannot have life in you." That is worth keeping in mind.

If our Lord says to us: "Come up higher" — up to the altar rail — that call need not frighten us. Rather it should make us attune our hearts to be one with Him. It is the intention of the Church that all who go to Mass should go to Communion sacramentally. True, she does not command it, but she does wish that we would do so. Did those Catholics, going to Mass yet staying away from Holy Communion, realize how much out of place they are, away from the altar rail, they would make up their mind to go to Communion as often as they hear Mass.

There are many solid reasons why we should go to Communion frequently. Most important of these are:

1. Because the Mass is not a sacrifice for the priest alone — it is also for the people, for all who assist at it. The Eucharist is a banquet, a sacrificial feast, where the priest is not the solitary communicant, but the faithful partake with him. Christ is come upon our altar in order that all may have life, and have it more abundantly. He, the Victim, is offered for the people as well as for the priest; indeed, for the whole Church. So the participation in the Victim, that is, receiving Communion, is equally desirable for people as for the priest.

2. We should not stand aloof from our Lord when we need His help, His grace, His life for our souls. "When," says Bishop Hedley, "the soul's intellectual, human, spiritual will is acted upon by the power of the body of Christ, then there is union, just as if a swiftly rising eagle caught in its grip some aimlessly drifting lesser bird, and bore it up out

of sight in the sky." Experience abundantly proves this, and the wise will heed. They that receive the Lord shall "renew their strength, they shall take wings as eagles, they shall run and not be weary, they shall walk and not faint" (Isaias xl, 31). Go often, then, to Holy Communion, where the Lord "satisfieth thy desires with good things: thy youth shall be renewed like the eagle's" (Psalms cii, 5). Back of much unrest of youth is a certain coolness toward our Lord in the Blessed Sacrament, an indifference toward receiving Holy Communion frequently. It is easy to see why many boys and girls are sad, selfish, unhappy. Their souls are heavy, half sick, in need of the divine Physician. They feel vaguely something is wanting. They have shut out the light of life, and get only darkness. They need to be stirred up by grace. They need to throw open the door of their soul and welcome their Saviour in Holy Communion.

3. Genuine devotion, remember, is firmness of the heart toward God, and the fulfilling of His holy will. The best way of increasing devotion is to come close to Christ in love, adoration, contrition, above all in Communion, which will intensify your heart's desire to love and serve Christ.

4. In the ancient custom of the Church, everybody who went to Mass went to Holy Communion. All who were present communicated — this fact is most clear in all the early accounts of Holy Communion. There were distinct orders for all who went to Mass to communicate. Nobody dreamed of going to Mass without going to Holy Communion, and the greatest care was taken to exclude from Mass all who were not fit to take part and go to Communion. Indeed the very rite of the Mass places the people's Communion immediately after the priest's Communion. Priest and people partake of the Holy Sacrifice.

5. Pope Pius X said, "Holy Communion is the shortest and surest way to Heaven." Get into the habit of going and you will feel in your innermost soul that this is true: nay more, that it is a foretaste of heaven. By frequent Communion you will understand how keen were the early Christians never to miss Communion when they went to Mass. It is true that the Church has let down the bars of discipline since these days. The reason, of course, is that many people abused this royal privilege, early fervor having cooled sadly. Again many were not able or willing to keep the long fast; their flesh was weak, their spirit not sturdy enough. Hence the Church's ancient discipline is no longer in effect. But we must remember what is her mind in this matter; namely, that the faithful unite with the priest in the great and holy action (the Mass)

DOMINE NON SUM DIGNUS

and share with him the Victim, in Holy Communion received sacramentally. This is to complete and perfect the great action in which it is our privilege to have a real part.

Nothing is more needful nowadays than to insist much upon the right viewpoint, so generally overlooked — to the loss of the interests of mind and heart and soul. Until we realize the essential part of Communion in the sacrifice of the Mass, and make up our mind to go often, the loss of many graces will be ours. It is good to see crowds at the Communion rail at every Mass, because that shows how many more are mustering in for the more active service of Christ, our Captain.

EARLY SYMBOL OF CHRIST

For our further instruction it is good to go back in spirit to the early days when Christians heard Mass and went to Holy Communion at the risk of their lives. What examples they left! What genuine heroism! Jammed up against them as they crowded into a catacomb might be a traitor or a spy, who had squeezed in to report what the Christians were doing. A constant happening, this. So, among the early Christians, one of the first acts was to watch the door lest a spy got into their meeting place. There is something stirring in studying the old documents portraying their acts.

Very ancient directions for receiving Holy Communion were as follows: After the sacrifice has been made, let each rank severally partake of the Lord's body and of the precious blood, approaching in rank and reverence and godly fear as to the body of a king; and let the women draw near with veiled heads, as befits the rank of women. And let the doors be watched, lest any unbelieving or uninitiated person enter. "By ranks" was understood the several orders of the clergy and ascetics, according to dignity, then laymen, then women (Apostolic Constitutions).

Do not fail to note the sacrifices these people made, the risks they ran of capture, imprisonment, and martyrdom, in order to hear Mass. The courage born of Christ was in their hearts. Secretly they forgathered in the Catacombs, in fastnesses, in private houses. They received Holy Communion day or night as the time was most propitious. Nightly Communions were common even in the third century. Tertullian (160 A.D.) tells of a heathen husband who would not allow his Christian wife to pass the night from home, lest she go to Mass and Communion. But when the Church received its freedom, set hours began to be appointed for Holy Communion. Usually one hour, nine o'clock, the third hour of the Roman day. Observe this was the hour in which Christ was nailed to the cross on Calvary. Centuries back Pope Telesphorus (127–138 A.D.) decreed *"ut nullus ante horam tertiam sacrificium offere præsumeret."* Thus it was in the early centuries of the Church before ancient discipline was relaxed.

A few more examples of early Church procedure will prove of interest. The Kiss of Peace was given before Communion as a sign of unity and fellowship in Christ. This was part of the Eucharistic service and occurred where we now say "The Peace of God be with you always. And with thy spirit." Then, too, the Host, while in some cases it was put in the mouth as now, in others was given into the hand of the one about to receive it; and women had to cover their hand with a white cloth, called the *dominicale.* When the precious blood was received, every one drank from the chalice, not touching it with the lips but by means of a reed or a tube of gold or silver, in order to prevent spilling.

For some time no lay person was allowed to receive in the sanctuary, save the Roman emperor.

What an inspiring thing is the story of those early Masses! They were said, and people went eagerly to Mass and Communion, even when persecutions raged. You can go back in imagination to those troublous times. Every one of us recognizes what courage and loyalty were possessed by those early Christians. Nobody with any knowledge of history would dare to deny the facts. We know how many heroes risked their lives daily to go to Holy Communion; for their comings and goings, their ways and words were closely observed by pagan neighbors, who called them "flesh eaters," "cannibals," "enemies of the empire." We also know that our Lord in the Blessed Sacrament gave them the courage, the joy, the spiritual resistance that made them the envy even of their persecutors. By the grace of God, their spirit was active, free, unafraid. Standing out boldly before their tormentors, these forerunners of ours in the Faith, often tender virgins, often mere boys, were stronger than Cæsar. What mastery they had over themselves! What moral courage! What spiritual strength! They were giants of God. We feel a fine thrill as we read what they said and did in the face of their foes. Often we wonder how they did it! The main fact is that they loved our Lord. The triumphant certainty is that Holy Communion gave them divine strength to defy the world. After all is said, that kind of strength is the one thing we need in our life. You can get it only by going often to Holy Communion. You will have good reason to worry if you neglect the great graces our Lord offers you, when He comes in the Mass and says: "Friend, come up higher!" It ill behooves us to neglect that invitation.

The best way to approach sainthood is by keeping close

to Christ. Make up your mind, then, to go to Holy Communion, sacramentally, as often as you go to Mass. If that is impossible, be sure to go spiritually; that is, make a spiritual communion. This is the union of your mind and heart with the sacred body of Jesus Christ. You can join your mind, will, affections with our Lord and ask Him to make you a more worthy child.

ROMAN SACRIFICES
Showing the ox led to the slaughter.

1. What is a religious vocation? 2. Now is the time for boys and girls to pray that God may make clear to them just what He wants them to do in the future. Does He will for them a vocation for the religious life or an avocation? If it is a vocation, then it is a great grace. To some our Lord says: "Come up higher!" Now this is a call in one's inmost soul. God wants to draw such a one closer to Himself. If, instead of answering that call one stays away and refuses the higher seat, then another will take it. Such is a lost vocation. Read Luke xiv, 7–11. No greater grace can come to a boy or girl than the call to the religious vocation, the invitation to serve God in a convent, in a brotherhood, or in

the priesthood. Look back and see whether the call has come to you. 3. Have you prayed hard to know just what God wants you to do? 4. Down to about the twelfth century the normal way of receiving Communion was under both kinds everywhere. Then the change came, and Communion in the Latin Church was received under one kind only. Do you know why? Is it still received under both kinds anywhere in the Catholic Church? Explain. 5. In the history of the Church could a lay person ever give Holy Communion? Would the Church permit you to do so under any circumstance? Look up the history of the administering of Holy Communion in the early Christian ages.

XXXV

COMMUNION

After the people's Communion, the priest replaces the ciborium in the tabernacle, makes a genuflection, and closes the door. Then the altar boy pours a little wine into the chalice and the priest drinks it, the first ablution, saying " Quod ore sumpsimus." The priest then goes over to the epistle side, where the altar boy pours wine and water over the priest's fingers into the chalice. That done, the priest returns to the middle of the altar, wipes his fingers, and takes the second ablution, saying the Corpus tuum. He next wipes his lips and the chalice. Having purified and covered the chalice, he goes to the epistle side of the altar and there reads the antiphon called Communion.

From very early days this prayer was sung. The Church resounded with joy all during the time of the priest's and people's Communion. At first the hymn was a psalm, such as "Taste and see that the Lord is sweet" (Psalms xxxiii). A dim memory of all that long-drawn joyous chant still survives in the short form used to-day. The priest, his thoughts and emotions fully occupied with our Saviour in his breast, murmurs the short prayer — Communio. It is full of joy. But no longer is it a whole psalm ; now we have only the antiphon or a fragment of the Scriptures, such as this one from the second Mass of Christmas :

Exsulta, filia Sion; lauda, filia Jerusalem : ecce Rex tuus venit sanctus, et Salvator mundi.	Rejoice greatly, O daughter of Sion; shout for joy, O daughter of Jerusalem : behold thy King cometh, holy and the Saviour of the world (Zacharias ix).

COMMUNION

The Sacrifice proper has come to an end when the priest receives the body and blood of the Lamb of God in Holy Communion. This is indeed the marriage supper of the Lamb. "Let us be glad and rejoice, and give glory to Him, for the marriage of the Lamb is come. Blessed are they that are called to the marriage supper of the Lamb. . . ." Precious truths, truths exceedingly precious, that we must make real for our soul. Never forget that it was for us that Christ offered Himself in sacrifice. Just before the first Mass, our Lord said: "With desire have I desired to eat this Pasch with you." And later in the Mass He said: "Take ye and eat, this is my body which is given for you." "And this is my blood of the New Testament": the eternal covenant of love and friendship, of the contract between the soul and its divine Spouse. Therefore St. Paul truly says: "He is the mediator of the New Testament, that by means of his death (the Lamb mystically slain on our altar and mystically consumed in Holy Communion) for the redemption of those trangressions which were under the former testament, they that are called (that is we ourselves) may receive the promise of eternal inheritance" (Hebrews ix, 15).

On this promise of the eternal inheritance our Lord gives the most outspoken statements. These are His words:

I am the Vine, you are the branches . . . abide in Me (John xv, 1-16).
With desire I have desired to eat this Pasch with you (Luke xxii, 14-20).
Except you eat the flesh of the Son of Man and drink His blood you shall not have life in you (John vi, 53-59).

So clear is our Lord's way of stating the truth of Holy Communion as to leave no shadow of a doubt. He proves this by a wealth of evidence. Nothing could be plainer.

What a wonderful love, then, is God's love for the soul! What a gift to us of Himself! The body of our Lord, the same that was sacrificed on the cross to glorify the Father, becomes the food of our souls; an assurance of the glory of heaven; a pledge of eternal happiness; a viaticum to help us on our journey heavenward. Well could St. Andrew exclaim: "We have an altar whereon day by day I offer up to God, the Almighty, the One and the True, not the flesh of bulls nor the blood of goats, but a Lamb without spot: and when all they that believe have eaten the flesh thereof, the Lamb that was slain abideth whole and liveth!"

Christ lives in the communicant, the communicant in Christ. "He that eateth my flesh and drinketh my blood, abideth in me and I in him." "As the branch cannot bear fruit of itself, except it abides in the vine, no more can you except you abide in me." Thus in Holy Communion one abides in Christ, becomes incorporate with Him. The soul clings to Christ, whose precious body and blood cleave to its affections. Christ's thoughts and feelings and ways and tastes intertwine with the soul's, like the vine with its branches, so close is the soul's union with Christ in Holy Communion!

It is those who go faithfully to Communion with this ever in mind—who get to know Christ better, love Him more and more, and keep His Commandments day in and day out. Of course none of us is really worthy. If we were waiting till we were worthy, why we should never go to Mass, or to Benediction, not to mention Holy Communion. The point is: Christ wants us to go. He has said so. More than that, He has put us at ease, made it less hard for us to go to Him, by veiling His Godhead under the appearances of bread and wine. None of us could see Him as He really is and live. See what happened to the mob in the

COMMUNION

Garden of Gethsemane when Christ faced them for a moment and showed them His preternatural power (John xviii, 4–9). It was the divine majesty of Jesus which produced that effect upon the mob that came with swords and clubs to capture Him. He did something like that, also, to the buyers and sellers in the temple (Matthew xxi, 12). In both cases they were foes who were thus treated. But our dear Lord does not want to overwhelm His friends with awe, let alone terror, when they come into His mystical presence.

Lastly, consider that Christ wants us to come, nay, tells us to come. And why? Because we need Him. Holy Communion is not a luxury, but a plain necessity, as necessary for our soul as food is for our body. Moreover, it is a medicine for the ills of our soul and body to receive the divine Physician into our hearts. He will cure us by degrees, just as a tonic taken regularly will restore our tired body to health and strength. By slow, insensible degrees, the tonic of Christ remedies your spiritual ills, enables you gradually to overcome bad habits, so that your soul grows strong in the grace of God, in love of Christ, and undying service in the keeping of His commands.

1. What is viaticum? 2. Just how would you prepare the table in a sick room when the priest is coming with Holy Communion? 3. Do you know what the candle symbolizes? How many are to be used at the various services in church? 4. Define "frequent Communion." 5. Why do we fast from midnight when we are to go to the Holy Table? 6. Explain the etiquette of going to Holy Communion, with reasons. 7. We often wonder how much time boys and girls give, outside church, to their preparation for Holy Communion. Surely we all feel that much time is due God, who is on His way to come under our soul's roof. That is a matter of Catholic hospitality. How much time do you give to tidying things up in your heart before He reaches there?

PART FOUR

XXXVI

POST COMMUNION

The Communion prayer having been said, next comes the Dominus vobiscum, finally the Post Communion, which is the last prayer read on the epistle side of the altar.

A Dominus vobiscum heralds the fact that we are leaving the heights of Calvary. The Mass now runs quickly on to the end. This finale of the great drama is very interesting. You cannot help noticing that the action and movement are swift as the liturgy draws to a close. There is also much joy in the prayer. Throughout the Mass, to be sure, there is noticeable a spirit of gratitude. The Mass theme is thanksgiving with constant variations; but in this last part of the Mass the spirit of thanksgiving becomes the vocal, the outstanding one, and receives additional variations. Study its theme — this fugue of prayer. The keynote having been struck in the Communion with its eternal inner message, the harmonious melody in praise of Emmanuel continues on. "Up vistaed hope it speeds." Dominus vobiscum follows quickly on Dominus vobiscum. The praise grows in fullness and harmony in the Post Communion; it continues in joyous rush as it reaches the Last Gospel with its vision of life, eternal beckoning and inviting; and its notes terminate gloriously in the Last Blessing, followed by the exultant expression, *Deo Gratias:* Thanks be to God.

Now let us study the Post Communion. Coming from the center of the altar where the Dominus vobiscum has just been said, the priest reads (or sings) this prayer, which generally contains an allusion to the Communion just received. Originally it was a thanksgiving prayer, so called because it came after the Communion (Post Communion). "*Oremus*" the priest says; that is, "Let us pray." The duty is implied of making thanksgiving for the great privilege of having assisted at Mass and received Holy Communion. The Post Communion, therefore, is a short theme of thanksgiving. It is also, indeed always, a petition — a prayer to be enabled to make good use of the graces of Holy Mass and to apply them in one's daily life. The following is the Post Communion of the Second Mass of Christmas:

Oremus:	Let us Pray:
Hujus nos, Domine, sacramenti semper novitas natalis instauret: cujus nativitas singularis humanem repulit vetustatem.	May this birthday renewal of this Sacrament ever restore us, O Lord, Whose wondrous birth hath banished human decadence.
Per eundem Dominum nostrum Jesum Christum, Filium tuum, qui tecum vivat et regnat in unitate Spiritus Sancti, Deus per omnia sæcula sæculorum. Amen.	Through the same Jesus Christ, Thy Son, our Lord, who liveth and reigneth with Thee in the unity of the Holy Ghost, God, world without end. Amen.

That is the spirit of the Post Communion. See how it is reflected in a famous Catholic. Some of the most beautiful Masses ever composed came from the pen of Joseph Haydn, the father of the modern symphony. This genius, without means, modest and retiring, lived in a wretched garret room. With an old worm-eaten spinet, which he managed to buy cheaply, he worked and played. But he had a heart full of the love of God, of joy and humor; and in this poverty-stricken room, when only eighteen years of age, he composed and played, in 1750, his first Mass. Think of that — at eighteen — high-school age! All through a long life a beautiful spirit of joy was his and he was known everywhere as the "cheerful-hearted" because joy fairly bubbled out of his words, his works, his music. A celebrated musical

POST COMMUNION

critic says: "With Haydn, humor is a prominent characteristic. He might well be characterized the father of humorous tone poetry. His humor consoles the disappointed and soothes the sorrowful. His faith was never troubled with doubts. Joyfully accepting the teachings of the Church, his religion was that of purest belief in an omnipotent and omnipresent Creator." In referring to the period of the composition of his creation, the great Catholic composer is reported to have said: "I never was so devout as then. Daily I prayed for strength to express myself in accordance with His will." All the scores of Haydn's most important works are subscribed "In nomine Domini" and conclude with "Soli Deo Gloria" or "Laus Deo." He was a true Catholic, one who from childhood was full of the Catholic spirit of joy. It is said that a friend once asked him why his church music was so full of gladness. He answered: "I cannot make it otherwise. I write according to the thoughts I feel. When I think upon my God, my heart is so full of joy that the notes dance and leap from my pen. And since God has given me a cheerful heart it will be pardoned me that I serve Him with a cheerful spirit."

Is that not the spirit every Catholic should have, and keep, and never lose? And with what joy can the Mass fill our heart! What consolation it brings to our soul! Well may we be glad! "Joy," says a thinker, "is the vivid pleasure or delight inspired by immediate reception of something peculiarly grateful, of something obviously productive of an essential advantage, or of something which promises to contribute to our present or future well-being." The Mass gives us all this — light, truth, grace. Hence we rejoice in the Lord; but we want to rejoice always. Thanksgiving is the spirit we want to keep all the day long, even as we possess it now at the end of Mass. Joy is something to which we now have a right. The satisfaction of being near our beloved Saviour, of having heard Mass, of knowing that "it is well with us" — all that is ours. And we do not want to lose it. Why should joy die away from young hearts? It need not. God gives it to our youth. "I will go unto the altar of God, to God who giveth joy to my youth," sings the Psalmist. Nothing save sin can rob you of your joy. Sin entered the Garden of Eden and spoiled life for Adam and Eve. Sin does the same to souls nowadays. Therefore we must be on the watch against sin in every form, especially in the form it takes to tempt youth and spoil joy.

There are three wily forms of sin — suspicion, spite, and small talk. They try to creep into the soul; if they succeed, they take all joy out of life. Note them well.

First, guard against anything that resembles *false suspicion*. Zacharias the Prophet counsels us: "Let none of you imagine evil in your heart against his friend" (Zacharias viii, 17). It is the spirited, cheerful, manly, honest boy, the sweet, amiable, open-minded, unselfish girl that give joy to life. Just as soon as the door of your mind is opened to suspicion its repose of confidence is shaken. Have a care, then, lest your soul become a prey to this sin of false suspicion. Look the truth in the face; do not trust your feelings. Some people are quick to feel and weak to hide their feelings and impotent to control them. They become meanspirited and suspicious. They never think that the fault is their own, not their friend's, and they will not yield in the line they have taken. Instead of removing the false impression or uprooting the suspicion, they cling to the view that others will play them false. Forthwith their confidence dwindles. That is to be untrue to oneself, unjust to others.

The oldest book on record dates back at least to 3500 B.C. It is of Egyptian origin and is now known as the Prisse Papyrus. The author's name is Pita-Hotep; he was a sage, wise and venerable. In his book he advises all to live and act with cheerfulness. "Let thy face be cheerful as long as thou livest; has any one come out of his coffin after having once entered it?" These are his words. They dimly foreshadow the duty of every Christian as taught by our Lord. Anything that chills cheerfulness chills Christianity. Suspicion does just that. So, if you find a suspicion growing in your mind, get at the root of it right away. Rid yourself of it at once. Combat the thought. Ridicule it out of existence. Give no place to it in your soul. If you do not do that now, the task will be all the harder later on, for suspicion is like a wild weed. It grows deeper and deeper every day. If you let rash thoughts go thus far, further misunderstanding and dissension will result. A long-smouldering suspicion will leap suddenly into well-defined purpose, and then, alas! the ill is done. Thus suspicion inevitably spoils friendship. Enduring friendship calls for unselfishness: isn't this just what we ask:

Give me for my friend one who will unite with me hand and heart, who will throw himself into my cause, who will take my part when I am attacked, and who wishes others to love me as heartily as he.

See, then, how real friendship casts out suspicion and jealousy. "Of course," said Cardinal Newman, "I wish as much as possible to agree with all my friends; but if in spite of my utmost efforts they go beyond me or come short of me, I can't help it, and take it easy." That is the right way.

So remember that suspicion is the index finger of selfishness. "It creates its own cause. Distrust begets reason for distrust." Is it any wonder that people of that type are prone to misunderstanding, bickerings, accusations, false judgments? Naturally they deprive themselves and others of peace and the joy of life.

Spite takes all joy out of life. Somebody crosses the spiteful person's path, then that person is hurt, peevish, sullen. His pride has been offended, a quick sense of resentment follows, and he awaits the opportunity to strike back. Now all that is sheer stupidity. It's stupid to be spiteful, just as "it is stupid to fight; it always spoils a good argument."[1] Worse than that, spite has a way of sapping at the spirit of joy, drying it up, and leaving in the soul a feeling of petty resentment and sullen dislike. Could anything be more joyless than that?

Moreover, spiteful people are always looking for trivial triumphs. These triumphs generally cause fresh irritations — more snubs, sometimes polite, sometimes insolent, then slights or grudges, smiles intended to wound, raised eyebrows, shrugged shoulders. These things spoil peace; they slay good will. Have you not often seen how ugly is the result of spitefulness? By degrees any desire for unity is cast to the winds, friendships are gone forever; for chilly reception makes an end of good will. What a pity! Some people will go for days carrying the venom of spite in their veins until a chance presents itself of venting it on somebody who has injured them. One evil never justifies a second.

Rid your soul of every temptation to be spiteful. Forget the pagan maxim: "An eye for an eye, a tooth for a tooth, a claw for a claw." That may be all right for brute animals; it is not for Christians. To be spiteful is the meanest form of narrow-mindedness. It is to keep the root of bitterness growing in the soul, ugly, hacked, twisted,

[1] G. K. Chesterton.

hideous. Spite in the soul is like the ill-smelling phosphorus that burns on the surface of water. Watch it float and give forth smoke and bad odor.

Small talk. By this is not meant witty and pleasant conversation. Nothing is more wholesome. Sometimes, however, girls or boys grouping together say bitter things about somebody, pass a harsh sentence, throw out the ill-reflecting word that hurts a companion. Of what Jack is said to have done. Did you hear this about Jill? Do you believe it? I heard that —— So it goes on. One may never check up and blue pencil each false idea or stay to see that it does not square with cold fact. Small talk is just this; to go on airing the abusive word, the cutting remark, the stinging comment, the nasty hint, the ugly chit-chat. That sort of talk is sinister. Some schoolgirls repeat evil reports on the slightest hearsay. And boys sometimes rake up the personal faults and defects, even the sins, of others; and they do not scruple to let their tongues run riot, like a fire. They express unfavorable opinions of others, seldom let them have a chance to speak for their own side, do not even give them an opportunity to defend themselves. That is not just. It is to turn "justice into bitterness and the fruits of justice into wormwood" (Amos vi, 13).

The great danger in small talk is that it is so often snap judgment, rash judgment, false judgment. And how often what is said is a lie! Now a lie is an ugly thing to have any part in. Do we ever think how much every lie gains in the telling? "Every man is bound to leave a story better than he found it." "For the tongue," warns St. James, no man can tame, an unquiet evil, full of deadly poison. Read the whole of Chapter III of St. James' Epistle. Scandalous tongues are long, incredibly long; they drip with poison, and they harm all they touch. There is just the danger of small talk. It is apt to, and generally does, debase itself into vulgar gossip, scandal, and calumny.

It is as plain as day. One glad pupil is worth a roomful of grouches. Joy and happiness and good nature are like perfumes, which spread their fragrance everywhere. You cannot pour them on those about you without getting a few drops on yourself. On the other hand, small talk takes the joy out of life, sets people at odds, engenders ill feeling. Beware, then, of using words that wound. Fight shy of the girl whose talk is a mere flow of cheap hints and comments, or the boy who, to use a phrase of Shakespeare, "is a very superficial, ignorant, unweighing fellow." Their words weave a dark cloud about your brain if you pay attention to them. Have you the courage to frown on that sort of thing? Make up your mind to avoid small-talkers once for all. You know how they break up friendship and spoil class spirit.

> If all the good people were clever
> And all that were clever were good
> The world would be better than ever
> We thought that it possibly could.
> But alas! it is seldom or never
> These two "hit it off" as they should
> For the good are so harsh to the clever
> The clever so rude to the good.

Notice how the saints, having avoided the above-mentioned failings, had the real spirit of joy, even when face to face with death. The darkest perils did not make their hearts afraid. They fought down all human fears. They were heroes, detached from the world and attached loyally to Christ. Certainly the rising generation should have clear ideas of those eminent people. Let us make the acquaintance of a few of them. The science of joy, gone

POST COMMUNION

farthest away these days, is the science of those saints. Let us also master their secret, and strive to imitate them even a little.

1. Name four saints known for the spirit of joy they possessed. 2. What characters has history noted down for their happy dispositions? 3. Do you remember five places in the Mass where the prayers are brimful of joy? Give them. 4. What do you think is the most joyous note in the whole Mass?

XXXVII

ITE, MISSA EST: BENEDICTIO

At the end of the Post Communion the altar boy answers, "Amen." Then the priest closes the missal, goes to the middle of the altar, turns to the people, and says " Dominus vobiscum." Comes next the Ite, missa est, said while the priest is still facing the people; after that the Placeat is said and the Last Blessing bestowed.

Communion having been received, thanksgiving and petition concluded, it is time for the dismissal of the congregation. The priest comes back to the middle of the altar and turns to the people, saying:

P. Dominus vobiscum.	P. The Lord be with you.
A. Et cum spiritu tuo.	A. And with thy spirit.
P. Ite, Missa est.	P. Go, the Mass is ended.
A. Deo gratias.	A. Thanks be to God.

The Ite, missa est is a most ancient formula of dismissal. For years many a mind was puzzled as to its real significance. What precisely do those words denote? Quaintly enough, they mean: Go, it is the dismissal. The custom was to proclaim the words *Missa est* when assemblies, civil or religious, were dismissed. "In churches and palaces and judgment halls the dismissal (*missa*) is proclaimed to take place when the people are dismissed from attendance" (Avitus, Archbishop of Vienne, A.D. 490).

The congregation is on the point of going. If, however, the day was one of penance, instead of the Ite, missa est the Benedicamus Domino with its Deo gratias was recited, and

ITE MISSA EST: BENEDICTIO

the people stayed in church to say more prayers. In olden times they used to wait for certain prayers, but when the Ite, missa est was said they were free to depart. But many did not leave the church then. Long after the procession they stayed to carry on their private devotions, just as in our own days many are found praying in church after Mass is over. By degrees those private devotions were crystallized into definite form; then they were added on as part of the Mass. Thus you have the Placeat, the Last Blessing, and the Last Gospel, late additions to the text of the Mass. So now the Ite, missa est is said, but the end is not yet.

There still remain three prayers. The first of these is the Placeat. Its origin is like the origin of so many prayers — an outburst of praise and thanksgiving. After the old Mass with its end in the Ite, missa est, the priest coming out of the sanctuary would be full of gratitude for the great graces of the Mass. Instinctively he would praise God in his heart, and even his hands were raised to bless all about him. A writer of the eleventh century relates how the priests blessed the people as they started to go out. Even before leaving the altar he would bend over and kiss the altar and would say a prayer before giving the blessing. This prayer became the Placeat tibi, and was finally accorded a fixed place in the Mass.

Placeat tibi, sancta Trinitas, obsequium servitutis meæ; et præsta, ut sacrificium quod oculis tuæ Majestatis indignus obtuli, tibi sit acceptabile, mihique, et omnibus pro quibus illud obtuli, sit, te miserante, propitiabile. Per Christum Dominum nostrum. Amen.	May the performance of my homage be pleasing to Thee, O Holy Trinity; and grant that the sacrifice which I, though unworthy, have offered up in the sight of Thy Majesty may be acceptable to Thee, and, through Thy mercy, be a propitiation for me and all those for whom it has been offered. Through Christ our Lord. Amen.

After this comes the Last Blessing. It was Pius V (1566–1572) who added the Placeat, this blessing, and the Last Gospel as part of the thanksgiving following the Mass. Hence, in this place, the priest, having turned to the altar and begged in the Placeat that the sacrifice just offered should be acceptable to Almighty God for bringing His people closer to Him, proceeds to give the Last Blessing. You notice that the priest bends down and kisses the altar. Raising his eyes to heaven, extending, raising, and then joining his hands, he next inclines his head, then turns round to the congregation. With his right hand extended he makes the sign of the cross toward the people, saying in a clear voice:

Benedicat vos omnipotens Deus: Pater, et Filius, ✠ et Spiritus Sanctus. Amen.	May Almighty God, the Father, Son, ✠ and Holy Ghost, bless you. Amen.

With these words the divine benignity is invoked upon the people at Mass. Thereupon, with deep devotion, we should bless ourselves. A beautiful blessing this, imparted from the very heart of our Holy Mother, and with all the weight of authority belonging to her who is the well-beloved spouse of Christ. So with this deep and efficacious wish of the Church for the spiritual and temporal good of her children, we are assured of the highest prayers and invocations on our behalf. This blessing, remember, is a rite performed in the name and with the authority of the Church by the priest, who invokes divine favor upon the people. Really it is Christ whose hand is raised over us in benediction, when His blessing is invoked. One with the Father and the Holy Ghost, He bestows upon us in the Mass that help and grace which He sees we need most.

The custom of giving blessings goes back to the very

ITE MISSA EST: BENEDICTIO

beginning of days. At the completion of the creative work of each day, God's blessing was forthwith pronounced. "And God saw that it was good. And He blessed —— " When Noah came out of the ark, "God blessed Noah and his sons" (Genesis ix, 1). Thereafter the head of each tribe gave his blessing, calling on God to preserve and grant peace to the object of his good will. In the Bible you can trace out, age after age, how this practice obtained everywhere among the Chosen People. "Blessed art thou," said David, "and it shall be well with thee." Thus was expressed the wish that all good fortune, natural and supernatural, should accompany a person.

Not otherwise was it in the New Dispensation. Any one must have observed how often our Lord blessed people: the little children, the lame, the blind, the lepers. And His Apostles did the same thing. Says St. Paul to the Philippians: "May the peace of God which surpasseth all understanding, keep your hearts and your minds in Jesus Christ; may He supply all your wants out of the richness of His goodness" (Philippians iv, 7).

CHRIST
(Cathedral of Amiens.)

As was to be expected, this custom so elevated, so ennobled by the Son of God Himself, was adopted by the Church. Blessings abound in the life of the Church. They fall from the lips of our Holy Mother on her children, on objects connected with religion, with daily life and sustenance. Nowhere, however, is the liturgical blessing so fraught with grace as in the Mass; hence when the priest pronounces it, be sure to bless yourself slowly and prayerfully, uniting your wish, your dearest hope with that of the celebrant.

Blessings, you will note, are closely associated with processions. The Church wants us to be mindful of both. They recall to us our Lord and His disciples going along the roads of Judea, Samaria, and Galilee. That is why the Church so loves them. In the old days, along with many blessings, there were many processions. Writing on this subject, Edith Pearson says:

We shall find they stand for so much, symbolize so many things, are an epitome of so much beauty of order, symmetry, recollection, worship, perfect deportment, of humble adoration, and are a manifestation of faith that shines afar.

The body of a procession is of no avail without the soul of it; it is but an empty show of display.

Is there any more impressive sight than a well-arranged procession of the Blessed Sacrament? It has a power to draw souls to humility and reverence, to wonder of worship, and adoration, in our churches or out in the gardens and streets. The King of kings passing the humblest of His children; the Lord of lords among His loving servants, the disciples of His love. Every effort has been made to make it (even so far off being worthy as it is) as perfect as human effort can. Flowers and lights, rich vestments, swinging censers, spotlessly clad choristers and acolytes, innocent little ones in snow-white muslin, old-time confraternities and devotional laymen; and all preceding the canopied, jeweled Monstrance held aloft by the chief priest as the notes of the "Pange Lingua" swell in the breezes of July, or through the Gothic arches of some stately cathedral as the organ peals, or in the village chapel or wayside city churches. No matter where, the effect is the result of love and worship.

There is another symbolic meaning, the adoration of Nature, the strewn petals at His feet, the beautiful shrines of flowers and lights as the procession wends its way, and our Lord stays to bless as He reaches the points of rest. The lighted torches of burning wax for the Light of the World; the wreaths of incense from the exotic trees; the richest silk for the vestments, and precious stones from the mountain's depths around

ITE MISSA EST: BENEDICTIO

the little Pyx: all come with one beat of love and adoration in the greatest procession of all.

Just as soon as the Last Blessing is bestowed we are near the end of Mass. The soul, made strong by grace, knows what to do with truth. Faith and hope work hand in hand. Joy is yet the keynote to which the spirit of worship is attuned. "The expectation of the creature waiteth for the revelation of the sons of God" (Romans viii, 20). Can we keep that spirit? Yes, but how? By loyalty to the Eucharistic Lord whose great blessings we have just received.

1. This part of the Mass is athrob with love and thanksgiving. Explain why. 2. Name two memorable processions that took place during our Lord's time. 3. Nowadays where do you meet with great processions? 4. On what days of the year does your school take part in outdoor processions? What decorum should then be observed? Define reverence. Why are such processions held out of doors? 5. Do you know the Pange Lingua Gloriosi? How many hymns in honor of our Lady do you know by heart? 6. Describe two miracles wrought by our Lord when He was walking along the roads of Palestine.

XXXVIII

THE LAST GOSPEL

Just as soon as the Last Blessing is given, the priest moves over to the gospel side of the altar. There he makes the sign of the cross, first upon the altar, and then upon his forehead, lips, and breast, and begins the Gospel, according to St. John. At the words, " Et verbum caro factum est," he genuflects. At the end of the Gospel, the altar boy says, " Deo gratias."

Standing once more, when the priest, having given the Last Blessing, goes to the gospel side of the altar, you read with him the Gospel of St. John. This is the last addition made to the ceremonial of the Mass. It is, as it were, giving final honor to Christ, hailing His words over again, in His own house, among His own kin. And that is why the Gospel is read, even after the people have been told that they may go away. The beginning of St. John's Gospel (John i, 1–14) was the object of special devotion from the time of the Fathers. St. Augustine tells of a man who wanted this text to be written in letters of gold in every church. In the Middle Ages there were all manner of curious, often extraordinary, practices connected with it. People wrote it on amulets and wore it as a charm. It was sometimes said at Baptism and at Extreme Unction. Then as a favorite devotion it was said by priests after Mass.

Thus, by steady degrees, this beautiful Gospel won its way into the Mass. Pope Pius V in 1570 admitted it as part of the Mass. You might say it was through the indefatigable persistence of priests and people who were fired

THE LAST GOSPEL

with love for this word of God. Surely that is just as it should be. If that was the mind and will of our forefathers in the faith, then it is for us to love and appreciate that Last Gospel. No ideas on earth are so true, so powerful as those it furnishes. It is so full of light from on high that in its light you can see the True Light. It is needed nowadays to draw men together in the spirit of Christian coöperation and brotherhood. It is also needed to guide us all in the way of truth and to inspire us with an unfading vision. As a prelude to the Last Gospel, we have:

P. Dominus vobiscum.	P. The Lord be with you.
A. Et cum spiritu tuo.	A. And with thy spirit.
P. Initium sancti evangelii secundum Ioannem.	P. The beginning of the Holy Gospel according to St. John.
A. Gloria tibi, Domine.	A. Glory be to Thee, O Lord.

Like a knot of love, tied ever so many times in the Mass, this last Dominus vobiscum binds our souls in a union, one with another, and all with Christ, about whom we are going to learn yet more in this Gospel. What way more fitting than this to terminate the Holy Sacrifice and do honor to Him who has come to the tabernacle to be among us. We do well to want to know more about Christ. Evidently there was great wisdom displayed by the Church when over three hundred years ago, she inserted this Last Gospel in the Roman rite of the Mass.

The Mass, to be sure, has made us know and love our Lord very much, in so far as we have tried to awaken ourselves to a vigorous and varied exertion of all our faculties: mind, heart, will, and affections, to draw near to the divine Master. Yet we want to know more and more about Him. It is true we can never fully master "'all about Christ': who He is, what He does." "But there are many other things which Jesus did, which, if they were written every one, the world itself, I think, would not be able to contain the books that should be written" (St. John xxi, 25). Nevertheless we want to grasp firmly the character of Christ, to fill our mind with "Jesus Christ and Him crucified," for He is the true light of every mind, the "First Sayer of our every true word, the First Thinker of our every true thought."

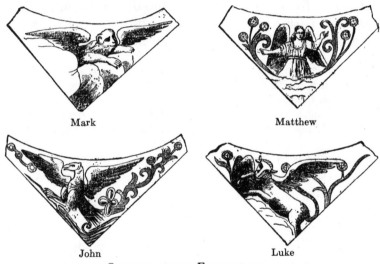

SYMBOLS OF THE EVANGELISTS

Besides, no time could be better than now for a holy retrospect. When a friend leaves us after a visit, we like to tell about him: who he is, where he came from, how long we have known him. Naturally we do the same with our changeless Friend. The Evangelists have told us a lot about Jesus, for which we love them dearly. We even have symbols for the Gospel writers which explain just what they tell us of our Lord. Thus the "face of a man" is the symbol for St. Matthew, whose first chapter describes the generation

THE LAST GOSPEL

of Christ. The Gospel of Mark opens with the prophecy of Isaias about John the Baptist proclaiming our Lord's coming. The Baptist, you know, was the voice in the wilderness, where he lived for thirty years amid lions and other wild beasts; because Mark begins with the Baptist, the second evangelist is often represented by the face of a lion. Luke's symbol is an ox, because of all the Gospel writers St. Luke treated most freely of our Lord's sufferings and death when He was offered as a sacrifice for our sins; and the ox, of course, serves as a symbol of sacrifice. Finally, St. John is pictured as an eagle since his Gospel flight is straight up into the bosom of the Godhead. Swifter than an eagle he takes us upward on wings of faith, where we learn "the truth that is in Jesus." In the beginning the Word was in the bosom of the Father, the same Word that was made of flesh and dwelt among us. In the revelation of the Word, John summons before us a marvelous series of events. Winged words, those! They rise up inspired, immortal from his pen. On them, as on pinions, we are borne aloft, and given an ever clearer presentiment of divine things.

"In the four Gospels," writes St. Augustine, "or rather in the four books of the one Gospel, St. John the Apostle, not undeservedly in respect of his spiritual understanding compared to the eagle, has elevated his preaching higher and far more sublimely than the other three; and in this elevating of it he would have our hearts likewise lifted up. For the other three evangelists walk with the Lord on earth as with a man; concerning His divinity they have said but little; but this evangelist, as if he disdained to walk on earth, just as in the very opening of his discourse he thundered on us, soared not only above the earth and above the whole compass of air and sky, but even above the whole army of angels and the whole order of invisible powers and reached to Him by Whom all things were made; saying, 'In the beginning was the Word!'" (Tractate xxvi on St. John's Gospel.)

In most Masses the Gospel of St. John is said. It is taken from the first Chapter:

In principio erat Verbum, et Verbum erat apud Deum, et Deus erat Verbum. Hoc erat in principio apud Deum. Omnia per ipsum facta sunt, et sine ipso factum est nihil quod factum est. In ipso vita erat, et vita erat lux hominum: et lux in tenebris lucet, et tenebræ eam non comprehenderunt.	In the beginning was the Word, and the Word was with God, and the Word was God: the same was in the beginning with God. All things were made by Him, and without Him was made nothing that was made: in Him was life and the life was the light of men; and the light shineth in the darkness, and the darkness did not comprehend it.

Next John tells of the mission of Christ's forerunner, John the Baptist, who was not the light, but whose mission was to bear witness to it, and to reflect it:

Fuit homo missus a Deo, cui nomen erat Joannes. Hic venit in testimonium ut testimonium perhiberet de lumine, ut omnes crederent per illum. Non erat ille lux, sed ut testimonium perhiberet de lumine. Erat lux vera quæ illuminat omnem hominem venientem in hunc mundum.	There was a man sent from God, whose name was John. This man came for a witness to give testimony of the light, that all men might believe through him. He was not the light but came to give testimony of the light; the true light which enlighteneth every man that cometh into this world.

Even before His Incarnation, the Word who is Light shone among all races, enlightened every man as he came into this world. For the Word who is in the beginning with God, was God and had manifested Himself even before the Incarnation, in nature, prophecy, conscience, and grace. Besides, the Word came unto His own, the Jews, at the

THE LAST GOSPEL

time of His Incarnation; but they received, that is, believed, Him not. Hence they lost the privilege of becoming true sons of God. But those who united with Christ received that sublime supernatural privilege:

In mundo erat, et mundus per ipsum factus est, et mundus eum non cognovit. In propria venit et sui eum non receperunt. Quotquot autem receperunt eum, dedit eis potestatem filios Dei fieri, his qui credunt in nomine ejus: qui non ex sanguinibus, neque ex voluntate carnis, neque ex voluntate viri, sed ex Deo nati sunt.	He was in the world, and the world was made by Him, and the world knew Him not. He came unto His own and His own received Him not. But as many as received Him to them He gave power to become the sons of God: to those that believe in His Name, who are born not of blood, nor of the will of man, but of God.

Now comes the statement of the wondrous fact of the Incarnation, the central mystery of our Religion. For Christ, our Saviour, is true God and true man. God's Son, whose glory and the spiritual splendor of whose life, seen even visibly by John in the Transfiguration and Ascension, revealed the nature and the glory of the Eternal Father.

Et Verbum caro factum est, et habitavit in nobis: et vidimus gloriam ejus, gloriam quasi Unigeniti a Patre, plenum gratiæ et veritatis. Deo Gratias!	*And the Word was made flesh* and dwelt among us: and we saw His glory, as it were the glory of the Only Begotten of the Father, full of grace and truth. Thanks be to God!

The Mass is over. What we need, then, is to understand this life — which is the light of men. When you understand that last Gospel, the closing message of the Mass, you are really in possession of the truest philosophy in the world. Begin now and ponder the words in your hearts until you know and thoroughly understand them.

St. John tells us about the life God bestows on us — the true life. Mark those words — true life. How often you hear that word "life." It is on the lips of every one in our day and generation. High-spirited boys and girls use the word, sometimes they misuse it; hence many trials and tragedies in school. Sometimes, too, you hear grown-up people express views of life that are gross, animal-minded, unworthy of decent Christians. Plainly their views are just pagan. Everybody knows, or ought to know, that there is a life to be kept alight in our hearts. Action and movement make up life, they dominate existence. But action whither? Movement in what direction? That is what counts. Not any sort of life, but the right life, true life. Not the life that is mean, silly, or self-centered. Not that which is sham, shallow, pretentious. Such life is nowise spiritual. Nay, it hinders spiritual life, which is bent upon battling strenuously and self-unsparingly for the will of God, for truth and justice, for the good of our fellow men. The right order of life is this: God; My neighbor; Myself. Or, as a great teacher once said, true Christian education should train, 1st, for God; 2d, for father and mother; 3d, for one's own life; 4th, for our country; 5th, for the trials of life.

If we follow our Lord's life closely, we shall learn how to fulfill our duties, and live our life. The Mass will instill in our heart the grace to do well. "For he that eateth hath eternal life, the life of love, personal and intimate; the love of Christ and all our brethren." It has been said that the heart that does not love is dead, a handful of ashes. Christ can bring all hearts to life, to highest life — eternal life. "This is eternal life, that you should know God the Father and Jesus Christ whom He hath sent."

What a wonderful study! St. John teaches us ever so

much on that subject. The idea he gives us is big, and, like all big ideas, simple. Anybody ought to be able to grasp it. You have been taught it since you were old enough to understand. You remember, when you were a tot, how our Lord was pointed out to you, in a holy picture, in the crucifix, in the church. You did not see Him, yet you knew how real He is. He made glad your heart, you prayed to Him. Later you learned about His life.— Bethlehem, Nazareth, Jerusalem, Calvary. All the time He was stirring the life of grace in your soul. The reward, when you coöperated with Him, was more life and having it more abundantly. That is the only kind of life eternally worth while. Never forget that it is from Christ that you learn what true life is. Life, true life, is the great desire of all of us. The glad tidings of the Fourth Gospel have to do with this true Life.

St. John the Evangelist
(Mosaic in Ravenna, cir. 547.)

Where shall we obtain it? Nowhere but from the Infinite Life, the Eternal Truth and Love (John iv, 8–16; v, 6–7).

God's truth and love are life in action, for they are of God who is life itself. God is love, God is life. God is spiritual life; therefore thought and will. In Him was life and the life was the light of men. The Mass generates that life, sheds that light. Worth-while Catholics show a genuine interest in their soul's salvation by drawing ever nearer their Saviour. That is why they love the Mass, and they do their duty. They know that the heights of Calvary can be reached and they go gladly toward it. If our Lord said: "Come to Me," He certainly meant to draw us to Him in the Mass. So go often to Mass. Keep your will near to the will of Christ and all will be well; then you need have no fear for the future. For you are called to be Christ's, and power is given you to be made sons of God. That power is grace, for grace is life. Make yourself more familiar with this life.

The two books which you can never dispense with are the book of the Mass and the book of the Gospels. "If all the spiritual books of all the saints were packed into one, they would not compare with one word of the Gospel. If you want to read, take the Gospels, read them, study them."[1] Then let it be our last resolve as we leave Mass to go often to the Gospel and learn more about the living and loving personality of Christ who cares for us so much, and visits us daily in the Holy Sacrifice. Let the Gospel be our guide book, the Mass our guide post. The Mass and the Gospel! Be assured that if we read the Gospel and hear Mass in the proper manner, we all of us will come out of church "joined together in one great noble body, with the ideals of Jesus Christ before us and the ideals of our mighty country beckoning us on; ready to bring back this world to that love and brotherhood which ought to be ours, to that fullness of life, liberty, and freedom that is the American ideal; and above all to that dream that fills all great hearts, the dream of peace and of unity and of love."

COLYMBION
An old vessel used for holy water.

[1] Bishop Curtis.

THE LAST GOSPEL

1. When were the prayers in English first said after Mass? 2. How many of them do you know by heart? 3. Why the prayer to St. Michael? 4. Do those prayers suggest anything as to private devotion? 5. Explain the etiquette to be observed on leaving the Church. 6. The prayers said at the end of Mass are but another appeal for help in the battle of life. Before leaving the headquarters of our Captain of Salvation, we pray that when we get into the line of fire, we may never waver or retreat into wrong. Whom do we ask for help? Why, the Mother of God, and St. Michael. Great names! They will arm us to cope with the powers of darkness; they surely can help us to win. To them then we pray, for we need their help. Every Catholic knows the *Hail Mary;* equally familiar should be the *Hail Holy Queen,* a prayer full of pathos and sublimity. And let us often bespeak the aid of St. Michael the Archangel, "the greatest warrior but One," who proved his power in celestial battlefields, and who will help us to wage a brave battle and never allow us to pass over to the enemy.

APPENDIX

THE VESTMENTS OF THE MASS

When the priest offers the Holy Sacrifice, he wears vestments, an official dress, which, costly or inexpensive, with or without ornaments, nevertheless signifies his office and priestly duties. Vestments are used in the Mass for several reasons:

1. They are in some cases very much like the clothes our Lord and His disciples wore at the Last Supper; still more are some of them like the street clothes commonly worn in the first centuries of Christianity. One can see, then, that they help give to Catholic worship its true historic message.

2. By an extended meaning, they hint, they imply, they stand for things. They convey a lesson, point a truth, and suggest a motive; for they are put on, as we shall see, with a prayer and worn with a thought of what they stand for. In fact, our holy Mother speaks to all, both priest and people, with her vestments. Hence they are not mere garments of an antique cut but are the official robes of the Holy Sacrifice, eloquent with meaning.

3. Being so many objects rather than words, they have a special way of teaching. They are rich, colorful signs which arrest thought and convey instruction far more vividly than words could do. They readily lend themselves to symbols and meanings that impress the religious sense. So the Church, always a wise teacher, employs them as a sign language — the oldest language in the world.

4. In their ancient and religious character they are meant to bring home to us the truth of the Church of the Ages: one, holy, catholic, and apostolic. As our earliest fathers did, so do we, is the whole idea. Under the Church's fostering care these vestments have been preserved to us; they are clung to as most sacred heirlooms and in their use no radical change is allowed lest they lose their ancient significance.

All these deserve close study. The vestments used at Mass will be seen to have a significance — historical, devotional, doctrinal. To study their origin gives one a panoramic sweep of the ages; and nowhere else could the intelligent observer be brought in closer vital contact with the remote past. It is true that the history of the Mass vestments dates far back to ages long gone. Once they were the costumes of a period or the daily dress worn simply to cover the body to protect it from the weather; or, again, the official vesture of an ancient minister of religion. Yet the Church clings to them, uses them on and on, age after age, with but slight change in their venerable patterns. The purest, richest cloths are used whenever possible. Nothing can be too good, too costly, too fair, for the house of God. All the wealth of silk and linen and jewels are worn in the Mass; they are laid, as it were, at the feet of our Lord, just as the Magi came and offered their gifts to Him. Who that loves God can help doing that?

Glorious things, therefore, are displayed and rightly so, in the Holy Sacrifice of the Mass. Catholics should make it their business to acquaint themselves with the names, history, and meaning of the vestments used at Mass. All have them before their eyes when at Mass. It will help to study them one by one.

THE AMICE

The amice (*amictus* = a covering) is a one-piece linen garment, about the size of a small shawl, which the priest places over his shoulders and then ties with long strings. This vestment can be traced back to the dim past. The Book of Genesis mentions a garb like this, worn in the primitive fashion:

APPENDIX 349

And the eyes of them both (Adam and Eve) were opened: and when they perceived themselves to be naked, they sewed together fig-leaves and made themselves aprons (amices) (Genesis iii, 7).

In the beginning, the very word *amice* meant a cloth, a covering, a dress of some sort. Such a garb was worn by ancient slaves toiling in the brick fields of Egypt. In Palestine, boatmen and wood sawers wore a similar covering, reaching down to the knees. Any outer garment came to be called an *amictus*. Vergil speaks of a toga as an amice; and the ancient priests used such a garment, made of fine linen with a purple border, when they were engaged in the act of offering sacrifice. When our Lord came, the garment was in common use. Evidently it was then a large sheet thrown around the body. On the night when our Lord was seized by the Roman soldiers in the Garden of Gethsemane:

> Then His disciples leaving Him, all fled away. And a certain young man followed Him, having a linen cloth cast about his naked body; and they laid hold on him. But he, casting off the linen cloth, fled from them naked (Mark xiv, 50-52).

Later on amice was the name given to the linen garment worn by women as a covering for their shoulders; a bride's veil was also called *amictus*. To this day the veil is worn by women everywhere in Eastern towns. Wide as was the use of the amice, we do not know just when the Church first began to use such a garment in the Mass. As early as A.D. 825, Amalarius of Metz speaks of the

AMICE
Adorned with embroidery.

amice as the first in order of the vestments of the Church:

primum vestimentum nostrum quo collum undique cingimus.
In those days, as now, the amice was worn round the neck and about the shoulders.

In form, it was an oblong piece of linen, sometimes (in the tenth century) ornamented with gold, sometimes (in the eleventh century) embroidered, even bejeweled. As it always touched the priest's throat, it was regarded as a symbol of due restraint of the voice. That meant that the priest, saying Mass, must observe the notes and tones of reverence and worship in the Holy Sacrifice. The sense of prayer was everywhere to be observed as the Mass was said, even from the time when the priest, like:

> Morning fair
> Came forth with pilgrim steps, in amice gray.

To-day the amice is the symbol of a helmet, the helmet of salvation. A piece of fine linen in the form of an oblong square, it is meant to be suspended over the shoulders of the priest. As the priest puts it on, first letting it touch his head, he recites this beautiful prayer: "Place, O Lord, upon my head the helmet of salvation." He is going to say Mass. He needs to be proof against vain, idle, or ill thoughts during those sacred moments; so he has to be spiritually protected. So he puts on the amice, symbol of the helmet of salvation. "Take unto you," says St. Paul, "the armor of God, that you may be able to resist on the evil day; take the helmet which is the hope of salvation." This the priest does as he puts on the amice and prays: "Place, O Lord, upon my head the helmet of salvation, that I may be armed against the attacks of the evil one."

PLAGA
An ornament fastened on the amice as a collar above the alb.

The Alb

The alb (*albus* = white) is a long white linen (or part lace) vestment reaching to the feet. It is worn over the amice and is secured by a girdle or cincture. Though not so old as the amice, a garment much like the alb has been in use among men from time immemorial. White dress of cotton or linen was very common in the East and along the shores of the Mediterranean where warmth of climate prevailed. Egypt and Syria sent linen to Tyre, as Ezechiel narrates in xxvii, 7–16. Indian cambrics were known to the Arabs as *Shesh-Hindi*. And we know that the cerecloths with which the Egyptians wrapped their dead were linen mummy cloths. "At all times let thy garments be white," says the preacher in the Book of Ecclesiastes. In his day white was constantly worn at feasts and was symbolic of cheerfulness. This is seen also in the days when Solomon's temple was first opened: "Both the Levites and the singing men, with their sons and their brethren, clothed with fine linen, sounded with cymbals and psalteries, and harps, standing on the east side of the altar" (II Paralipomenon v, 12).

Among the Romans this long white tunic was known as *alba tunica*. As early as A.D. 265, the Roman Emperor Gallienus sent Claudius an alb made of silk interwoven with some other material. This gift was called *alba subserica*, or a tunic from Seres. Now Seres was the name of an Indian people from whom the Romans got their first silk. One can easily fancy what a gift that must have been!

Being a street dress in the early days of Christianity, the alb lent itself to religious ceremonies. In the Church, however, the alb was a full-flowing white garment with large sleeves of white linen only. None were allowed to wear this robe save bishops, priests, and deacons. As time went on the alb was enriched with ornaments and colors. Oblong patches (*paraturæ*), richly colored, were added; but not until a very late date was lace used.

To the faithful, an alb is a symbol of purity. Those who serve at God's altar needs must have clean hands and pure hearts. The priest robed in white is soon to stand at the very altar where the Lamb without stain is to be sacrificed. What could be more fitting than that pure lily-white vestment. Does it not tell how the ancient darkness is transformed by the Light of Life, our Lord? And does it not speak of purity of faith and practice? A revelation received by St. John in the Isle of Patmos reads thus:

ALB
Showing oblong patches or *paraturæ*.

> But thou hast a few names in Sardis, which have not defiled their garments: and they shall walk with me in white because they are worthy.
>
> He that shall overcome shall thus be clothed in white garments, and I will not blot out his name out of the book of life, and I will confess his name before my Father, and before His angels (Apocalypse iii, 4–5).

So Christ speaks to St. John in the Apocalypse. No wonder, then, the priest robes himself in a pure white alb for the Mass where the Sacrificial Lamb of God is mystically slain. Now we understand why the Church took that street garment and made of it a vestment for the sanctuary. While putting on the alb, the priest prays thus: "Make my soul white, O Lord, and my heart clean that, purified in the blood of the Lamb, I may possess eternal joy."

The Cincture

The alb is confined with a cincture. This is a long thick cord, silk or linen or cotton. Whatever the material, the cincture itself has been in use for ages. Isaias, speaking of the coming of a Saviour, says: "And I will clothe Him with thy robe, and will strengthen Him with thy girdle, and will give thy power into his hand" (Isaias xxii, 21).

As it was the ancient custom to wear long flowing robes, it became necessary to secure them with some sort of belt. That was the *cingulum*, or girdle. Follow history and you can see how the cincture winds its way down the ages from the earliest days to our own.

Women wore such a girdle both as an ornament and when they wanted to draw up their hanging skirts and brace themselves for prolonged exertion. The Eastern women are hard workers. "The housewife, having got up at daybreak, sets her house in order. She rose before the others, swept the house in and out, and sprinkled about water and sand." Of such an active good woman the Hebrew proverb says: "She hath girded her loins with strength and hath strengthened her arm" (Proverbs xxxi, 17).

Soldiers wore a sword belt round their waist. This the Greeks called *zona;* the Romans, *cinctus*. Often a dagger was suspended from the belt or put into it for security. Later on the belt was worn upon the armor and supported the kilt.

Workmen who found the long tunic in their way had to gird it up by means of a cincture; thus they were braced for strenuous activity and their clothes did not impede them in their toil. "They shall not slumber nor sleep, neither shall the girdle of the loins be loosed, nor the latchet of their shoes be broken" (Isaias v, 27).

Ancient priests, offering sacrifice, also wore the girdle. And when they came to the solemn part of the act, the girdle was loosed and the folds of their dress allowed to hang to the feet. Jeremias, himself a priest of the high God, speaks of the wicked people in the very term of the girdle which he wore.

This wicked people, that will not hear my words, and that walk in the perverseness of their heart, and have gone after strange gods to serve them and to adore them; and they shall be as this girdle which is fit for no more use. For as a girdle sticketh close to the loins of a man, so have I brought close to me all the house of Israel, and all the house of Juda, saith the Lord (Jeremias xiii, 10–11).

When John the Baptist came to preach the advent of the Saviour, he wore a raiment of camel's hair secured by a leathern girdle of undressed hide, such as Elias had worn ages before. That belt of John's was typical of an austere preacher of repentance and of the hard work he was doing for the good of souls. His very words bear out his workmanlike appearance. "Prepare ye the way of the Lord, make straight his paths. For now the ax is laid to the root of the trees" (Matthew iii, 3, 10).

Also, above all, our divine Saviour Himself at the Last Supper, laid aside His outer dress, took a towel, and girded Himself. After that, He poured water into a basin, and began to wash the disciples' feet, and to wipe them with the towel wherewith He was girded (John xiii, 4–5).

St. Peter, asleep in his prison, was wakened by an angel sent to aid him in making his escape. The angel commanded: "Gird thyself!" And St. Paul writes: "Stand, therefore, having your loins girt about with truth" (Ephesians vi, 14).

The girdle continues to be used in the East, even to this day. Bedouins of the desert dress with shirt and belt exactly as did the Arabs five thousand years ago. A high Eastern official wears the cincture like a sash wound round the waist and falling to the feet, the ends richly ornamented in silk and gold — a badge of his office.

Both in the East and the West, from the earliest days of Christianity the cincture formed part of the monastic dress. It indicated chastity and signified the beauty wherewith Christ girds Himself on entering into His kingdom. Those meanings have long been attached to the use of the cincture and they continue so to this day. When the priest puts on the cincture for Mass, he follows the old idea of the soldier of pure purpose getting ready to face a foe apt to tempt him at that most holy time. Such a foe is sin. Now in order to fight sin, the priest must be pure and strong. Purity and strength come from God. "Thou hast girded me with strength unto battle and hast subdued under me them that rose against me" (Psalms xvii, 40). The power of chastity comes from God, too, and it is similarly symbolized by the cincture. St. John once saw angels "come out of the temple, clothed with clean and white linen, and girt about the breast with golden girdles" (Apocalypse xv, 6). If angels were so costumed, coming out of the temple of God, the need of the priest being strong in virtue is still greater. For he has to offer the Holy Sacrifice and worthily. Otherwise God will say to him as He said of old: "I am the Lord, and there is none else: there is no God besides me: I girded thee and thou hast not known me" (Isaias xlv, 5). The priest plainly needs God's invisible support; so when he puts on the cincture with the idea of fighting evil and the hope of withstanding evils, he asks God to enable him to preserve his chastity.

"Gird me, O Lord, with the cincture of purity, and extinguish in my loins all evil desire, so that the virtue of continency and chastity abiding always in my heart, I may the better serve Thee."

The Maniple

An ornamental vestment marked with a cross, the maniple is worn like a band over the left arm and falls in equal length on both sides. The word *manipulus* means "folded together," just as you would fold a pocket handkerchief or a hand towel. The original purpose of this piece of cloth was a practical one. Long before the Church employed it as a vestment, people in Eastern countries wore it on their arm and used it much as we do a handkerchief. The maniple of old was nothing more than a handkerchief. Naturally the ancient maniple was very necessary in climates where heat and dust were great. Even to the present day such a cloth is used to wipe the face and the back of the hands. Indeed, the Palestinian not only carries the handkerchief but also folds (*manipulare*) the cloth around his neck to keep the sweat and grime away from the collar of the outer garment. To-day the Easterner carries a *manipulus* on the road, in the vineyard, or at the plow, to wipe away the perspiration from the face. The Jews are said to have used this cloth for keeping their money secure. Very likely it was a *manipulus* in which the lazy servant in the Gospel wrapped up the pound trusted to him. Instead of using aright his Lord's money he put it in his sweat cloth where it lay idle.

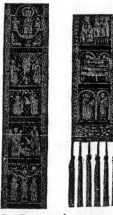

St. Bernulf's maniple
XIth century.

And another came saying: Lord, behold, here is thy pound, which I have kept laid up in a napkin. For I feared thee because thou art an austere man: Thou takest up what thou didst not lay down, and thou reapest that which thou didst not sow (Luke xix, 20–21).

Then, too, the article mentioned in Acts xix, 12, may have been nothing else than the maniple.

And God wrought by the hand of Paul more than common miracles.
So that even there were brought from his hand to the body of the sick, handkerchiefs and aprons, and the diseases departed from them, and the wicked spirits went out of them.

"Apparently," says a commentator, "the handkerchief and apron used by the apostle as he worked at his tent were frequently begged from him and used as a precious garment, which conveyed the supernatural gift of healing which the wearer exercised."

Quintilian, a Latin author of the first century, calls the *manipulus, sudarium* — that is, sweat cloth — and describes its use to wipe off perspiration from the hands and face. No doubt, too, this folded cloth took on ornamental features and was carried more for show than for utility. As an ornamental handkerchief it was employed by the Roman consul to give the signal for the commencement of the games. It is true the Romans called it by another name, *mappa*, but it was merely a fancy handkerchief.

Whatever were the uses of the *manipulus* during early ages, when the Church first took it over in Rome for her ceremonies, she had a good reason for so doing. In the sixth century we read that it was worn by priests and deacons in Ravenna; four hundred years later its use was universal in western Europe. There is to-day in the museum of Durham Cathedral a maniple with an inscription embroidered on it telling how it was made for the Bishop of Winchester by order of Queen Æthelflæd (c. 900). By the late Middle Ages the maniple was made of silk, and often was jewel-studded, and adorned with gold and silver. All along the ages the Church has retained it as one of her vestments. That the maniple is still put on for Mass need not surprise us. It has its value for instruction and is an incentive to prayer. Any one can see that it hints of work, of sweat, of trial. Just that is in the mind of the Church when she uses it, though now it be but an ornament. In the Mass the maniple symbolizes a handkerchief intended to wipe off, not the body, but the mind and the heart; to banish sloth, which is fear of labor; and to inspire a love of good works. The maniple, therefore, is the mark of spiritual strenuosity. On his arm, it reminds the priest of the duty that is his when discharging his sacred ministry, of the path in which he must go if he is to follow his divine Master who came on our earth

To preach the gospel to the poor, to heal the contrite of heart. To preach deliverance to the captives, and sight to the blind, to set at liberty them that are bruised, to preach the acceptable year of the Lord, and the day of reward (Luke iv, 18–19).

Enough has been said to show that the maniple suggests the cares and sorrows of life. That is why the priest when fixing it on his left arm prays that he may be able to labor with patience amid toil and trial in view of a heavenly reward.

"Let me merit, O Lord, to bear this maniple of tears and sorrow so that one day I may come with joy into the reward of all my labors."

The Stole

The stole is a vestment composed of a strip of material, usually silk fabric, about eighty inches long and from two to four inches wide, and may be white, red, etc., according

APPENDIX 359

to the liturgical color of the day. The early origins of the stole are dim and uncertain. Its use among the ancient Romans is thought to have been much like that of the maniple; viz., a kind of handkerchief. At first a thing of utility, it became in time a badge of honor. The Church looked upon it as a mark of sacred powers; and it indicated both dignity and duty. This idea is beautifully brought out in the ordination of a deacon. When the bishop puts the stole on the left shoulder of the deacon, he charges him as follows:

Receive from the hand of God the white garment and fulfill thy duty, for God is mighty enough to give thee His grace in rich measure.

At first the stole was worn by deacons when serving at the altar. There it may have been used as a liturgical towel. Indeed, many regard it thus and speak of it as sacred to the memory of the cloth with which our Lord is alleged to have wiped away the sweat from His face as He passed to the crucifixion. But whatever its purpose, certain it is that the stole had a special place in the liturgical service of the early Church.

Until the fourth century, however, nothing is recorded of the stole as a liturgical vestment. We know that deacons in those days wore a stole together with an alb or colobium. A deacon was regarded as a sailor or a boatswain on the ship of Peter, whose apparel must not be too floating, since he had to be an active helpful server. So with his stole worn like a sash, the deacon's duty was to assist the priest. All the early writings on this point stress the ideal of the deacon as one of duty, of steady service.

STOLE

> How graciously thou wearest the yoke
> Of use that does not fail.

Helpfulness, therefore, at the altar where the priest needed him was the essential duty of the deacon, a duty designated by the very garb he wore — the stole. Perhaps that is why the stole was allowed him, as a badge of service. Daily the deacon wore it as he served at God's altar.

St. Chrysostom, 347–407, seems to stress that idea. In a vision he saw ministerial angels engaged in the service of the altar; on them rested the stole, of fine linen, that floated over their left shoulders. The rule of the Church was that when deacons wore the stole, it should be over the left shoulder, the right being left free so as to permit quick dispatch in the discharge of their sacred duties at the altar. No one except priest or bishop might carry it over both shoulders.

Undoubtedly this vestment continued to be employed by priests in the Holy Sacrifice, although spare mention occurs in the earliest writings of the West. Under Church adoption, we know that its use by the priest conveyed the self-same idea of service at God's altar as it meant for the deacon. *Amare et servire!* Indeed, our Lord when washing His disciples' feet told them that they should be full of lowly service, one to another. And he who was highest among all men put Himself to the lowest. "The Son of Man is not come to be ministered unto, but to minister and to give his life a redemption for many" (Mark x, 45). This is the spirit in which the stole is worn.

By the seventh century priests saying Mass were in the habit of wearing the stole crossed in front of the breast. The Synod of Baraga so ruled in A.D. 675. The accompanying illustration of the stole found in St. Cuthbert's tomb may possibly date from this period. Time and the art of new ages wrought minor changes and adornments in this as well

APPENDIX 361

as other vestments. It is a pity that we have so few records touching this subject. Perhaps the very widespread use of the stole as an article of vesture is the reason why it is so little mentioned in the manuscripts. At any rate we have enough evidence here and there to show how it was worn during the early centuries of Church history.

After the ninth century, frequent mention is made of the stole. A priest was obliged to wear it on a journey as a badge of his calling, much like the Roman collar is worn in our day. In those days also the custom was to ornament the ends of the stole with tassels or little bells. Some time later, in the eleventh and twelfth centuries, the stole was very long and extremely narrow. It is true, perhaps, that in the Middle Ages the stole, like so many other vestments, was ornamented with embroidery and heavily jeweled.

STOLE FOUND IN ST. CUTHBERT'S TOMB

One can understand why the stole was so valued, since the giving of it to a candidate implied not only devotion to the ranks of the clergy but also entrance into the service of the Church.

Lastly, notice that the Mass stole has a cross embroidered on the collar, which the priest kisses before putting on. The vestment is then placed round the neck across the shoulders, falling to the breast, where the two halves cross each other over the alb and are fastened securely with the cincture. Thus worn, it reminds the priest of his daily duty of expending his energy enthusiastically for the cause of Christ. Now enthusiasm springs from love, and service born of love reveals itself in self-sacrifice for the sake of the Master.

"Athletes!" says St. Basil, "workmen of Jesus Christ, you have engaged yourselves to work for Him all the day, to bear all its heat. Seek not repose before the end; wait for the evening, that is, the end of life, the hour at which the Householder shall come to reckon with you and pay you your wages."

The one thought, then, in the priest's mind when putting the stole on should be service. And that he may serve God with clean hands and a pure heart he prays for that innocence and immortality which man had when he came from the hands of his Creator. "Return to me, O Lord, that stole of immortality which was lost to me by my first parents and though all-worthy I approach Thy great Mystery, nevertheless grant me to merit joy eternal."

Chasuble

The amice, we saw, was a development of a very ancient garment, which is also true of the chasuble. The outer vestment worn by the priest at Mass is to be traced to the band or fillet which bound the brow of the priest and victim in an ancient sacrifice. It was called *infula* and also *vitta*. Its bands were commonly made of red and white stripes.

> Stans hostia ad aram
> Lanea dum nivea circumdatur infula vitta.
> (Vergil, Georgics, III, 487).

In time this head decoration developed into a sort of hood. Then the word came to be used of the head covering of Christian priests; then it signified the whole outer vestment. Thus *infula* came to mean *casula*, or chasuble. No really satisfactory knowledge is had of how these changes came about. As we have seen, certain garments worn in

APPENDIX

pagan days were appropriated to Christian purposes. The daily clothes of the old Roman were not only the outdoor garb of the clergy, but even the vestments of the altar. Certainly, one of the most striking instances of this is found in the history of the chasuble. About the time the Church put it to her own uses, it must have been simply an old-time garment. Doubtless it had a hood, and was called *casula* (diminutive of *casa* — a hut) because it covered the entire person, like a hut conceals one who was within. Philo Judæus (born 25 B.C.) speaks of this garment made of goatskins commonly worn in his time; it resembled a portable house, serving that purpose for travelers, soldiers, and others, who were obliged to be much in the open air.

CHASUBLE OF THE YEAR 1387

This garment, therefore, was a very humble garb, generally of sheepskin, or wool, made in one piece throughout, without sleeves, and without slit or opening in the front. Nowadays we should describe it as a mackintosh or an immense hooded sweater without sleeves coming down loosely to the knees. Obviously it was both a hat and a cloak in one, and was worn by peasants and artisans as their ordinary outdoor dress, for protection against cold and wet. St. Augustine in the fourth century tells of one Florentius, a working tailor of Hippo, who lost his *casula* and had no money to buy a new one. It was worth fifty folles. But the tailor was economical, and figured that he would buy some wool and have his wife make the garment as best she could. The Bishop of Hippo further mentions the *casula* as a garment which any of his congregation might wear, if it were a good one. An interesting record tells how St. Cæsarius, Archbishop of Arles, in Gaul (A.D. 540) used to wear a *casula* on his walks about the city. Again, Abbot John, a Persian, came to Rome in the days of Pope Gregory to visit the tombs of Sts. Peter and Paul. "I was standing in the middle of the city," he relates, "when who should come across toward us but Pope Gregory. The Pope came close up ... then embracing me with much humility, he slipped three pieces of money into my hand, and desired that a *casula* should be given me, and everything else that I required."

By degrees, however, the *casula* grew to be a more pretentious outer garment. Indeed by the seventh century we read of *casulæ* of finest materials, brilliant colors, costly silk. Boniface III sent King Pepin (A.D. 606) a *casula* formed partly of silk and partly of fine goat's hair.

Gradually the hood disappeared. The garment was taken over for Church purposes so that the priest at the altar was dressed as in civil life, but the custom doubtless was to use newer, cleaner *cas-*

CHASUBLE

ulæ than were worn on the street. The clergy, from the priest to the archbishop, wore this ecclesiastical costume. A most curious as well as ancient allusion to the *casula*, as worn by priests in the Mass, is to be found in the prophetic utterance of the Druids. Before St. Patrick came to Ireland (A.D. 440) the Druids circulated this order:

> Adze-head (that is the peculiar form of tonsure) will come with a crook-head staff (crosier): in his house head-holed (that is, chasuble) he will chant impiety from his table (that is, altar): from the front (that is, the eastern) part of his house all his household (attendant clerics) will respond, 'So be it! So be it!'

What a curious description of the Mass were those ancient pagan priests giving to the world!

The historian can trace the use of the chasuble in the sanctuary with various modifications as to form, material, ornament. The *casula* in the earlier times consisted of a big piece of cloth, in the center of which a hole was made; through this the head was passed. With the arms hanging down this did indeed cover the whole figure and must have looked like a hut. The shape, however, varied with the material. Likely its altar use started very early; for from the fifth century on, in Italy and Spain, we know it was employed for the super vestment worn in the Mass. In the eleventh century, besides being made of very costly stuffs, it was often shaped to fall in graceful folds. Often, too, it was made of thickly embroidered cloth of gold, and was oval in form.

The chasuble, we know, is the principal vestment of the Mass. It nearly covers all the others; but no longer is it the big, broad capelike garb with ample folds, rather is it a convenient vestment nowise impeding the use of the arms; it has a large cross on the back, and it symbolizes the yoke and burden of Christ.

Take up my yoke upon you, and learn of me, because I am meek and humble of heart: and you shall find rest to your souls. For my yoke is sweet and my burden light (Matthew xi, 29-30).

That yoke, says St. Augustine, is like the plumage of a bird — an easy weight enabling the soul to soar heavenwards. Hence the priest, putting on the chasuble, seeks to pattern his heart after the meek and lowly One who can teach us all truth; the vestment even carries His cross which is His yoke. Now the cross is light, the burden sweet for those, and only for those, who are like Christ, meek, lowly, loving, and obedient to the will of God. That he may be just that, the priest prays as he puts on the chasuble:

"O Lord, Who hast said: 'My yoke is sweet, My burden light,' fix it that I may be enabled to so carry that yoke and burden as to earn Thy grace. Amen."

Clad with these vestments, three of linen (amice, alb, and cincture), three (maniple, stole, and chasuble) of some other material colored according to the day, the priest goes to the altar. He carries in his hands, under the veil with its burse, a chalice, paten, pall, and purificator. In the burse atop the veil, lies the corporal which is placed over the altar stone upon the priest's arrival at the altar. With the altar itself prepared, candles lighted, the credence table set with water, wine, and linen, and altar boy ready, the Mass begins.

THE MASS OF THE CATECHUMENS

It is helpful to review the first part of the Mass. Observe how it has risen steadily from the Confiteor to the splendid culmination of the Gospel and the Credo with their dramatic intensity. Then view this part in its historic background — the Mass of the Catechumens. At the end of the sermon the Mass of the Catechumens was over. All the Catechumens, Gentiles, Jews — in fact, all those who were not of the faithful (*fideles, i.e.* baptized) — had to leave the church, for now the "Sacred Mysteries were about to begin with the Offertory." "Take notice," says St. Augustine, "after the sermon the dismissal of the Catechumens takes place: the faithful will remain." The formula of dismissal was, "If there be any Catechumen here let him go out." It is instructive to note that the Oremus after the Credo still points out the place where prayers, now omitted, were once said over the Penitents before they were dismissed from the church. For until they had been restored to full membership in the Household of the Faith they could not be present at the more sacred mysteries, the Mass proper. The Catechumens, remember, were converts still under instruction and not yet baptized. One of those, Theophilus, was instructed in the main facts of the Gospel, and St. Luke inscribes his Gospel to him (Luke i, 3). Notice how the instructions were sometimes given in brief: to the Ethiopian (Acts viii, 36) and to the Philippian jailer (Acts xvi, 33). In fine, St. Paul gives a hint of the kind of instruction generally considered necessary for those new converts (Hebrews v, 12–14). Later on, of course, the Councils of the Church prescribed conditions for the instruction and reception of Catechumens into the Church.

Notable also is the fact that St. Paul, twenty-four years after our Lord's ascension, tells us something about that

BAPTISTRY OF AQUILEIA

Notice the steps up and into the hexagonal *piscina* where people were baptized.

Mass of the Catechumens. The Apostle gives us a little glimpse of what the early Christians did in this part of the Mass. You will find it in the First Epistle to the Corinthians, that letter which is an inexhaustible mine of Christian thought and life. "How is it then, brethren?" asks St. Paul, "when you come together, every one of you hath a psalm, hath a doctrine, hath a revelation, hath a tongue, hath an interpretation: let all things be done to edification" (I Corinthians xiv, 26). You can see here the whole structure of the Mass of the Catechumens. You can still trace every part in our Mass. Even the very order St. Paul describes is still preserved.

I.	The Psalm	Judica me Deus
II.	The Doctrine	Confessio (Confiteor, Holy Trinity, etc.) Lection or the Epistle (doctrine)
III.	The Revelation	Gradual, Tract and Versicles
IV.	Tongues	Gospel, the gift of applying vocally and *ad rem* the teaching of Christ's Holy Spirit (Acts ii, 4)
V.	Interpretation	The sermon preached on the Gospel

When the early Christians were thus assembled with the Candidates, or Catechumens, a psalm was on their lips; a doctrine or instruction useful to all was pronounced; an apocalypse or revelation was proclaimed, bringing to light some hidden truth or mystery of the Scriptures; tongues, *i.e.* certain ecstatic utterances under the inspiration of the Holy Spirit, such as we read of in Acts x, 46, and xix, 6; finally, interpretation of some truth (Gospel) already delivered. How beautifully St. Paul touches on the Catechumens' Mass! Just a few lines and — a picture! What a precious insight into the life, the fervor, the fidelity of the first Christian congregations.

A few more facts about what went on will be welcome, we feel sure. Naturally, we want to know more and more of the doings of those early Christians when they assembled for Mass. Father Fortesque tells us: "There were readings from the holy books, as among the Jews (Acts xiii, 15). St. Paul tells Timothy to read as well as to preach (I Timothy, iv, 13); his own letters are to be read out to all the brethren (Thessalonians v, 27; Colossians iv, 16). Evidently Christians read their own books as well as the Old Testament. After the readings came sermons, expositions of what had been read (I Corinthians xiv, 26; Acts xx, 7). They sang psalms

(I Corinthians xiv, 26) and hymns (Ephesians v, 19; Colossians iii, 16). The two are obviously distinct in these texts. There are fragments of rhymed prose in St. Paul which are supposed to be examples of the first Christian hymns (Romans xiii, 11–12; Ephesians v, 14; I Timothy iii, 16; II Timothy ii, 11–13).

There were prayers said publicly for all kinds of people (I Timothy ii, 1–2; Acts ii, 42). At the meetings, collections of alms were made for the poor (Romans xv, 26; I Corinthians xvi, 1–2; II Corinthians ix, 10–13). These elements, readings, sermons, psalms, hymns, prayers, and the collection of alms we know to have been those of the Synagogue services. Together they formed the normal Christian morning service, as distinct from the Eucharist. To this picture of the morning service we can add details. The people prayed standing, with uplifted hands (Philippians i, 27; Ephesians vi, 14; I Timothy ii, 8). This was the Jewish position (Psalms cxxxiii, 1; cxxxiv, 2; Luke xviii, 11, 13; Matthew vi, 5; Psalms cxl, 2; lxii, 5; cxxxiii, 2). The men were bareheaded, the women veiled (I Corinthians xi, 6–7). Women were not allowed to speak in church (I Corinthians xiv, 34–35). There was a kiss of peace (I Thessalonians v, 26; Romans xvi, 16; I Corinthians xvi, 20; I Peter v, 14), a public profession of faith (I Timothy vi, 12). The people continued the use of the old Hebrew formula Amen as an adverb, 'certainly,' 'truly'; so, constantly in the Old Testament (Deuteronomy xxvii, 15–26; Psalms xl, 14, etc.) as the sign of their assent after a prayer (I Corinthians xiv, 16) it occurs in the archetype of all prayers, the Our Father (Matthew vi, 13). We may suppose other formulas that occur constantly in St. Paul to be well-known liturgical ones in the Church, as they had been in the Synagogue. Such formulas are 'for ever and ever'

APPENDIX 371

(again a Hebraism, Romans xvi, 27; Galatians i, 5; Hebrews xiii, 21; I Peter iv, 11; Apocalypse i, 6). 'God blessed for ever' (Romans ix, 5; i, 25; II Corinthians xi, 31). Such doxologies and blessings as II Corinthians xiii, 13; Romans xi, 36, and the form 'Through our Lord Jesus Christ' (Romans v, 11, 21) have the look of liturgical formulas."[1]

[1] Adrian Fortesque, "The Mass, A Study of the Roman Liturgy," pp. 3-4. Longmans, Green & Co.

BAPTISMAL FONT
(Romano-Byzantine)

Along the ages, art has spared no pains to render fitting tribute to the "Laver of regeneration and renovation of the Holy Ghost," Titus iii, 5.

INDEX

Abel, sacrifice of, 92
Abraham, 93
Agape, 263
Agatha, St., 232
Agnes, St., 233
Agnus Dei, 283–296
Alb, 351, 352
Altar, 27, 209; various kinds of, 27; in World War, 26
Altar Stone, 20–28
Amice, 348–350
Anastasia, St., 233
Andrew, St., 273, 316
Angels, 209–211. *See Seraphim*
Aramaic, in Gospel, 36

Babylon, 11
Barnabas, St., 230
Bells, 197
Bigotry, 162
Bishop, seat of, 23; prayer for, 160
Blessings, 236–241, 330–335
Brotherhood, 205–207, 249–250, 274

Canon, 140–141, 155–158
Canonization, 172
Catacombs, 5, 216–219
Catechumens, Mass of, 367–371
Cecilia, St., 233
Centurion, 298–300
Chalice, of Antioch, *frontispiece;* early type of, 97–100; meaning of, 100
Chasuble, 362–366
Christ, Our Lord, Captain of Salvation, 226–235, 309; Divine Physician, 300, 317; Elder Brother, 274; Giver of all, 239–241, 244, 262, 274; Good Shepherd, 179–185; great High Priest, 187; Lamb of God, 288–290; Prince of Peace, 290–296; remembrance of, 201; Teacher, 247, 255–256; teachings of, 32, 79, 205, 206, 260; True Life, 342–344; symbolized by the altar stone, 21; used the Psalms, 32–34
Church, 202, 205, 213, 256, 291; age-old customs in, 24; an army, 223–235; and the age, 73, 132–133, 141, 160, 202, 259, 292; and the Gospel, 67–75; wise Mother, 15, 164–165, 214–216, 246, 332; numbers of, 162
Ciborium, 126–127, 196
Cincture, 353–356
Collect, 54–57
Columba, St., 31
Columbus, 28
Commixtio, 276–282
Communicantes, 169–174
Communion, 243, 297–317; frequent, 307–308; holy, 204, 262, 264, 297–313, 321–329
Communion of Saints, 171–184, 203–206
Conduct, 47–52, 75, 111–116, 260
Confession, 14, 17
Confiteor, 10–20
Consecration, 186–198, 243
Contrition, 111
Cowardice, 223, 228, 259, 262
Credo, 77–87
Cross, 3–9; use of, 69, 159; varieties of, 4–5
Crucifix, 7, 158

Dialogue, 138–139
Diptych, 167, 216
Domine Non Sum Dignus, 297–313
Dominus Vobiscum, 44–53
Doxology, 241

INDEX

Drama, 65–66, 120–121, 146, 155, 180, 193, 242, 246, 274
Duty, 131–132, 204, 254, 257, 262, 266

Education, 47–52, 75, 80, 112
Elevation, 188, 195–197, 241–245
Epistle, 58–61
Evangelists, 36, 338–339
Example, 48–51

Fatherhood of God, 205, 250
Felicitas, St., 231
Forgiveness, 16, 265–267
Fractio Panis, 276–282
Frequent Communion, 307–308
Friendship, 325

Genuflection, 8–9
Gloria in Excelsis, 40–43
Gospel, 67–76, 336–345
Grace, 264–267
Gradual, 62–66
Greek, used in Mass, 35–37

Hanc Igitur, 175–185
Heaven, 169–171, 250–253
Hebrew, used in Mass, 35–37, 55, 63, 148
High Priest, 128
Holy Communion, 204, 262, 264, 297–313, 321–329
Holy Ghost, 103
Homage, 193
Humility, 101–102, 109, 288–289, 301
Hymns, in the Mass, 32

Ignatius, of Antioch, 230
Incarnation, 341
Innocence, 106, 110
Intercession, 160, 174–177, 217, 273
Introit, 29–34
Ite, Missa Est, 330–335

John, the Baptist, 228, 340
John, the Evangelist, 339, 343

Joy, 40–43, 322–329
Judas, 281–287
Justice, 112–113

Kingdom of God, 181, 203–205, 254–258
Kyrie Eleison, 35–39

Languages, used in Mass. *See Latin, Greek, Hebrew*
Last Supper, 80, 109, 165, 186, 244, 276–277
Latin, used in Mass, 35–38; language of the Church, 37–38
Lavabo, 104–117
Libera Nos Quaesumus, 272–275
Lucy, St., 232

Magdalene, Mary, 15, 109
Maniple, 356–358
Marcellinus, St., 230
Martyrs, 228–235; relics of, 22–23; works of, 82–87; sufferings of, 84–86
Mary, 273
Mass, definition of, 96, 211; in early ages, 309–311; fruits of, 131–132, 280
Matthew, St., 36, 229
Melchisedech, 92
Memento, for the living, 164–168; for the dead, 213–220
Milton, on the Nativity, 72
Miracles, 25
Missa Fidelium, 92
Missal, 71–72
More, Blessed Thomas, 3
Mystical Body, 45, 171

Nazareth, 63, 74
Newman, Cardinal, on the Mass, 56
Nobis Quoque Peccatoribus, 221–235

Obedience, 46–47, 258–262, 294
Oblations, 25, 96, 180
Offertory, 91–103, 238
Orate Fratres, 125–133

INDEX

Passion, of Our Lord, 3
Passover, 289, 290, 295
Pater Noster, 246–271
Peace, 162, 180–181, 280, 310
Per Ipsum, 241–245
Per Quem, 236–240
Popes, and the Mass, 54, 119, 162, 230, 248, 332
Post Communion, 321–329
Postures, 8, 17
Praise, 129, 249, 253
Preface, 138–145
Processions, 334–335
Prophets, 30, 33
Psalms, of Exile, 12; Judica me, Deus, 10; worth study, 19, 32–33; used in Mass, 18, 29, 319

Real Presence, 76, 186–198, 200
Relics, 22–25
Religion, 204–205, 217
Repentance, 101–102
Resurrection, 201, 280
Reverence, 9
Ruskin, John, on Catholic prayers, 55; on education, 112; on reverence 9,

Sacrifice, of the Mass, 96, 211, 213; in old Law, 95, 207–208, 237; the essence of, 95, 96, 141, 297; in early days, 92–94, 103, 302
Saints, 174
Sanctus, 146–154
Satan, 183, 269
School, Catholic, ideals of, 48
Secreta, 134–137
Sequence, 64–66
Seraphim, 148–149
Service, 51–52

Seven Last Words, 33, 120–121
Silence, great, 119–123, 134–137; value of, 121–122
Sin, and forgiveness, 10–19, 275, 281, 300–302
Soldiers, of Christ, 221–235, 269–270
Spite, 326
Stephen, St., 83, 229
Stole, 358–362
Success, 75, 260
Supplices te rogamus, 208–212
Supra quae, 207
Suscipe Sancta Trinitas, 118–124
Suspicion, 324–325
Swearing, 114

Teachers, 76
Te Igitur, 159–163
Temptation, 227, 267–270
Thanksgiving, 236–245, 321–329
Tract, 64
Tradition, 68
Transubstantiation, 199
Trinity, Holy, 118–124, 241, 249

Unde Et Memores, 199–212
Unity, 125

Vanity, 112–113
Veil, of the altar, 127–128
Vestments, of the Mass, 347–366

Washing of hands, 104–110, 304
Wilderness of Judea, 123
Will of God, 258–262
Wine, used in Mass, 97–100
World War, Chaplain in, 26
Worship, 249

Zangwill, Israel, on prayer, 43